BEN

TRANSFORMERS

GHOSTS OF YESTERDAY

1

Standing taller than a thirty-six-story building and weighing six million, seven hundred thousand pounds, in the year 1969 the Saturn V moon rocket was the biggest man-made object ever sent into space. Representing the epitome of human research, it was a technological marvel that awed even those whose dedication and long, hard labor had come together to make it a reality.

No one on Earth suspected that there were forces at work throughout the galaxy, good as well as evil, to whom the massive rocket was nothing more than an oversized firecracker.

Though not the first Saturn V to be launched from Kennedy Space Center, *Apollo 11* was special. The three astronauts waiting patiently in the capsule atop what was, after all, little more than a gigantic but hopefully domesticated flying bomb had trained long and hard for the coming mission, but they were still human. They were not machines, and they were certainly not robots. All three of them had families and lives they fully intended to return to. No one doubted the success of the forthcoming venture, but that did not mean they had no qualms. The tons of explosive fuel waiting to be ignited just aft of their backsides were enough to induce second thoughts in even the most highly trained individual.

Too late for any kind of thoughts now except those essential to carrying out the launch. Switches were thrown, readouts checked and rechecked, the primitive computational devices of the late 1960s engaged. Over the craft's internal speakers the three waiting astronauts could hear the composed voice of Mission Control.

"T minus thirty seconds and counting." Simple words for some of the most complex coordinated activities humankind had ever attempted. The men on board responded as they had been trained to do.

"Astronauts report all systems check out," the controller announced. "T minus twenty-five seconds and counting."

While the men onboard devoted their full attention to their respective instruments, they still managed to find time for personal thoughts. Uppermost among these was the certain knowledge that if the launch failed and the rocket blew, they would likely never know what had happened to them.

"T minus fifteen seconds. Guidance going to internal." The briefest, most significant of pauses, then, "Twelve, eleven, ten, nine, ignition sequence start, six, five, four, three, two, one, zero. We have ignition of the Saturn Five, we have ignition."

The kind of rumble one experiences only beneath the center of a supercell thunderstorm erupted from the base of the rocket. It was as if half a dozen tornadoes had been recorded spinning around a common axis. Those observers not stationed at a distance and not wearing suitable protection hastened to cover their ears.

"All engines running."

Slowly, with a ponderous grace that was at once a wonder and an impossibility to behold, the entire enormous cylindrical shape began to move. Rising from the launching pad, slowly picking up speed and trailing streamers of white, the Saturn moon rocket climbed skyward with an agonizing steadiness that was a tribute to the thousands of individuals who had worked to make it a reality.

"Liftoff!" The controller was not quite able to contain himself. "We have a liftoff! Thirty-two minutes past the hour, we have liftoff of *Apollo Eleven.*" Realizing that he had not been cleared to express personal enthusiasm, the controller restrained himself. "The tower has been cleared."

Outside, man-made thunder sent wading birds in the nearby shallows fleeing in all directions. Bemused alligators ducked underwater while swamp rodents of various species scrambled frantically for cover. Within Mission Control, a new voice and a new controller took over.

"Okay, we've gone to roll program."

Still a third voice added with becoming calm, "Neil Armstrong reporting that we are in the roll-and-pitch program. *Apollo Eleven* is now on a proper heading, destination—the moon."

Same year, same day, same time. While the attention of the world was focused on a spit of low, sandy land on the east coast of humid Florida, something remarkably similar was taking place nearly half a hemisphere away. Far, far to the north of thc Saturn V launching pad. So far to the north that it was ignored. No one paid any attention to such places. They were the habitat of polar bears and seals, narwhals and arctic hares, howling gales and blinding blizzards.

Located in the high Arctic on an island so rugged and isolated and difficult to reach that it was shunned even by itinerant Inuit hunters, something extraordinary was taking place. At first glance it involved a base and a launching site that would immediately have reminded a startled visitor of the historic event currently unfolding far to the south in Florida. Closer inspection coupled with a little knowledge of rockets and astronautics, however, would have indicated that the major components involved were very different indeed from those located on the Atlantic shore. They looked like nothing that had ever been premiered in magazines such as *Aviation Week* or *Sky & Telescope* or even *Analog*.

Some of them, in fact, looked downright alien.

The ship currently standing on the single camouflaged launching pad resembled the hulking Saturn V moon rocket about as much as a child's balsa wood glider resembled a jet fighter. It was sleek and winged and boasted only a single stage instead of the Saturn's three. Assorted decidedly unaerodynamic bulges and accoutrements protruding from its sides hinted at a technology that was tens, perhaps hundreds of years in advance of the best that the Florida facility could send skyward. Even the monitoring equipment within the single low, snow-covered structure that served as local Mission Control was far in advance of anything in use at Kennedy.

Identification of any kind was noticeably absent both within the heated confines of the control station and on the ship itself. Anyone standing outside in the frigid, snow-whipped arctic air might have seen a name on the side of the silently waiting ship: GHOST 1. A concise designation whose full meaning anyone not intimately involved with the highly secret project would have been unable to grasp.

There was a small sign, almost an afterthought, on the main entrance to Mission Control.

ALPHA BASE—SECTOR SEVEN

Not very informative, that signage. Deliberately so. Not that any unauthorized pedestrians were likely to wander in off the frozen Arctic Ocean and inquire as to its meaning. At least one element of the forthcoming furtive launch would have been familiar, however. Already decades old, the traditional countdown could not be improved upon.

"T minus thirty seconds and counting. SS *Ghost* reports all systems good to go." Fighting the chill wind, outdoor observers made last-minute checks of their instruments.

"T minus twenty-five seconds. T minus fifteen seconds. Guidance systems online. Drive system initiation . . . five, four, three, two, one, zero."

The sound that emerged from the stern of the strange ship was silkier than that produced by the liquid-oxygen–based propellant that powered the Saturn V. This ship was propelled by an entirely different combination of reactants. It showed not only in the different pitch of the engines but also in the fact that there was less fire and smoke. Something radically new was lifting this ship aloft. Something special, secret, and derived from sources outside of and unknown to NASA's exclusive group of scientists and engineers.

"Propulsion system is a go. We have liftoff." Even the controller's voice differed markedly from that of his counterpart at Kennedy. It was as if he was not only an engineer but something more as well. A member of a branch of government whose interests included specialties and endeavors beyond the exploration of space.

"*Ghost One* is off," the man declared coolly. "Thirty-two minutes, sixteen seconds past the hour, we have liftoff of *Ghost One*." A moment later he added, "The tower is cleared."

From the remarkable, rapidly accelerating craft a male voice responded, "Roll program engaged."

Within the tightly sealed structure, so very different from mission control in Florida, a technician seated at his monitor declared, "Captain Walker is reporting that *Ghost* is into the roll-and-pitch program."

Watching his own screen, the tech next to him murmured softly, "If all preparatory calculations prove out, that should put *Ghost One* on a heading and departure well away from *Apollo Eleven.*"

Standing between them, an older man let his attention wander from one monitor to the next. He was nodding to himself as he spoke. "So far, so good. While the world is transfixed by *Apollo*, our ship will slip away unnoticed." He smiled. "Like a ghost through the atmosphere. Every telescope on Earth will be watching the moon rocket." Straightening, he called across to another technician. "Inform headquarters the baby bird that hatched last year has finally spread its wings. Send the relevant details maximum-encrypted."

There was a lot more room on the advanced prototype called *Ghost* than on the *Apollo*. Smothered in their launch seats, the three astronauts presently bound for the moon would have been astonished at the other vessel's comparatively spacious interior. Blasting through the atmosphere, the clandestine craft left behind the familiar bounds of Earth as it soared spaceward.

Every possible precaution notwithstanding, a pair of amateur astronomers did take notice of the launch. One was located near Kiruna, Sweden, and the other just outside Moose Jaw, Canada. The first was convinced he was drunk and disregarded what he saw through his telescope. The second received a visit from several members of a branch of the Royal Canadian Mounted Police that by all accounts did not actually exist. There was talk of meteors. There was mention of a visit to a certain mental institution. Something was said to both sky-watchers about confiscation of equipment in the name of national security.

Nothing further was heard from either man, ever.

Ghost's unique propulsion system shut down as it glided toward the stars. The craft was now free of much of Earth's gravity. On board, sighs of relief from the crew mixed with awed exclamations as the view out the forward port steadied.

So that was what the homeworld looked like from space, each of them mused silently and separately. Blue and white and beautiful. And small, oh so small.

Sam Walker would enjoy the view later. As mission commander his time for sightseeing, such as it was, lay well in the future. His free time being inversely proportional to his responsibilities, he would be lucky to have a moment or two entirely to himself—and that moment was not now. Leaning forward slightly, he directed his voice toward the nearest pickup.

"SSAB Command, this is *Ghost One*. Temporary orbit achieved, and we're positioning for the first solar directional burn. All systems are green."

Though he knew he sounded calm and confident, that was nothing more than his professional self operating on instinct. The truth was that he had never been so tense in his life. Part of it came from the strain attendant on managing a successful liftoff. A lot was due to the knowledge that the grand journey he and his crew had embarked upon could wind up becoming a suicide mission, though not planned officially as such. Part test, part reconnaissance, *Ghost 1*'s mission was to first determine if the ship was truly spaceworthy and then explore the solar system for any signs of beings similar to the Ice Man. Sector Seven wanted to know if an attack might be staging on the far side of Jupiter. Using the advanced technology of *Ghost 1*, they should be able to complete the mission and return to earth within six months. Though the odds were largely against completing a successful round trip, Walker had believed from the first time he had been exposed to the applicable calculations that the ship *could* complete its targeted journey and still make it safely back.

Privately, he had made it his primary mission to get his crew home. That was not what he told his superiors, of course. Experience had taught him that not only was it unnecessary to commit his personal intentions to paper, often it was best not to even mention them to anyone else. Yes, he had his official orders. Their mission was to get out to the edge of the solar system before attempting to return home. And yes, he had his own priorities. If all went optimally, he would be able to fulfill both. *So far, so good,* he told himself.

Besides, there were precedents for this kind of mission. Columbus, for example. Tell the queen and king one thing and when they're no longer looking over your shoulder, shift your responsibility to your crew.

Rotating his seat, he scrutinized the carefully picked team. Like him, every one of them was a volunteer. Like him, they had read and signed the pertinent waivers. Each of them knew the deal, knew what they were getting into (as much as anyone could know). All were aware of the risks the mission entailed. Thrown together in haste and compelled to work and study overtime, they had melded into an efficient team during the simulations. If getting back to Earth was a long shot, well, so was just getting successfully off the planet. And they had done that. He thought of Columbus again. That was another long shot that had panned out.

Despite making no attempt to conceal the risks, there had been no shortage of applicants. Life was short, and the number of highly trained specialists ready to give up TV and movies, dull food and duller conversation, for a chance to push the boundaries of human knowledge was extensive. As the first one to be officially assigned to the project, Walker was not surprised. He was one of them.

The voice of Mission Control was already starting to

show signs of breaking up. Static crackled as those on the ground manipulated their instrumentation in order to maintain contact. "Sounds good, *Ghost One*. Everything looks fine from here, too. Stand by."

The smooth voice that spoke up softly behind Walker was full of jaunty resignation. "You do know there's a good chance we're all going to die out here, right?"

Walker turned around and narrowed his gaze as he glared at Craig Clarkson. "Do you mind?" he snapped. "You prepared for this just like the rest of us. It's a little late for second thoughts, and if now you're feeling a morbid turn of mind, do the rest of us a favor and keep it to yourself." He paused briefly for emphasis. "You can feel however you like as long as you do your job. Just keep it between your ears."

The systems engineer looked properly abashed. "I'm sorry, Captain." Clarkson mustered a wan smile. "Guess I'm more nervous than I thought I'd be. You think about how you're going to react, you talk to the psych boys about it, but there's really no way to prepare. Not for something nobody's done before or might ever do again. Being first is one thing. Getting yourself ready to be the last is something else." Looking past Walker, he stared out at the nothingness that made up the view out the foreport. "Making it back—it's all theoretical. Not like *Apollo*, where the paradigms are known. This trip is based on a bunch of advanced math and new physics that hold up okay on paper but might not do so in reality."

"That's what we're here to find out." Walker did his best to project confidence. "Once again—everyone was apprised of the risks before they signed on for this mission. As systems engineer you ought to be more familiar with them than any of us." He mustered a smile. "It's all going to work, just like the theorists laid it out before they started design on the *Ghost*. It's going to work—and we're going to make it back."

"I am delighted to hear that you think so." Clarkson paused. "No spacecraft has ever been tested under the kinds of conditions that we're going to be subjected to on this mission. There's no way to simulate them. A wind tunnel is one thing, interplanetary space another. I'll do my best to keep my opinions to myself, but forgive me if I'm a little skeptical."

Walker looked past him, peering around the cabin and meeting the expectant stares of every member of the crew. The only one who ignored him was the second-in-command, Jacob Thompson. A damn fine pilot, as the Academy would say. At the moment he was concentrating on his station's readouts and gauges. Thompson was quite content to let Walker talk while he monitored the ship.

Farther back, Michael Avery was in figurative if not literal heaven. The mission's chief science officer, Avery had recorded enough new information between the time of liftoff and now to keep him busy for years—and they were just starting out. He'd been part of the team that had developed the initial *Ghost 1* project. He was all scientist, to the point that he wouldn't care if they failed to make it home so long as he had enough time to transmit the knowledge he had acquired in the course of the journey. If the science survived, he considered himself expendable.

And of course, there was Maria Gonzalez.

In addition to handling communications and having to fend off the by-now-tiresome references to her as "Uhura," she was responsible for chronicling everything that happened on the journey and making sure the information was successfully transmitted back to Mission Control. She was efficient and good company. As commander, Walker prized the latter attribute as much as the former.

They were a good mix, he told himself. Each

exceptionally competent in their chosen field. Maybe not perfect, perhaps not the very best, but given the constraints and requirements of the most unusual mission in the history of the covert Sector Seven space program, certainly the best to have made themselves available.

Once he was sure he had everyone's attention, including Thompson's, Walker leaned forward and dropped his folded hands between his spread legs, adopting as informal a pose as he could manage in the absence of gravity.

"Well, we've made it this far." Relieved laughter and the isolated edgy glance greeted his observation. "Not too bad for a groundbreaking mission."

"Atmosphere breaking," put in Avery, essaying a weak attempt at a joke.

Walker appreciated it, even if nobody laughed. "We've each of us spent years preparing for this. I don't need to reiterate that if we're going to get through this mission successfully, we've got to rely on one another. Everyone assists everyone else. There are no polymaths on this ship, but each of you has at least some experience in more than one area of expertise. Or to put it in non-technical but entirely relevant terms, everybody watches everybody else's back. There's no turning around now." Though it was hardly necessary to do so, he paused a moment to let that sink in.

"This ship *will* perform. It will perform not only because those who designed and built it intended for it to do so, but because this is the best possible crew to make it work. It will perform if we have to get out and push. I just want you to know, each and every one of you, that you have my solemn promise: no matter what happens, no matter what unexpected challenges and difficulties we may encounter, no matter what the instruments say, I will find a way to get all of us safely home again."

Except for the soft humming of equipment, it was dead silent in the cabin. Someone might have led a cheer, except there was no time. Mission Control was on the horn again and would not be denied.

"*Ghost One,* this is SSAB Command. We're all set down here and ready to track you on the first solar burn. Running final systems check."

Walker ignored the call. "If anyone is consumed by doubts, now's the time to dump 'em." He did not look in Clarkson's direction. "We're privileged to be on the most advanced, the most complex, and the most safety-redundant spacecraft mankind has yet built. It can do amazing things. Things I wouldn't have dreamed were possible if I weren't a direct part of the project. We're going to complete our mission and then we're going to go home. Is that clear?"

This time the voice from the ground did not interrupt. Everyone chorused their agreement—albeit some more energetically than others. It was enough.

"Good." Swiveling his seat, Walker turned back to the main console. "Now let's do this, and go where no man has gone before."

"Or woman," Maria added definitively.

Walker smiled to himself. He had deliberately left her the opening and, sure enough, she had jumped on it. Highly trained technicians were more predictable than most.

"SSAB Command, this is *Ghost One.* All systems are green, we are a go for first burn on my mark." He glanced at Jake, who nodded.

"Mark in five, four, three, two, one—mark!"

Careful not to let anyone see him, Walker let out the tiniest possible sigh of relief when the engines successfully fired anew. Everyone was pushed back into their seats. Maybe one day, he thought, there would come a time when onboard computers were advanced enough to allow a crew to relax entirely. But that time was not yet, and Thompson kept a firm grip on the controls. While this was not the time for making manual course corrections, there was no harm in being prepared to do so should the need present itself. Besides, Thompson was a pilot, and pilots disliked handing over the flying of their craft to a machine. Probably always would, Walker mused. Anyway, if the burn set them slightly off course it should be easy enough to correct. Headed outward from Earth, their first target would be hard to miss.

With its unprecedented engines firing smoothly and in concert, *Ghost 1* headed straight toward the sun.

Construction of the Sector Seven High Arctic Base had demanded the utilization of America's finest cold-weather engineers, the implementing of new technology, and a ton of money funneled through various congressional "black" appropriations. The base was not yet finished and might never be. It had been a work in progress ever since the discovery of the alien frozen in the ice. The bulk of its facilities were underground—everything from fuel storage tanks to food prep areas. Those facilities that by their nature and purpose could not be buried had been carefully designed so that the visible portion of the complex resembled a typical Arctic research station. The launching pad with its attendant paraphernalia was located on the most inaccessible part of the island, concealed from casual sight on three sides by high, steep-sided mountains.

An astute observer stumbling on the complex might, if he or she were particularly perceptive, note that for a research facility there was a substantial military presence. Much more than might be needed, say, to safeguard any new information recently obtained on the reproductive habits of the arctic hare, or on the migration patterns of the right whale.

Intricate and large as it was, the launch complex had also been designed to be, if not truly portable, at least capable of being rapidly erected and disassembled. It was the latter process that was under way at the moment. Swarms of technicians operating Big Machines were disassembling the tower, communications, fueling facilities, and much more. Even the blast pad was swiftly and efficiently camouflaged so that from the air it would look like nothing more than a landlocked chunk of ice. Huge sections of gantry, lengths of conduit, prefabricated chunks of support structure were taken apart like the components of a giant Erector set and trundled underground or packed neatly into cavernous waiting bunkers. Those engaged in the difficult, dangerous, and well-rehearsed task feared accident more than the wind or cold.

Though he, too, was presently functioning belowground, Colonel Thomas Kinnear was gazing out through a wide, triple-paned window. Beyond, teams of technicians scurried about like termites in the vast subterranean chamber as they prepared to move the Ice Man—also known among those charged with protecting and preserving it as "that damned alien monstrosity." Over Kinnear's vociferous objections the government had determined to relocate the Ice Man and the bulk of the team assigned to studying him to a new facility in the lower forty-eight.

"A major mistake," Kinnear had insisted when the possibility of the move was being debated. "We're damn near invisible up here. What with the day-to-day weather, the storms that blow in without warning, and the isolation, no one comes anywhere near us. Never mind Inuit. Probing reporters prefer big hotels with warm bars. The same thing goes for curious reps working for other governments. Aside from being able to more easily maintain secrecy and security, there are scientific issues that I don't think have been fully addressed. For example, we don't know what moving the Ice Man might do. He might be affected by the mere process of movement. What happens if something goes wrong and he thaws out?"

Given his status within the project Kinnear's concerns had been taken seriously, examined in detail—and promptly dismissed. Too many anxious (overanxious, Kinnear felt) researchers had wanted to speed up their progress on reverse-engineering the alien. That deliberate process had already led to a number of important breakthroughs in at least three fields. The *Ghost 1* was only the most prominent and dramatic consequence of that work. Too many scientists and their political patrons believed that the only way to accelerate the progress they were making was to relocate the Ice Man to a place where research could be carried out without the need to shuttle scientists back and forth to one of the most remote regions of the Arctic.

They were also anxious to observe him in the same facility and with the same instruments that were being used to study a certain peculiar otherworldly Cube that bore markings similar to those that had been found on the frozen bipedal entity.

"Then bring the damn Cube to our Arctic facility!" Kinnear had bellowed at the panel that was charged with discussing the move. "It's a far safer and more secure location, and the Cube would be a lot easier to shift than the Ice Man."

"Not necessarily," he had been told without explanation. The members of the panel had been adamant. "The Cube can't be moved." What was more infuriating than anything else was that despite his high security clearance, nobody would tell him why.

Tom Kinnear had been in the military all his adult life. That had not prevented him from questioning orders he did not understand or believed were unsupported by evidence and logic. When he had been approached about heading up a secret government project doing extremely classified work the likes of which he had never heard of, he had jumped at the opportunity. Most of the time he was proud of what took place under his command. The operation in the Arctic operated on the cutting edge of military and scientific technology. Boundaries were probed and exceeded every day. The recent successful launch of *Ghost 1* had been a high point, the culmination of years of hard work and experimentation.

Today, however, left a lot to be desired. If the higher-ups in charge of the project valued his opinion so highly, then why had they chosen to ignore it this time? He did his best to set his anger aside, even as his opinion had been set aside.

At least he couldn't fault the steps that had been taken to ensure that the Ice Man remained frozen for the difficult, clandestine journey south. The special container that had been built to hold him had been designed to look from the outside like nothing more than an oversized shipping container. For the duration of the journey it would be accompanied both within and without by technicians familiar with the artifact's unique requirements. In addition to standard refrigeration, continuously recycled liquid nitrogen would be used to ensure that the body remained frozen. The scheme had been constructed with backups for the backups.

Watching from the office as preparations continued, Kinnear prided himself on knowing not only the names but also the backgrounds of every one of the officers and technicians assigned to the project. It was an ability that would stand him in good stead should he ever follow through with a lingering desire to enter politics. Given his professional history, that was a possibility that would always be slim.

"What is your background, Colonel Kinnear?"

"Can't tell you that, sir."

"Well then, what was your specialty during your time in the military?"

"Can't tell you that, ma'am."

"Can you tell the voters *anything* that you've accomplished over the past ten years?"

"Well, I was hooked on cigarettes—but I'm off them now."

No, much as he might wish to consider it, a public life was one that was probably closed to him.

Not to everyone who had worked in Sector Seven, however. He found himself focusing on one of the busy supervisors below: Lieutenant Jensen. Good man, fine soldier. Always upbeat, always ready with a smile. Knew not only his own assignment but usually those of everyone he was working with as well. Kinnear suddenly found himself frowning at nothing in particular. Always curious about others' specialties, Jensen was. A sign of exceptional intelligence, or something else?

In the space of a couple of minutes he had gone from admiration of Jensen to the first stirrings of suspicion. It was part of his job, of course. But it hinted at a paranoia that stretched beyond the professional. That could happen to someone who spent too much time working for Sector Seven. Kinnear was sharp enough to recognize the signs, and he didn't much care for the way they made him feel.

He'd already made up his mind. If the powers that be weren't going to take his advice, then there was no point in knocking himself out to provide it. As soon as the Ice Man move was completed and that portion of the high Arctic facility closed, he was going to apply for retirement. The government owed him a healthy pension, and he was still young enough to enjoy every dollar of it.

He had it all planned. Thinking about it had helped him through some difficult times at the base. He was going to move to the Virgin Islands. No more relentless cold and ice and wind. No more enigmatic frozen, alien bodies. Buy a fishing boat, run charters, sip rum, maybe even meet someone and get married. When you couldn't tell anyone where you worked, what you worked on, or when the government might call you away to some far-off land with more consonants than vowels in its name, you didn't have much of an opportunity to develop a social life. When he was younger, he'd had one. He still remembered what it was like, and he was looking forward to resuming where he had left off in his twenties.

One thing that would ease his mind was if the Russians would quit snooping around. As far as they were concerned the Arctic was their personal backyard. Reports of flyovers by high-altitude spy craft were unconfirmed, but they recurred with a nagging regularity. He couldn't do anything about such rumors. Just as he couldn't do anything about the Soviet atomic-powered icebreaker that had "strayed" dangerously close to the island where the station was located while engaged in purely "scientific" research.

Well, he'd be done with it all soon enough. Thoughts of warm weather, cold beer, and fighting fish pushed images of glowering, vodka-swilling Soviet agents out of his mind. They made him as gloomy as the subject matter. Why not concentrate on something positive, like the launch? It had gone faultlessly, even to the fortuitous presence of the intervening storm front that had masked events from any eyes that might have been turned north from the nearest communities. The social as well as the physical aspects of the project were proceeding as planned. While the population of the planet was transfixed by the flight of *Apollo 11, Ghost 1* had taken off in the opposite direction entirely unobserved.

The several monitors mounted in the console off to his right showed various locations in Mission Control. All was comparatively quiet. The last flurry of activity and anxiety had accompanied the ship's first burn, which had gone off as smoothly as the launch itself. It was time for exhausted technicians to lean back, relax, and exchange notes and observations.

Staring into the hangar, he watched as dozens of technicians operating a raft of machinery prepared to shift the Ice Man. One day they'd know exactly what the artifact was, maybe even where it had come from. One day. Perhaps this mission would help bring some enlightenment. Having spent so much time in the company of the frozen alien, he would like to share in those eventual revelations.

But not at the expense, he told himself, of zipping over blue water in a fast boat with the sun warming his face and friends at his side who had stars in their eyes instead of on their shoulders.

"Captain, we're on final approach for slingshot." Thompson spoke without looking up from the console. "If you wish to abort, the determination needs to be made in the next couple of minutes."

Walker looked around at the rest of his crew—Clarkson, Gonzalez, Avery. Everyone was relaxed, attentive at their respective stations, and waiting for his response. Expectation flavored the air inside the ship.

"All elements green, all indicators positive. Nobody has to go to the bathroom?" He smiled, and was rewarded in kind. "I'd say we're good to go." Turning forward, he clicked TRANSMIT and addressed the pickup. "SSAB Command, this is *Ghost One*. We are approaching coordinates for slingshot and all systems are go."

They were far enough out now for there to be a noticeable time-response delay. Static bedecked the response but did not garble it. "*Ghost One,* this is SSAB Command. We copy. Everything looks good from down here, too. You are a go for slingshot. Following burn and concurrent with rotation we anticipate a communications blackout of approximately six standard hours. Good luck, and we'll talk to you again on the other side."

"SSAB Command, this is *Ghost One,*" Walker repeated. "Thanks for the good words. We'll talk to you soon." He turned to Thompson and nodded. "Let's see if this thing can make the kind of speed the math boys have claimed."

Internally, he was far more nervous than he let on. No human-built craft had ever come anywhere near the velocities the *Ghost* was about to attempt. Compared with what they were going to try during slingshot, the *Apollo* spacecraft on its way to the moon would appear to be standing still. He was less worried about a failure of the unique propulsion system than he was about the fabric of the ship holding together.

"And try not to mess up the angles," Clarkson was saying, "or we're all going to come out the other side as crispy critters. If we come out at all."

"Can we toss him out as we go by, Captain?" Thompson's attention never wandered from the controls.

Walker chuckled. "Naw, Jake, we'll keep him for ballast. Besides, we wouldn't want to be without our engineer, now, would we? What if something really critical like the food prep system were to break and someone actually had to do some work on this thing?"

His comment broke any remaining ice. *Ice,* he mused. *Hold that thought.*

"True enough," the copilot conceded. "Ready for burn on your mark."

Walker closed his eyes briefly, considering what they were about to do. If the calculations were off by even a tiny amount, they would find themselves caught by the

Sun's massive gravity field. *And me without my sunglasses,* he reflected. If those who had run and rerun the relevant computations back on Earth had misplaced a cosign or a decimal, he and his crew would perish unknown and unrecognized, a qualified footnote in the history of Sector Seven. If the calculations were correct but the ship failed to function as intended, they would still die. The opportunities for a lingering and unrecognized demise were manifold. Truly a mission fraught with possibilities.

A little late, he reminded himself, to second-guess having put in his name when the system had originally asked for volunteers.

Opening his eyes, he smiled across at Thompson. The copilot was staring at him. "Sorry, Jake. I was trying to remember if I'd brought along my suntan lotion."

Thompson nodded somberly. "I've got some extra. With cocoa butter."

Walker grinned back. "Okay, let's do this. On my mark in five, four, three, two, one . . . mark!"

Thompson flipped three switches in rapid succession. Engines that previously had existed only in the imagination of science-fiction writers came to life, and *Ghost 1* accelerated at incredible speed toward the far side of the sun.

The cosmos is—big. Incredibly, inconceivably, mind-stretchingly big. Not all of its parts are congruent or easily assessed. There exist expanses never observed, entire immense stretches humankind has yet to examine in any kind of detail, places where the familiar does not and never has existed. In these regions roam organisms who know nothing of Earth and its bustling, self-centered people. Entities with interests and demands of their own. They operate according to laws unto themselves. Some are benign, while others would brush aside the moral conventions and needs of human beings as effortlessly and thoughtlessly as a person would flick an ant off a table.

Sight of the *Nemesis,* for example, would not be reassuring to a human observer. Enormous, dark, and intimidating by design, it represented the epitome of Decepticon science. For all that, the black and gray metal and composites of which it was constructed were not those of a warship but of a transport. It carried representatives of an order that had dedicated itself to the total destruction of its enemies. The war in which they were engaged had gone on now for millennia. That did not trouble those on board. Composed of inorganic components, powered by energies far longer-lasting than those that gave life to simple carbon-based life-forms, they viewed time itself from an entirely different perspective. They did not find unusual a war whose length would have appalled far shorter-lived humans.

The conflict would finally end only when the last of their adversaries had been eradicated.

The bipedal shape that sat in the command chair was sleek, powerful, and resembled nothing living on Earth. Call him Starscream. At the moment he was doing his best to ignore the continual harping and bickering of his fellow Decepticons. For more centuries than he cared to think about they had scoured the galaxy, searching for the Allspark and for their long-lost leader, Megatron. At least, that was their stated objective.

In reality, the Decepticons were no group mind. For example, as far as Starscream was concerned the *Nemesis* was engaged in a fool's errand. He was convinced that Megatron was long dead. There had not been a signal or a sign from their erstwhile leader for thousands of years. His hope was that, given time, the others would come to realize that he, Starscream, was and always had been more powerful than Megatron and should be acclaimed their new superior. That hope had yet to materialize. Despite the considerable amount of time that had passed in fruitless searching, the other Decepticons on board insisted on continuing the quest for their lost leader. Logic dictated that they were wasting resources as well as time. Far more sensible to terminate the search and return to Cybertron. Or perhaps find a new world to conquer.

To Starscream this persistence in the face of reason suggested not strength but weakness. He had come to the conclusion that the only way to snap his fellow Decepticons out of their tunnel thinking and draw them away from futile hoping was to give them a visible, important victory over their hated enemies, the autonomous bots. To be as effective as possible it should be a triumph as brutal as it would be decisive. He, of course, would be the one to conceive of and lead them to that conquest. Afterward, while they were celebrating his leadership, he could concentrate all their efforts on finding the missing Allspark. Once the autonomous bots had been eliminated and he had possession of the Allspark, his ultimate rule of Cybertron could commence. Only then would memory of Megatron's reign recede into Decepticon history.

One who was consistently fractious even by Decepticon standards turned from where he was sitting in another mammoth chair. The designation *Barricade* more than fit his personality. For the moment, though, he was more focused on carrying out his assignment than in fighting with anyone or anything within reach.

"Starscream, we have locked onto a signal that appears . . ." He hesitated—a mental condition unusual in its own right for a bot. "It would seem to be almost Cybertronian in origin."

Startled out of contemplation of his own nascent wondrousness, Starscream looked over at his fellow Decepticon. "Cybertronian? In this sector? That's highly unlikely. Can you be more specific?"

"It is a beacon of some kind, on the move." Barricade studied the readouts, absorbing far more information in a few seconds than any human could have in a similar span of months. "The wavelengths being employed are more akin to our standards than anything else that we have come across in a very, very long time."

"Location?" Though he kept his tone carefully neutral, Starscream was less than overjoyed at the report. Not *now. Not after all these years . . .*

"It is still in motion." Barricade continued to scrutinize the multiple readouts. "The source is a great distance from here, barely within range of our deep-field sensors. Now it is . . . " His voice trailed off.

"It is *what*?" Starscream demanded to know.

"It's gone." Barricade ran a hurried recheck. He did not expect the original information to change, and it did not. "Based on a final distortion of wavelengths, the source of the signal appears to have entered a wormhole. The drop-off in strength was consistent and unswerving, so it must be presumed to have been deliberate."

No need for presumption, Starscream decided. "Besides us, there is only one group of beings capable of entering a wormhole with the intention of utilizing it for navigation: Autobots." He voiced the concision with undisguised disgust.

"Only one group that we are *aware* of." Barricade was always ready to argue. "It is a significantly large galaxy, and we have explored only a small portion of it."

Starscream was not in the mood. "Spare me any revelations of the painfully self-evident. Is there any way to track the signal source?"

Barricade considered this for a moment. "Through a wormhole? Not the signal itself, but it is possible that the source might leave behind a trailing energy signature. It depends on how long and how strong the latter lingers."

"Then you'd best not waste any more time in indifferent discussion," Starscream informed him curtly. "If it ties to the Autobots, we shall pursue and destroy. Too long have they evaded ultimate destruction."

"And what," exclaimed the voice from behind them of the one called Blackout, "of our abiding search for the Allspark and Megatron?"

Starscream allowed himself a moment of manic amusement. "Did you not hear what Barricade just pointed out? It is a large galaxy. However, I am always open to productive suggestion. I presume you have a precise notion as to where we might search for either of the aforementioned?"

Blackout looked away. "Not at this time," he admitted unhappily.

"Then contain yourself and conserve your energies for useful pursuits." Through voice and energy Starscream dominated his surroundings. "I lead the Decepticons, and I will decide our path."

"As you command, Starscream." Blackout instantly reverted to modified deferential conversation mode. "Of course."

Ignoring the subtly sarcastic tone of his subordinate, Starscream turned his attention back to Barricade. "Track that signal source. Do not lose it, wormhole or no wormhole. Here is a perfect opportunity for you to display your mastery of physics. Curiosity needs slaking—we must identify whatever it was that was transmitting."

Barricade readily indicated agreement and turned back to his instruments.

Aware that Blackout was still hovering behind him, Starscream murmured, "You may leave, Blackout. Unless you have something more to contribute beyond the same tiring arguments concerning what we should be or should not be doing."

"No, Starscream." The other Decepticon performed a stiff little half bow. "I have concluded my input." Turning, he departed.

Starscream waited impatiently for Barricade to respond with further evaluation. Or even better, a series of coordinates. Track and follow, track and follow. The same vastness that was interstellar space made it easy to run down a target once it had been located. If indeed it was the wandering Autobots, those disgusting mechanoids would offer the perfect opportunity for him to assert his true leadership once and for all.

These fools will eventually realize that Megatron is not coming back from the dead, he mused. Patience, he counseled himself, was simultaneously one of the most effective and most overlooked tools of leadership.

That, and cunning.

The presence of large dollops of dark matter and other arcane fragments of physical reality notwithstanding, the galaxy was largely void. Even at inconceivable velocities, the principal characteristic of traveling through such emptiness was extreme tedium. Only occasionally was this interrupted by episodes of intense danger. On the long-range viewer before him, Optimus Prime gazed at stars that streaked and flared and seemed to move. They didn't, of course. It was only the *Ark* that moved.

The ongoing distortion he was looking at was nothing more than an optical illusion. When traveling through a wormhole it was the universe without that appeared unnatural, when in fact it was the objects doing the journeying that were terrifically distorted. He looked down at himself. His metal body and the deck below his feet appeared perfectly normal. That was because his senses and perception were as distorted as everything else that was traveling inside the physical anomaly. What the *Ark* and its contents looked like from normal space no one knew. No ship or instrument could get close enough to a wormhole to have a good look inside without succumbing to its gravitational effects.

Under the direction of his fellow Autobots, the *Ark* stayed in the center of the wormhole. Stray too far toward the gravitational periphery and it could be torn to bits, reduced in an instant to a brief flurry of subatomic particles. He was not concerned. His companions were the best of their kind, the most skilled at their various tasks. They did not need supervision from him.

The *Ark* was, and had been, their home for a long time now. Existing solely on a ship as they scanned the galaxy in search of something that sent out a signal only once every thousand years—a limited signal at that—had been wearying. At least the *Ark* had been conceived and built with space sufficient to comfortably accommodate its chosen crew. While the spherical vessel was a refuge from the uncaring and often hostile universe outside, no matter how many modifications were performed to its interior it would never be home.

They had visited myriad worlds. Some had been wondrous, some welcoming, others blasted and empty, a few openly hostile. Those traveling on the *Ark* had acquired an extraordinary amount of new knowledge. For all of that, what Optimus and his crew wished more than anything else was simply to return home. Even if Cybertron, their homeworld, was now little more than a shell of its former splendid self. Devastated by its inhabitants in the course of unnecessary and unending warfare, it had ultimately been abandoned altogether when the Allspark, the source of life itself, had gone hurtling off into the cosmos. That had been—too many years ago, he reflected.

Even after the Allspark was located and recovered—and it *would* be found, Optimus insisted to himself—and brought back to Cybertron, countless additional centuries of work awaited the war's survivors. The conflict that had raged between the Autobots and the Decepticons had ravaged the entire surface of the planet. Whole cities had been laid to waste and millions of individual sparks extinguished. All that, he knew, could be laid at the feet of one particular Decepticon: the malevolent, power-crazed Megatron.

Thankfully, that dangerous demagogue had long since vanished into the depths of interstellar space. He had rushed off Cybertron in pursuit of the escaping Allspark. Had he found it, Optimus was certain that he would have returned long ago. Precisely what had happened to the self-declared dictator of Cybertron no one knew. In his haste to recover the Allspark, it was entirely possible Megatron had paid insufficient attention to mundanities like navigation. He could have intersected orbits with an asteroid or a comet. All things were possible. Maybe, Optimus mused, the maddened despot had encountered a lifeform even more evil and more powerful than he had been. It was a big galaxy, and not even sentient bots knew what lurked in its deep corners or out among the stars of its spiral arms.

Despite Megatron's continuing silence Optimus remained wary. Weary of the seemingly interminable search. A part of him was more than ready to admit that Cybertron's most dangerous denizen was most likely dead. The burden of being Prime, the responsibility of overseeing all the Autobots, combined to weigh heavily on him. But now was not the time for mistakes.

Especially not when there was a vague possibility they might be close.

The ship quivered slightly and began to slow as the field of stars that had moments ago been sliding past like streaks of paint started to resemble a more normal stellar environment. The *Ark* was emerging from the wormhole near its intended destination: a cluster of stars from which a faint but distinctive signal speeding across the reaches of deep space might be the echo of a long-ago call from the Allspark. It was certainly a more convincing indicator than any they had detected thus far.

Searching an entire star cluster—even a small one, even at the speeds they could travel—was a time-consuming process. He chose to hold out hope that the signal they were currently tracing might mean the conclusion of their journey rather than merely another dead end.

"Ironhide, Jazz, Bumblebee." Optimus locked ocular lenses with each of his associates as he named them. "Once we are fully clear of the gravitational effects of the wormhole, we will leave the ship on the edge of this star cluster. You three will depart with me; we will then split up to scan the cluster one quadrant at a time. Ratchet, I want you to remain with the ship and continue to monitor the echoes of that signal."

"As you decree, Optimus," Ratchet rumbled.

Their leader was agreeable to additional discussion, but none of his colleagues volunteered any objection to the plan. With nothing more to be said, they headed for the bay located at the base of the *Ark*. There they would transform into their cometary protoforms and begin the process of scouring the indicated quadrants for the source of the inscrutable signal.

Cybertron, he thought as he led the others downward through the great ship. *By now it was little more than a memory.* With luck, and perseverance, and an enormous amount of effort and hard work it might one day be again something else, something more. A place of life and study and awareness. Something that again belonged to those who had evolved and developed on its once benign, welcoming surface.

Even a sentient machine can get homesick.

On the far side of the sun, *Ghost 1* achieved the kind of speed hitherto thought only theoretically possible. Exploding from the star's surface, a solar flare reached outward for the minuscule vessel that had already shot on past. Given an immense gravity boost, the *Ghost* continued to accelerate beyond bounds thought intolerable—and then faster still. Faster even than had been predicted.

While it represented an extraordinary achievement for all mankind, that particular development, Walker realized, wasn't good. Something was not right. They had not only achieved a hoped-for goal, but exceeded it. Kicking one's car up to a couple of hundred miles an hour might also be considered by some to be a great accomplishment—unless the road one happens to be testing it on dead-ends at a cliff.

And there was something else. Another development he could detect without having to check readouts for confirmation.

Through the port he could see the light from distant stars begin to blur and bend, as though the universe around them were somehow being stretched like a rubber band. Stars should be pinpoints or dots of brilliant light—not longitudinal streaks.

"What the hell . . . ?"

"Captain, we've exceeded all predicted maximums!" As frightening as were Clarkson's words, even more unsettling was the fact that the usually phlegmatic engineer had raised his voice. "This—" He made one more disbelieving check of the instrumentation. "—this rate of acceleration is unsustainable! The ship will tear itself apart."

"Jake, is it holding together?" Walker was amazed at his own self-control. He stared hard at his copilot. Thompson's fingers were dancing over the main console, trying to make sense of the impossible. He was utterly focused on his job, locked in as effectively as if someone had thrown a switch in his brain. Fine for work, but bad for interpersonal communication.

Clarkson wasn't the only one who could raise his voice. "Jake!" Walker growled loudly. "I need a structural analysis, stat."

Inconveniently, the ship chose that moment to give a sudden and unpleasant shudder. Since there was nothing to affect it externally, the source of the tremor had to be internal. Outside, the stretched stars continued to make nonsense of normality.

Lifting his hands from the instrumentation, Thompson slowly leaned back in his seat.

"We're still in one piece. I think. As the math boys

predicted, engaging maximum acceleration simultaneously activated artificial gravity." Reaching into a pocket, he removed a small stylus, held it out parallel to his chair, and dropped it. It promptly hit the floor. "Cool. Talk about your significant side effects . . . "

"That's what I need," Walker muttered. "Convincing absolutes. Vector? Are we still on course to swing out and return to Earth?"

"I have no idea, Captain."

Walker frowned at the man he expected to supply him with comprehensible answers. "What do you mean, you have no idea?"

Thompson turned to face his superior. He looked dazed. "We're heading out of the system at an angle about eighty degrees to the ecliptic. Not toward Earth. Not toward any of the planets. No way are we going to be able to slingshot around Jupiter the way it was planned for the return home."

Walker struggled to digest this. It made about as much sense as the fractured starfield visible outside the ship. "That," he replied slowly and carefully, "doesn't make any sense."

A thin, humorless smile creased the copilot's face. "Excellent. We're in full agreement."

Walker resisted the urge to smack his second-in-command hard across the mouth. Thompson was not being hysterical—just incomprehensible. "Okay. Okay," he repeated, as much to calm himself as any of his stunned crew. "If we're not on vector, if we're not heading home, then where are we headed—and why are we heading whatever way that is?"

Thompson, infuriatingly, just shrugged. "No idea."

"What do you mean you've got no idea?" Maria shouted from her rearward position. "We're indisputably heading *somewhere*. Do the math."

"I'm afraid that won't suffice."

Everyone turned to look in Avery's direction. His deep voice was strangely calming in light of the current situation, like a father reading a bedtime story to a child.

"You see, according to the instrument readings we are presently in a state where theory takes precedence over knowledge." He gestured forward, out the port. "Note the distortion of the visible spectrum. Wherever we are and regardless of where we are heading, we are no longer in normal space. Incidentally," he added by way of an afterthought, "our astrogation instrumentation lost sight of the sun about five minutes ago."

"I don't consider that an incidental," Walker snapped. "If you have any idea of what's happened to us, Mike, don't keep it to yourself." Though he was developing an intense dislike for the way the conversation was evolving, Walker saw no choice but to continue it. For as long as they stayed in one piece, anyway. If they were going to die, it would mitigate their demise at least a little if they knew why.

"We are traveling under the influence of and have fallen into a gravity well of unprecedented dimensions," Avery explained. "Under its sway the *Ghost* will continue to accelerate until we either come apart or—" He broke off, his attention focused forward.

"Or?" Walker prompted him.

"Brace yourselves," Avery murmured, his voice still remarkably calm. "I postulate that the 'or' is about to eventuate."

"What's the 'or'?" Thompson glared at the scientist. "The notion of being torn apart while trying to decipher a riddle doesn't much appeal to me."

"That." Raising an arm, Avery pointed forward.

Everyone had been watching him. Now they turned back to face the main port. Beyond in the blackness, all hints of color had vanished. The cosmos had shifted entirely into gradations of white and black. Immediately in front of them and growing larger and more massive by the second was a swirling nexus of indescribable radiance.

"What in God's name is that?" Walker heard himself whispering.

"I believe it just might be a wormhole," Avery declaimed.

"Which means that we're dead. We, the ship, everything, will be crushed down to little tiny subatomic particles." Leaning back in her chair, Maria studied the approaching cataclysm with a sudden resignation born of a complete absence of alternatives. "Well, we learned a lot in a short time. Pity we won't be able to pass it along back to Earth. *Así es la vida—y la muerte.*" She looked around fretfully.

Idly, Walker wondered how fast they were traveling as they approached the event horizon. Faster than any human-built device had ever traveled before, certainly. Faster than any human had ever traveled before. Since everything else was moving at incredible speed, with luck death would arrive just as fast. He intended to keep his eyes open and maintain consciousness for as long as possible. Who knew what last-second wonders he might see?

Gravity, however, had other ideas.

I hope that when the end comes, it's not cold, he thought. He'd spent far too long in the Arctic, training and preparing. He was sick of cold. He thought briefly of home.

Then consciousness fled and he blacked out.

III

"By the Allspark itself—what is that?" Staring at the viewer, Starscream could not believe his optical receptors. Though every component of his being was functioning normally, what he was seeing and running through his central logic processors made absolutely no sense.

Barricade was focused intently on his console, collating and evaluating the various scans picked up by the *Nemesis*'s multitude of external sensors. "It's—it appears to be a small ship of Decepticon design," he declared. "But it is not one of ours. Not only does it not emit any of the standard recognition values—it does not emit very much of anything at all."

"I didn't ask what it appears to be, you fool," Starscream snarled. "I can see for myself what it *looks* like. I asked what it *is*."

"I am scanning it now," Barricade replied hastily. "It is clearly a vessel of some kind, but the design is—odd. One might almost call it uniquely primitive. Scanners specify the absence of anything resembling a normal life-form."

That caused Starscream to hesitate. "What do you mean, 'normal'?"

Barricade contemplated the information that was rapidly filling his monitors. "Although there are no

Cybertronian beings on board, there are indications of another kind of life-form."

No Megatron. Starscream was relieved. "Don't be obtuse. What kind of life-form?"

Placing the question on hold, which he often did when it suited him, Barricade continued with his analysis. "There is something else. Something incongruously familiar about the overall design."

"What about it?"

The husky Decepticon was uncertain. "I cannot say—it is incongruous. Scans have now verified that the craft is indeed a primitive space vessel of vaguely Cybertronian design. My first thought is that it is the result of what might be called parallel evolution in engineering. It is almost like something we ourselves might have created if we had evolved with significant physical and mental differences."

"This is not a scientific expedition." Starscream's impatience threatened to terminate the dialogue altogether. "We have not come all this way in the service of gathering irrelevant information. As long as the craft poses no threat to us, then it is hardly worth taking the time to evaluate. Though I confess to a certain modicum of curiosity. Therefore I restate my earlier query. If not Cybertronian, then what kind of life-forms occupy the vessel?"

"Their specific makeup is unfamiliar to our analyzers," Barricade explained. "There is no record of the particular species in our data banks." He looked over at his leader. "Though an unusual occurrence to be sure, given the vast nature of the universe it is not unexpected that we should occasionally encounter the ship of another spacegoing species very different from ourselves."

"Any nonCybertronian intelligence capable of interstellar travel is a potential threat." Blackout had reentered the bridge. "I say we eradicate whatever they are *and* their puny ship and move on. We have more important things to do than waste time investigating obscure mysteries."

That was more or less what Starscream had already said. The fact that it had been emphasized by Blackout, however, meant that in order to reclaim the initiative for himself, Starscream felt compelled to order the opposite.

"And I say that we *will* investigate until we are certain of what it is we are dealing with. Once we have ascertained for certain that this unknown species truly poses a threat, *then* we will destroy their vessel and resume our search."

Blackout appeared ready to argue the point, but wisely demurred. "As you command, Starscream. A thorough and proper examination cannot be conducted at this distance. Who will lead the expedition from the *Nemesis*?"

"I will," Starscream replied without hesitation. "You, Barricade, and Frenzy will accompany me. I value your input." The best way to reduce the threat from a potential rival, he knew, was to co-opt him. Flattery was useful and cheap. "The rest of the crew will continue on station, monitoring the area for any potentially unsettling surprises."

"Then we should probably hold off leaving the ship and commencing the proposed study." Barricade was once more alert to his instruments.

"Why?" Starscream made no attempt to conceal his irritation. "Given the archaic design and construction of their vessel, I am confident these unknown beings pose no threat to us."

"I am sure that they do not," Barricade agreed. He enhanced the image on the main viewscreen. "But *they* do."

A stellar distortion appeared in the distance beyond

the small craft they had been examining. Something massive, artificial, and of decidedly sophisticated design was materializing. Starscream cursed to himself as he recognized the manifestation. There was no mistaking its lines, or the very real threat it represented.

No Decepticon possessing a hint of spark could fail to recognize the *Ark*.

"Autobots!" The peculiar little alien vessel was immediately forgotten. "Barricade, snap-time maneuver! They are in the process of emerging into normal space. It may be that their sensors have not resolved yet. We have a chance to surprise them."

Active on station, Jazz was monitoring the same functions that would have required the full and undivided attention of a dozen highly trained human engineers—who would not have understood the operational elements involved anyway.

"Emergence is on site and on schedule."

"Very good." Optimus was staring at the main viewer. "Let's have a look and see if we can figure out what was emitting that atypical signal."

"The source itself is within range of our optical perceptors. I'll put it up on the main viewer." Ratchet's voice came through the ship's com to the bay. "We came out as close as could be realized."

Imagery of distant stars was replaced by a view of an unusually small vessel. Uncharacteristically, it was Ironhide who offered the first opinion. "That's a Decepticon design," he declared. "I'm sure of it. No, wait." Internal data conflicted with the visuals he was receiving. "Now I'm not so sure. I speculate."

"Jazz, what's the latest from our sensors?" Optimus asked.

"There is no question that the object is the source of the signal. Ironhide is right. It does resemble something the Decepticons would put together. The key term is *resemble*. It is most certainly not a standard Decepticon design." He checked his readouts. "And the materials, the presumed construction methodology, are entirely foreign. Whatever it is, it did not originate from Cybertron."

"Are you certain?" Optimus stared, fascinated, at the mystifying object.

"Ninety-nine point eighty-seven percent," Jazz replied. "It's *extremely* primitive. If I may inject a personal opinion, I don't believe a vessel of such shoddy construction could possibly have survived the journey intact all the way from Cybertron."

"If it is not a Decepticon ruse and it is not Cybertronian in origin, then what are we dealing with here?"

"I am as anxious as you to know," Jazz replied frankly. "My instinctual programming insists it cannot be good. However superficial the external similarities, it is clearly Decepticon-derived, and nothing good ever comes of anything ever associated with them."

Optimus pondered hard as he contemplated the baffling image on the viewscreen. The longer the conundrum lingered both in his eyes and his mind, the more the encounter began to feel like a trap. At the same time it seemed a little too obvious to be a Decepticon maneuver. In any case, it would do no harm to exercise normal caution.

"Maintain distance, Ratchet. If it should angle toward us, take us out of weapons range immediately. We'll have a closer look, but only with the *Ark* at a safe distance."

Bumblebee nodded in excitement. Of all those confined to the ship, he had suffered most. Seeing Optimus staring reprovingly in his direction, he gave the robotic equivalent of a shrug.

"I beg a moment's consideration, Optimus." Ironhide might keep a lot to himself, but he was not afraid to speak up when he felt there was something that needed to be said. "You're intending to leave the *Ark* for the purpose of conducting a hands-on exploration of that thing? Whatever the source of the signal it's generating, it is clearly not the Allspark. Prudence dictates we should probably just leave it alone and move on." He indicated the object on view. "An absurd enigma like that, drifting alone out here, makes no sense. Unless it is some kind of snare."

"Perhaps it is," Optimus conceded. "I have already considered the possibility. But I feel we should take a closer look anyway." His occasional dry humor came to the fore. "It's not as if we do not have the time. There's something singular about all this. Something almost familiar. The discrepancy nags at me. We might be able to unravel the ambiguity if we investigate further. You, I, and Bumblebee will go. Jazz and Ratchet will stay with the ship."

"Optimus." Ratchet's voice sounded clear on the bridge.

"Listening." All four Autobots in the bay were attuned to the voice of their compatriot.

"Analyzers have colluded on two new factors." Ratchet continued. "The first is that there apparently are life-forms of some kind on the unidentified vessel. Life-forms whose activities, insofar as I can discern them, hint at intelligence, albeit limited. More importantly, they are not in our database."

"And the second revelation?" Optimus queried.

"It does appear to have some martial capabilities," Ratchet informed him.

"How do you know that?" Ironhide asked. "Its appearance is wholly innocuous."

"Not anymore." Jazz pointed toward the central viewer. "It has begun to divulge what is clearly weaponry. It's some kind of compacted warship!"

All optics locked on the main screen as the exterior of

the bizarre little alien ship began to unveil some primitive defense systems. Though clumsy and slow, the procedure itself was unmistakable. As were the weapons that began to reveal themselves in the process.

"I knew it was a trap!" Ironhide exclaimed.

"Autobots, prepare for battle," a disappointed Optimus ordered. "Jazz, join Ratchet. The two of you keep the *Ark* safe until our return. Bumblebee, Ironhide, come with me." Whirling, he headed for the core egress.

If they were going to have to fight, better to do so as far away as possible from their sole means of returning home.

"Captain, wake up, damn it!" Thompson was yelling.

Blinking, feeling every muscle in his body screech in protest at the sudden movement, Walker cracked open his lids and stared up at his pilot. "What—what's the matter?" he asked dumbly, like a drunk coming out of a bad hangover. "What's our status?"

"I'm still trying to figure out the details, but without getting overly technical, I think I can safely say that *that* can't be good." Thompson pointed forward.

Gazing out the port Walker saw what was unarguably an artificial construct. Whether it was some kind of ship he could not tell. Certainly it looked nothing like the *Ghost*. At the risk of anthropomorphizing, he came to the snap decision that the object was at the very least a little threatening. Better, he decided, to be safe than sorry.

"Holy mother of . . . I think we'd better activate the defense system. Get the others up."

Thompson nodded. Moving fast, he rushed through the cabin, waking the rest of the crew. Walker could hear them muttering behind him, struggling out of sleep.

Defense system, defense system. Like nothing that had ever been built on Earth. Working fast, Walker fought to recall as many details as possible from a complex system it was hoped he would never have to engage. His fingers keyed a bank of controls set off to one side. When he felt he had done everything that was required, there remained one last command to be entered. In keeping with the best that security engineering could devise, it employed superior available voice recognition technology.

"Walker, Samuel L., Captain commanding." He spoke clearly and distinctly into the pickup. Tired as he still was, this was no time to slur his words. "Authorization Gamma Six Alpha. Defense system activation."

The ship's primitive artificial intelligence replied without wavering. "Walker, Samuel L., Captain commanding: recognized. Defense system will be deployed on receipt of final authorization code."

Walker rubbed his eyes, momentarily worried that he might not be able to recall the necessary sequence. It had not been a priority, because no one had really expected it would ever need to be utilized. Then it came to him. "Authorization code zero, nine, eleven, two, Delta, Whiskey, Bravo."

"Command authorization code accepted," the AI responded evenly. "Crew prepare for weapons system deployment."

Walker turned, scanned the cabin. "Is everyone okay back there?"

"Yeah, where are we?" Clarkson's voice was a soporific mush, as if he were trying to talk with a sock stuffed in his mouth. "What's going on?" He sat forward slowly. "Are we headed back to Earth?"

"Not exactly," Walker told him. "Jake, get back up here. I want you at control while we're undergoing this systems adjustment, or whatever the hell is going to happen. We might have to operate on full manual."

"You got it," Thompson told him as he resumed his seat. "But I sure wish I knew what I was going to have to operate."

"You've got a minute or two to figure everything out," Walker informed his copilot. "Just get us the hell away from that!"

From behind he heard the others gasp as they saw the massive alien artifact. Maria Gonzalez swore quietly in Spanish. Walker would ask for a translation later. Any lingering vestiges of sleepiness had vanished from his brain.

"Look at the structure, the general outlines, the overall configuration." Avery's analysis of the oncoming object might have been quick, but it was well considered. "It looks—like our Ice Man has relatives."

"Big ones." Thompson checked his readouts. "Weapons systems are online."

"Everyone be ready," Walker admonished them. "I don't know where we are and I don't know what's going on, but we need to be prepared to talk or fight however the situation dictates." His tone was solemn. "The Ice Man wouldn't have been equipped with weapons if he hadn't had a need for them. The implication was that he was at least occasionally expected to fight. Fight what, the tech folks were never able to establish." He indicated the enormous object that now dominated the view forward. "Maybe that's full of his friends. Or maybe it's packed with his enemies. Not knowing if we qualify as the first or the second, we have to be ready to be seen as one or the other."

"There's a third choice," Clarkson pointed out. "We could run for it. Running is always an option."

"Got beat up a lot in high school, did you?" Thompson commented. "Where would we run to? If we just take off wildly we may never get back to where we are now. And while we don't know where we are now, we do know that it's at the end of a vector that one way or another leads back to Earth. Run from it now and we might never find it again." He turned to Walker. "Weapons systems are yours, Captain."

"Understood." Walker's tone was grim. Of all the unique apparatuses on the ship, a combination of human- and alien-based weaponry was the last he thought he would ever actually be expected to activate and operate. "I hope we're not going to need them."

"Tom, it looks like we've got a slight problem."

Kinnear looked up from the mission report he was reviewing and cocked an eyebrow at the figure of the lieutenant colonel standing in the doorway. Nolan was mission director for the Sector Seven space program, and the only staff member on the base who felt comfortable addressing Kinnear by his first name. They had been together in the service for a long time. Over the years the two men had earned each other's deep respect. Any early need for formality had been dropped during a fairly hazardous black ops program in the jungles of Southeast Asia.

Broad-shouldered, heavyset, hair tending to gray and waistline toward the equatorial, Nolan was no longer a man who felt comfortable jumping out of a chopper a hundred feet above the water in full scuba gear. His last few years had been spent diving into nothing deeper than a desk drawer, and it was starting to show. Though both men regularly made light of the change, at heart Kinnear did not approve of those who effortlessly surrendered to the onset of age. Especially those in the military, where it was reasonable to expect more exacting standards to apply. Personally he could not rationalize such weakness. Not when doing a few sit-ups each morning might one day mean the difference between life or death. Nolan looked especially sloppy today. He made a mental note to speak about it later with the man.

"Phil, this is Sector Seven. We never have 'slight' problems." Kinnear ran a hand through his hair. It, too, was in better shape than Nolan's. "What have you got?"

"Trouble with *Ghost One.*" Nolan's current unhappiness was personal as well as professional. At one time or another he had worked closely with everyone who was presently on board the ship. "It could be a communications glitch, but the techs don't think so. Every minute that passes and we don't hear from Gonzalez, they're more and more convinced of it. And they don't want to be."

Kinnear looked at the clock on the wall and then turned to a stack of papers on his desk, shuffling through them until he found the one he wanted. The stats he perused only confirmed what Nolan was telling him.

"They should have reestablished communications almost an hour ago, right?"

"Actually, the revised estimate puts them back in effective range nearly two hours ago. But we haven't heard a peep."

Kinnear's lips tightened. "Like I said. Not a slight problem."

"Okay, so I was understating. Call it wishful thinking." Nolan indicated the paper his friend was holding. "Everyone's trying not to overreact. It *could* be a simple programming problem. Or circuitry. There's a couple of hundred years' worth of advances packed into the *Ghost*, and we're not even sure what all of it does. Some instruments could be working at cross purposes, or maybe somewhere there's a circuit that didn't close. Simple, basic, but enough to shut down communications as effectively as if someone deliberately repositioned the main antenna." He waved his hands. "It could be any number of things."

"But the techs don't think so," Kinnear murmured softly.

"No. They're already postulating that maybe something went badly wrong at the end of the first burn. Or maybe during it. For example, despite the ship's advanced radiation shielding, if it took a hard enough hit from an unpredicted solar flare, *that* might have been enough to fry communications." He shrugged. "Of course, that's just what the communications techs are saying. They clearly want to blame the engineering guys."

"And the engineering team?"

Nolan managed a doleful smile. "They're saying it's probably a communications problem."

"Some things can't be changed even by the most advanced technological developments. You're mission director. What's your opinion, Phil?"

The other officer pinched the bridge of his nose and closed his eyes. "Right now I'd say it's about fifty–fifty. We just don't know enough to make an accurate determination one way or the other."

"Why am I not surprised?" Kinnear held up a hand. "Don't answer that. Okay, so the only thing we do know at this point is that *Ghost One* should have been back in range and reestablished communications approximately two hours ago."

"That's correct," Nolan conceded.

"What about the alien ranging beacon?"

Looking downcast, Nolan shook his head.

"That's not good enough." Kinnear turned pleading. "Phil, I can't just call the Old Man and tell him that the ship is missing. Blown up, sun-crisped, off course—*that* I can convey. But 'missing'? You know as well as I do that we need more than that."

Nolan sighed heavily. "I know, Tom. We're working around the clock. I should have some updated reports for you within the next hour. And, of course, we'll keep trying to raise them on audio."

"I know, I know. Do your best." Suddenly the Caribbean was looking as far away as one of the "seas" on Mars. "Anything else?"

"That's everything for now." Nolan managed a hopeful smile. "I'll keep you informed."

"Phil, you've got to reestablish contact with that ship."

"Tell me something I don't know. We'll find it, Tom. I'm sorry I wasn't up here with better news."

Kinnear gestured for him to leave. "So am I. Go and find us some."

Nolan nodded before turning and exiting the room. He was moving more quickly than Tom had seen his old friend move in quite a while. The door shut behind the other officer, and Kinnear was alone again. Usually he enjoyed his solitude. Not now. Not anymore.

So much for getting through these last couple of months without a hitch.

In the stillness of his office, he tried to conjure optimism. It was far too soon to give in to despair. Unless the ship had actually been caught by and fallen into the sun, *Ghost 1* was still out there somewhere. Hopefully suffering nothing more serious than a malfunction of its radical new communications gear. He allowed himself a private shudder. If it was hard on him and the others at the base, one could only imagine what effect the complete lack of contact with Earth was having on the ship's crew, professional and highly trained though they were.

It was too quiet in the office. Picking up the walkie-talkie lying on his desk, he dialed in a frequency. "Lieutenant Jensen?"

A brief crackle of static, then, "Yes, sir."

"Kinnear here. Come up to my office, please. I want a status report on your section."

"Yes, sir. I'm on my way." Another crackle of static, this one more prolonged and irritating.

Kinnear grunted. They could reverse-engineer alien science to build a spaceship that among other things was capable of transmitting the signal of a locator beacon across millions of miles of empty space, not to mention that the same vessel also incorporated armament-guidance systems and other elements from the Ice Man, but they couldn't come up with a portable radio that eliminated static. Not for the first time he found himself wondering about the sometimes weird roads scientists tripped down and the decisions they made as to which ideas to develop and which to ignore.

The sharp rap of boots on the metal staircase that led to his office brought him back to the present. The rap on the door was as perfect and precise as everything else about Jensen.

"Come in, Lieutenant."

Jensen entered, halting at a perfect parade rest in front of the desk. A little too formal for Kinnear's taste, though the colonel could hardly upbraid the man for being military.

"At ease, Lieutenant. Take a seat. You must be worn out. From what I can tell, your team has been running nonstop."

"Yes, sir. We are a bit fatigued, sir." Jensen sat down in the padded, gray metal chair in front of the desk. "You requested a status report?"

Kinnear nodded. Something to take his mind off the uncommunicative *Ghost*. "Where are we with the Ice Man?"

"Everything is on track and moving along fairly well, sir. We're actually slightly ahead of schedule, and the methodology for keeping him frozen while in transit appears to be working as advertised. I can tell you that the tech staff is delighted. Actually, we're due to load him onto the transport approximately thirty minutes from now. As soon as the shift is complete, the insulated panels will be raised and sealed around him."

"Any problems?" Nolan inquired hesitantly. "Not that I want there to be any. It's been a rough day as it is."

Jensen nodded. "I know, sir. Word has gone around.

As to my section, nothing adverse to report that I'm aware of at this time. When the time comes to move out, however, there's a chance weather may become a factor. You've seen the latest reports?"

Kinnear pointed at the stack of papers on his desk that contained good news, bad news, all the news. "Yes, I've got them. Possibility of a storm. Not that that's any kind of surprise up here. At the moment they're forecasting that the low is going to move north of our location. With luck it'll miss the coast entirely."

"Hopefully, sir," Jensen agreed. "But we'll be keeping an eye on it, just the same. Wary of the usual changeability. Maybe one day we'll have a satellite system sufficient to keep track of all the storms that race through up here."

"Don't count on it," Kinnear muttered. "Keep me closely informed of your progress from here on out, will you? I've had enough surprises for one day. I don't need any more."

Jensen chuckled, then realized that the colonel was not being funny. "No, I suppose not, sir. But however much we dislike them, it seems like there are always surprises."

Kinnear snorted. "Maybe the next one will turn out to be pleasant. Thank you, Lieutenant. You're dismissed."

"Yes, sir." Rising, Jensen sketched a quick salute before pivoting on his heel and heading for the door.

Hard to fault the man for being disciplined, Kinnear told himself. Better than a lot of the unruly pension-snatching desk sitters he had encountered over the years. He made a quick note to himself. If everything involving Operation Ice Man went smoothly, Jensen was most likely going to earn himself a promotion.

Make a fine commanding officer, too, he mused. Jensen had the smarts to do it, even if he was still only a lieutenant. Had something held him back? Kinnear shrugged the irrelevant thoughts aside. In his spare time he could request a look at the younger officer's records. In his spare time. Right. Reshuffling the papers on his desk, he turned his full attention back to the most recent *Ghost 1* documents.

The ship *had* to be out there somewhere.

Didn't it?

IV

The small moon was just one more part of what was a normal solar system. The world it orbited held on to an atmosphere, of sorts. So did several of the other twelve planets that circled the unnamed sun in the unremarkable section of the galaxy an unimaginable distance from Earth. The moon itself was dead and airless.

That did not mean it was utterly useless to certain visitors.

Hovering near the satellite's equator among high mountains and deep craters, the *Nemesis* drifted with the lifeless gray sphere as Starscream and his fellow Decepticons gathered on the ship's enormous bridge. They looked on in puzzlement as the eccentric little alien vessel began to blister with primitive weaponry, even while the *Ark* and Autobots began to back away from it.

No one spoke until a startled Blackout pronounced, "It's definitely Cybertronian. These primitive creatures may have some knowledge of Megatron's whereabouts." If his eyes had not been fixed in his head, they very well might have widened.

Everyone responded at once, confused voices filling the chamber.

Despite a rising sense of panic, Starscream did his best to stay calm. "Do you have backflow on your logic circuits?"

Barricade was studying the readout on the main viewscreen intently. "It is not inconceivable."

"Perhaps Megatron is also somewhere in the vicinity," Frenzy suggested thoughtfully.

"Everyone shut up!" Starscream slammed a fist into a nearby panel, denting it.

As they complied, everyone turned to stare at him. In the brief moment of silence that followed his outburst, Starscream pondered why he had ever held any desire to lead this bunch of conflicted ambulatory heaps of metallic sludge. He took a figurative deep breath. "Megatron cannot be nearby," he reiterated slowly. "Our sensors would have picked up his signal."

"Then what of the Cybertronian connection?" Blackout wondered aloud, not unexpectedly.

"Who can say?" His tone turning sarcastic, the current leader of the Decepticons eyed Barricade. "As has been *repeatedly* pointed out, it is 'a significantly large galaxy.' For all we know it is possible that Megatron was terminated by the very lifeforms that occupy the vessel before us. We could debate the relevant issues for days, but one thing I believe is not open for discussion: its vaguely Cybertronian derivations are enough to mark that ship as a clear threat. It should be destroyed as soon as possible."

These beings cannot know Megatron's location, Starscream thought furiously. *Not after all these years.* Megatron had simply been missing for too long.

"And what about the Autobots?" Barricade indicated the larger view being supplied by the *Nemesis*'s advanced sensors.

"It is evident that they have not detected us yet or they would have reacted to our presence. We deal with one threat at a time." Turning away from the view, Starscream headed for the departure bay. "I will deal with the alien craft myself. Once it has been eliminated, we will purge the Autobots."

"If Megatron has allied himself with these life-forms, you're going to get your Spark handed to you," Blackout couldn't resist pointing out. "Painfully."

"I will tolerate no more discussion of this. All of you will remain here while I go to eliminate the alien ship that for unknown reasons somewhat *resembles* Cybertronian technology. When I return, we will deal with the Autobots together." Glancing back, Starscream gestured at the viewer. "Monitor closely their position and movements so that they do not surprise us."

"Use caution, Starscream," Barricade advised. "My scans show that while it is currently in flux, the small wormhole the alien vessel came through is still active. In your protoform, a trip through the wormhole would be—unpleasant."

A curt nod from Starscream indicated that he had heard and acknowledged the unnecessary warning. Turning to his fellow bot, Blackout snarled, a deep and unpleasant mechanical rasping. "Had to remind him, didn't you, Barricade?" Blackout was plainly unhappy. "If Megatron were here . . . "

Rising to his full height, Barricade glared hard at Blackout. "Megatron is *not* here. Whether we like it or not, Starscream is our leader. Without him, our collective strength is diminished and our overall ability to find the Allspark is minimized."

Immediately suspicious of this sudden outburst of loyalty, Starscream paused. "And it goes without saying that without me your hope of ever locating Megatron is also lessened."

Barricade turned to him. He was respectful but not intimidated. "True enough," he admitted. "I have chafed under your leadership, Starscream, and it would give me no small amount of pleasure to watch Megatron reduce you, piece by piece, to your basic components. But if we are to find him, it is highly probable that we will need your abilities. Until that day, you lead." He paused, then added, "It remains possible—I admit unlikely, but possible—that the beings on that alien vessel are indeed aware of Megatron's whereabouts. Perhaps our long-lost leader is even somewhere nearby. Should that turn out to be the case and a confrontation ensues, I do not expect you to return. Either way, you will have fulfilled your purpose."

"Do not count on it—'either way.'" Turning, Starscream stomped heavily from the bridge.

He had an alien ship to dispose of. He intended for the forthcoming termination to be as thorough as he could make it. It would not be enough simply for the mysterious arrival to vanish. To achieve the desired effect, it would have to be obliterated as memorably as possible.

Anything less would only lead to more questions regarding his fitness to command.

"That's no warship." Maintaining his position in free space, Optimus studied the alien vessel as he and his companions remained at a safe distance. "But its limited defense systems still bear a slight Decepticon resemblance. I'm loath to admit it, but there's a small possibility that these creatures may have come into contact with Megatron.

Next to Optimus, Bumblebee gave a nervous shake of his head, clearly not pleased with the notion.

While drifting, Optimus conducted a final evaluation of the unprecedented situation. Excepting himself, if there was anyone who would not want to see Megatron again it would be Bumblebee. Back on Cybertron, during the raging battle of Tyger Pax, Megatron had smashed Bumblebee to the ground and ripped out his vocalization module. Only a last-second intervention had prevented Megatron from destroying Bumblebee utterly. Unfortunately, they had still not been able to find an adequate solution to his lack of vocal instrumentation. The thought always filled Optimus with sadness and regret.

Optimus continued to contemplate the bizarre ship that for unknown reasons featured technologies likely derived from Cybertronian sources. While there was no denying it did look slightly Cybertonian, at the same time it was patently primitive. He wondered again whether Megatron or any of his Decepticon counterparts were involved.

He continued to vacillate. Before they moved in, they needed to know for certain what they were facing.

"Jazz, what do your sensors show?"

"I concur that it looks Cybertronian," the other Autobot responded from his position on the *Ark* with Ratchet, "but every reading I take insists that it's not. And it's obvious that there are alien life-forms inside."

"Very strange," Optimus admitted. "It is something almost beyond contemplation."

Ratchet had his own point to make. "The weapons that have been deployed are also not identical to anything on Cybertron. Even at this range there is evidence that they are considerably more primitive. Is it possible that what we are seeing is merely coincidental?"

"Or it could be a clever ruse. It is not for nothing that our old adversaries are called Decepticons." Ironhide spoke from his position alongside Optimus. "It doesn't matter. It hints a Decepticon pattern, so there must be some kind of Decepticon involvement. Let's just blow it out of normal space and be done with it."

Bumblebee suddenly grabbed Optimus and pointed excitedly.

The alien ship clearly was bringing weapons to bear.

"Jazz, give us details, fast—what kind of weapons are we dealing with?" Optimus asked.

"Astonishingly primitive, as Ratchet says," the studious Autobot responded. “There are a number of hollow cores containing explosive devices that I deduce are powered by simple combinations of combustible chemicals. I would call them playful were it not for their actual, if modest, destructive potential.”

“Let’s get ready to finish this.” Optimus turned to Bumblebee and Ironhide. “Spread out and assume a traditional attack configuration. Be prepared for anything. This display of ‘archaic’ weaponry may itself be a trick.”

“I don’t think that’s going to be necessary.” Ratchet’s voice was calm and controlled. “The alien craft is not preparing to strike. It is attempting to flee.”

Fixing his attention once more on the ship, Optimus perceived that it had engaged its drive and was indeed heading away from them. “Unexpected,” he murmured. “Even if it represents some kind of trickery, I would have anticipated an attack.”

“I concur.” Jazz’s voice drifted back over the com. “Where do you think it’s going?”

“What does it matter?” Ironhide was about out of patience. “Let’s end this right now. We don’t need whatever kind of Decepticon mechanism it happens to be materializing unexpectedly behind us. We have enough to do trying to locate the Allspark without having to worry about a possible ambush.”

Optimus shook his head. “After much thought, Ironhide, I have come to the conclusion that what we are confronting is not an independent entity at all. It may be that another alien race somehow managed to acquire a small portion of Decepticon technology, and used it to construct this vessel. If they had any formal contact with our enemies, it could not possibly have resulted in a positive experience for them. I suspect that they are retreating because they do not want a confrontation.”

“You don’t know that for certain,” Ironhide objected.

"Not enough to take a chance of leaving such a mechanism unchallenged, to work possible mischief at some future date."

"He's right, Optimus," Jazz chimed in. "We should not risk it."

Like any good leader, Optimus Prime valued the opinions of his companions. Despite the small resemblance of the alien craft to Decepticon design, however, it struck him in this particular instance as unnecessary to engage in battle without provocation. Jazz's and Ironhide's concerns notwithstanding, there would always be an opportunity to deal with the possible problem later.

"No. We will wait and see what develops. Whatever the alien ship is, I am convinced it is not interested in engaging us."

"So we're just going to sit here and wait." Jazz conjectured. "You can't be serious. I know it looks like it's retreating, but—"

Optimus laughed. "No, my friend. We are not going to wait for anyone to attack us." He pointed to the planet that the alien vessel was descending toward. To contact others of its kind? Or to conceal itself and wait for the *Ark*'s departure from this system? He was more convinced than ever that delaying conflict was the correct course. There were too many unanswered questions. As he looked on, the peculiar craft began to enter the outer reaches of the as-yet-unanalyzed atmosphere.

"Bumblebee, I have a mission for you."

"Name it." Bumblebee nodded unhesitatingly.

"We are in agreement that the design and structure of the vessel in question are disturbingly familiar. I certainly will not argue that. But familiarity is not the same as conclusive classification. In lieu of battle, let's try to collect additional information about it. I want you to follow it down and reconnoiter. See if you can get close enough to the ship to make a positive identification.

Confer with Jazz digitally, over your com. Hopefully you will also be able to discover something about the unknown life-forms the vessel carries within it."

Bumblebee waited patienetly, knowing that Optimus was not finished.

The leader of the Autobots added an admonishing word. "Bumblebee, I've had to caution you about this sort of excursion before. I need you to be a scout, not a soldier. There is always time for battle. The intelligent know that difficulty lies in avoiding combat, not seeking it. Right now we need information, not a fight."

Bumblebee nodded again, this time more solemnly.

"See that you are careful," Optimus murmured. "We all want you back. Go now, and find out what you can."

Executing a neat little half bow, Bumblebee proceeded to transform into cometary mode. A glow grew at his terminus as he activated his propulsion system. A moment later he had left the group behind as he sped toward the planet below.

"He's always been a good one," Ironhide declared as he and his companion turned in space and headed back toward the *Ark*. "I would sorrow if anything ever happened to him."

"Bumblebee is clever and observant," Jazz pointed out. "Better suited to a mission such as this than any of us."

Optimus looked over at his old friend. "Getting sentimental, Ironhide?" But he knew that Jazz was right. Bumblebee might be impulsive, sometimes to his own detriment, yet he was a brightness in the shade of their travels: always positive, always willing to help with the most tiresome work, always there when a friend needed companionship or just some quiet conversation.

Ironhide let out a sharp buzz, the bot equivalent of a dismissive snort. "No, not sentimental, Optimus. Sensible. Our strength is already much reduced. We can't afford to lose anyone else."

"True enough," Optimus admitted, a bit wistfully. "We cannot."

"Besides which," Ironhide added, "what else would we do for a scout? Send Jazz?"

Optimus returned the laugh. "A fine scout he would make. Silence is not one of his virtues."

"I heard that," Jazz sputtered. "Or did you two forget that all communications channels remain open?"

"Not only did I not forget," Ironhide shot back, "but I also made certain of it before rendering my opinion. Otherwise how could I be sure you would overhear?"

"Funny," Jazz muttered sarcastically. "Very funny. Would that all your circuitry were so artfully aligned."

Ratchet's voice suddenly cut in. "Curb the idleness! Optimus, scan the coordinates that I am about to feed you."

"What is it?" The Autobot leader was suddenly alert as he prepared to receive.

Ratchet's clarification was as ominous as it was terse. "*Starscream.*"

If the readouts on *Ghost 1*'s instrumentation were accurate, the ship had emerged in a region of space boasting not only an alien sun but at least two potentially habitable worlds. Having passed beyond shock and confronted now by uncommunicative, potentially hostile alien machines, Walker wasn't about to get fussy when it came to a choice of potential refuges.

Gazing out the viewport as the *Ghost* began its approach, his expression hardened. As revealed on the ship's monitors, the new world growing below them did not exactly qualify as one of the galaxy's choice vacation spots. But it was unquestionably the best available alternative to the alien monstrosities that were waiting for them out in interplanetary space.

At least it was for now.

"Maria," he barked even as he joined Thompson in adjusting their atmospheric entry, "is that alien communications system still working? Any chance of getting a message back to Earth?"

"How should I know?" she retorted. "This reverse-engineered apparatus has never been tried at distance. Hypothetically, it's supposed to be able to at least send simple code back and forth through something the techs called 'nonspace.'"

"I don't care if it goes by quantum Pony Express! Try it!" He looked over at Thompson. "I want you to be two people, Jake. Keep guiding us down, and also keep an eye on this ship's innovative sensor system. Whatever those things are out there, they didn't look or act any friendlier than the Ice Man back home."

"The Ice Man?" Thompson spoke without taking his gaze off the main console. "Are you kidding me? He's one of a kind."

"Not unless he was put together by elves and fairies. Someone—or some things—had to contribute to his construction. Three more not unlike him left that big ship and were heading straight for us until they stopped in midspace. I'd swear on my mother's grave they looked just like him, or enough like him to be close relatives. Mammoth metallic machines, bipedal, bisymmetrical shapes, recognizable heads and limbs—and these weren't frozen in a block of ice, and they sure as hell weren't lifeless."

" 'Relatives'?" Clarkson wondered aloud. "Think about that a minute, Captain. I know that it was suggested in our briefings that we might find evidence of these beings, but what are the odds we would find them here, when we don't even know where here is? And if they are as advanced as they give every indication of being, why haven't we had contact with them before now?"

"Who says we haven't?" Walker shot back. "None of

us, regardless of our individual security clearances, has access to all of Sector Seven's secrets. For all we know there's another entire government agency responsible for doing nothing but corresponding with alien intelligences. Also, need I remind you that there are one or two other governments besides ours that possess a certain degree of technological sophistication, and that we have no idea what their equivalent covert agencies may be up to? There is one thing I *do* know for certain, though." He shot a look back at his crew, all of whom were intent on their respective stations.

"We're not going to get out of this if we waste our time and energy on arcane speculation."

He had their complete attention now. And no idea what to do with it. So he considered. *Keep calm. Reassure. When in doubt, review and reassess.* As it plunged through alien atmosphere the *Ghost* bounced once, helping to prompt his response.

"All right. Consider our present status. We don't know where we are. We don't know where *Earth* is, or if we can communicate with it. We do know that our ship seems to be fully functional, and that both our flight and offensive capabilities are operational. We can fight if we have to. We also know that there is some kind of alien vessel out there, and we don't know anything about its occupants' intentions."

"A helpful summary, Captain," Avery murmured, "but not an especially encouraging one. As W. C. Fields once said when asked how he felt about death, 'On the whole, I'd rather be in Phil-a-del-phia.'"

It relieved the tension. Everyone started laughing, and Walker overlooked the slight insubordination. If there was one thing Walker could be sure of, it was that they were going to need a lot more of Michael Avery's wry humor in the coming days.

When the laughter had subsided, he added, "True

enough, Mike. Let's do our best to try to improve the situation. Right now we're not fighting anybody. Let's make use of that time. I want a full systems check. However we got wherever we are, we have to assume that it's at least theoretically possible to go back the way we came. Everything's recorded. Every pulse of the propulsion system, every coordinate we've passed through. If we can retrace our steps . . . " The possibility hung tantalizingly in the closed, recycled air of the cabin.

"And we need to be on guard. Whatever we saw out there might decide they want a closer look. If they do turn out to be the Ice Man's cousins, we're liable to be in serious trouble."

"Captain?" Gonzalez's tone was not encouraging.

He shifted his gaze to her station. "What is it, Maria?"

"I can—I can pick up their communications. They sound like . . . " Her voice trailed off momentarily as she fine-tuned instrumentation. "Like this."

The cabin was filled with a high-pitched screeching: modulated static that, if one had a degree in advanced physics and was tripping on bad acid, might almost be imagined to form words.

A fascinated Avery listened intently. "I wonder what they're saying."

"Nothing good, I bet." Clarkson had also turned slightly in his seat to take note of the raucous electronic shrieks. "Nothing that sounds like that could possibly be good."

Avery chided his fellow crewmember gently. "You're anthropomorphizing."

"Damn right." The engineer was unrepentant.

The landscape was less than appealing. It reminded Bumblebee entirely too much of the battle-scarred surface of Cybertron. Upon entering the atmosphere, he had used his sensors to locate where the alien ship had set down. Swooping in well to the south, he was careful to descend low and far enough away so that he was unlikely to be detected. Nor did choosing a landing site present any difficulty. The barren, wide-open, rock-strewn plateau offered plenty of acceptable options.

The problem was maintaining cover in the course of his descent. He saw himself dropping through the gray atmosphere, an easy and exposed target for any Decepticons who might be monitoring his progress from above or waiting down below. Forcing himself to set such concerns aside, Bumblebee tracked farther away from the alien ship than he had originally intended. Once he was safely on the ground his bipedal protoform would enable him to utilize the broken, craggy surface and unusual rock formations for concealment. The downside was that it would take him longer to reach the alien vessel's landing site.

Well, won't that be half the fun? he decided. Ironhide's evaluation had been spot-on: alone among the surviving Autobots, Bumblebee was forever positive. Settling on a landing site, he rechecked his sensors one more time. The alien ship remained where it had landed, a significant distance away near the planet's equatorial line. As he settled surfaceward, Bumblebee transformed anew to land with his feet on the ground. Without pausing to investigate the interesting particulars of the surrounding geology, he immediately moved to the cover of the nearest large rock formation.

From orbit and in the course of his descent he had picked up no evidence of an indigenous civilization. It was a desolate world, the most developed form of life apparently a limited assortment of organic growths based on simple carbon molecules. Colors of both growths and rocks tended to muted grays and yellows with splotches of brighter red indicative of strong oxidation. Located at a considerable distance from its sun, the planet was too cold and too harsh to give rise to a varied organic brew.

His necessarily hasty survey from orbit had also led Bumblebee to the conclusion that even if there were any spacegoing species in the interstellar vicinity, this world would not be a first choice for colonization. Certainly there was no sign that anything even as insignificant as an automated survey device had ever touched down here.

Not the kind of place I'd want to call home.

He reopened his digital communications channel and rapidly entered a message. "Jazz, are you there?"

"Where else would I be but where I am?" Jazz replied vocally. "What's your status?"

"Everything acceptable so far. I've landed on the surface of the planet. Nothing much to see. I'm about to start heading toward the alien ship."

"Be careful and stay on full sensor alert," Jazz told him. "Once you're ready to take off from there you'll want to track out of the atmosphere and back to the *Ark* as near as possible to the way you went in."

"Why the compulsory precision?" Was there some reason Jazz should be so concerned about his departure being witnessed by the occupants of the alien vessel?

"Sensors indicate that the wormhole that ship generated in order to arrive at this point in space is still present. It's slowly collapsing, and in the absence of any available matter to draw in, it is not spawning any associational luminosity. Its movement indicates that its generation was nonspecific. As a result, it keeps moving around even while it's in the process of shrinking. When you leave, you don't want to get sucked into a wandering space-time distortion, far less outside the protection of a ship."

"Understood." Bumblebee gave a slight mental shiver. According to his personal store of knowledge, no Autobot—or Decepticon—had ever survived such a journey.

"There's one other thing." Jazz managed to sound even more concerned than previously.

"'One other thing' invariably means trouble. What is it?"

"Very serious trouble," Jazz informed him. "We've got Decepticons up here. Don't know where from. They materialized out of nowhere. There's a skirmish looming for sure."

"I'll be as quick as I can." Bumblebee was already moving, working his com simultaneously. "You're going to need me."

"No," came the response, more assured this time. "Optimus wants you to take care of your mission down there. We'll handle any difficulties up here. I'm no more pleased at the current separation than you are, but if that small ship is some kind of new or unique Decepticon, despite its primitive appearance and the presence of an internal organic population, it is imperative that we determine its capabilities and intent."

Bumblebee mulled over his friend's response before conceding that the logic made sense, though he hated not being available to assist his friends in the possible forthcoming battle. He had no idea as to the Decepticons' strength, and Jazz had not filled him in. All he could do was carry out his own assignment as quickly and as efficiently as possible while hoping that Optimus and the others came through unharmed.

"All right," he replied, although the digital nature of his response could not convey his reluctance. "Let me know as soon as you can if you need me up there. Otherwise I'll be in touch again as soon as I have concluded my task and am headed back to the *Ark*."

"Safety and preservation," Jazz responded before terminating the communication.

Isolated among his stark surroundings, Bumblebee

headed off in the direction of the alien ship. He did not travel in a straight line or take to the exposed sky. Instead he advanced from one concealing geological formation to the next, forcing himself to utilize caution and tactics despite his impatience to be over and done with the work. He had no reason to suspect that anyone had seen him touch down, but neither was there any need to unnecessarily announce his presence.

Though he concentrated on the task at hand, he could not keep from wondering if they all had been wrong. Decepticons had been sighted by the *Ark*. What if, despite their preliminary analyses, the beings on the alien ship did prove to know something about Megatron. No matter where he might be, Megatron would always be the same within. Nothing could change that. As an entity he was power mad and pure evil, a being of enormous strength forever teetering on the edge of insanity. He stood for everything that Bumblebee hated.

He found himself hoping that the deceivingly innocuous alien vessel actually was the work of Megatron. It would give him and his companions the opportunity to remove from the civilized galaxy the handiwork of the most malicious Decepticon who had ever existed.

If he didn't remove them first, of course.

"Starscream is gone," Blackout announced. "And if Megatron really is in league with that primitive vessel and Starscream attacks it, chances are our erstwhile leader will not be returning." He eyed his fellow Decepticons. "I say we take this chance to give Megatron a welcome-back gift: the destruction of the Autobots and the *Ark*."

"And I say we wait," Barricade countered.

"Then it is a fortunate thing we are not listening to you." Without hesitation, Blackout seized the opportunity that had been presented to him. "We have all of us been following Starscream around for centuries and it has gotten us nowhere. We have not located the Allspark. We have not found Megatron on our own." He shoved a long metallic finger at Barricade. "This is not the kind of honored existence Decepticons are destined to live. We are conquerors." The finger turned to gesture at the main viewscreen. "Our enemy is right out there, standing its noxious ground. We should strike while we have the chance."

"Starscream said to stay here," Barricade countered once again. "Forget it not: as long as Megatron is not present, Starscream remains in charge and we take our orders from him."

"While not disagreeing with your summation, I believe Blackout's point is well taken," Frenzy put in. "Who can say when this chance might again present itself? I say we move quickly to crush the Autobots."

"Thank you." Sensing indecisiveness, Blackout eyed the others. "Anyone else wish to come along, or will the rest of you stay here and do what Starscream, that most egotistical of all Decepticons, wants us to do—which is nothing!"

"I will come." The hulking form of Bonecrusher had just entered the bridge. "Squatting here recycling useless information is boring and pointless. It has been too long since we have engaged in honest combat."

"So will I," Frenzy added. "It is time to fight, not time to pace endlessly around the ship, waiting for Starscream to come back and tell us we need to enter stasis for another century or two."

"Do as you will. I will make no effort to restrain you. Folly is a spark that burns brightly unto itself." Barricade struggled to contain his exasperation. "I will remain here. I will not risk the *Nemesis* on behalf of such recklessness."

"No one is asking you to do so. We do not need the *Nemesis* to defeat them," Blackout sneered.

"Perhaps not," Barricade replied, "but even you must admit that Optimus Prime is no weakling. If he is indeed out there with the *Ark*, then you will be lucky to come back with your limbs intact." He paused briefly. "You will be lucky to come back at all."

"So many words signifying nothing," Blackout responded condescendingly. "Clearly we are different, you and I. Myself, I was made for action—not idle prattle. Besides, we have a surprise for them." He looked to his left. "Don't we—Scorponok?"

The much smaller multilimbed Decepticon standing nearby did not reply. He was not a talker. He did not need to be.

There was nothing left to say. Turning, Blackout led his eager followers off the bridge.

"Captain, our subsidiary communications system—the one derived from studies of the Ice Man—appears to be fully functional. I can try to send a message, though given our, um, somewhat remote location it's doubtful whether it will reach Earth." Gonzalez gave a slight shrug and gestured eloquently with one hand. "It's not like we even have any idea how far away we are. Of course, none of the engineers who put it together pretends to understand exactly how the system works. As you know, the main components of the receiving complex back on Earth are derived from ongoing studies of the same alien science. Physics as metaphysics, some of the techs liked to say. I'll give it a try, and we can hope for the best."

Thompson smiled encouragingly, first at her, then at Walker. "The power requirements aren't onerous. What do we have to lose?"

"Nothing we haven't probably already lost." Walker nodded to his communications officer. "Go ahead, Maria—let's give it a shot."

She stared back at him. "What are you going to say?"

"I'm not sure yet. Just tell me when you're ready."

Twisting in her seat, she performed some final adjustments to the unprecedented communications instrumentation, then alerted the waiting Walker with a brief nod. "Ready as can be without the Ice Man here to offer suggestions."

Walker had one more notion. "As long as the gear doesn't react adversely, keep resending as a loop."

"Will do, for as long as nothing objects," she told him.

"Good," he replied. "Let's do it."

"Ready when you are, Captain."

Turning to the console pickup, Walker took a deep breath before starting.

"This is Captain Samuel Walker, commanding *Ghost One*, calling SSAB Command. Our current position is unknown; crew are safe. Request position assistance using alien-derived locator beacon. Postsolar acceleration propelled ship well beyond database. Transit wormhole or other unknown astrophysical distortion probable. Present location extrasolar. I repeat, extrasolar. Subsequent visual-only contact made with multiple alien artifacts that, while different, possess marked resemblance to Ice Man. Visual indication of possible hostile reaction to our presence. Please advise as to course of preferred action. Meanwhile will react and respond as circumstances dictate. Walker out."

"'Visual indication of possible hostile reaction to our presence'?" Thompson was unable to restrain a chuckle. "That's kind of an understatement, wouldn't you say? Did you get a good look at those things?"

"I can't confirm that they're aggressive until we have incontrovertible evidence of intent," Walker countered. "Mere appearance isn't sufficient. That doesn't mean we can't ask for advice."

"All right, so what do we do now?" Thompson asked.

"Sit here and wait? Hope our message gets through before the aliens find us and do whatever it is that aliens do to foreigners who show up in their backyard unannounced and uninvited?"

Walker glared at his friend. "That's exactly what we're going to do. Lie low, hope that cockamamie cobbled-together alien transmitter actually works across interstellar distances, and wait to see if SSAB Command gets back to us. Unless you have any better ideas?"

Aware that he might have framed his concern in an unnecessarily provocative manner, Thompson lowered his voice. "Actually, yes—I believe I do."

"Well, don't keep it all to yourself." Walker gestured impatiently for his copilot to continue. "Let's hear it."

Thompson shifted awkwardly in his seat. "Look, we don't know if our message will get through. We don't know if the aliens are going to pursue us down here, ignore us and go away, or maybe just—I don't know, implant us with little baby Ice Men or something. But there's one thing we do know reasonably well, and that's this ship. We've got sophisticated weapons and evasive capabilities. What we don't have is a good secure position. Let's try to conceal ourselves as best we can from external observation. Then, if we're blown to bits later, we might at least have a little time to avail ourselves of the unprecedented opportunity to be the first of our kind to explore an alien planet." He nodded at Gonzalez. "If the alien communicator works, even if we don't get back ourselves, the information we could gather and pass along would be invaluable."

"I second that." As the expedition's science officer, Avery would have been expected to support Thompson enthusiastically .

"And me," Clarkson added bare seconds later.

Walker nodded slowly, considering his copilot's words. His friend was right on both counts. They needed to be as prepared as possible for whatever might come next, and at the same time seize the initiative in their responsibility to science and humanity. He grinned.

"You heard him, people. Let's get moving."

"Captain, wait." Eyeing his instruments, Clarkson sounded suddenly concerned. "I just picked up something on sensors. It's pretty big, and heading our way."

Walker's expression tightened. "So much for scientific exploration. Get our weapons ready, Jake. It looks like we're about to have company."

Kinnear picked up the phone on the first ring.

"Colonel, this is Simmons. Switch to a secure line and call me back."

No *hello,* no *how are things?* The connection clicked briefly before going dead.

"Ah, hell," Kinnear mumbled. The Old Man never called unless something was really bothering him. Had he already heard that *Ghost 1* had gone missing? Why else would Simmons bother with a closed call?

Easy, he told himself. *Don't buy trouble. You've already got enough of the free variety.*

Switching to the red phone, he punched in a number—one of those special sequences of digits that was not scrawled on any notepad or typed into his Rolodex. Certain numbers had to be memorized. Not that it was unobtainable by persistent and persuasive enemy agents, but it was one they would have to work a lot harder to filch.

Few people knew the inner workings of Sector Seven. Those in the know were aware that despite the absence of any formal rank, Walter Simmons was the real power in the agency. Occasionally that lack of military experience troubled Kinnear. He himself was a full colonel. He had come up through the ranks in 'Nam, had fought in combat that did not make the evening news, had seen men and women die messily and alone in action. On one occasion he had been forced to leave behind a fatally wounded officer, a good man and a good friend. The regs were glass-clear on how to deal with such situations. He could have ordered a subordinate, a grunt, to do the job.

Kinnear had administered the necessary final shot himself. The man had been *his* friend.

Given the blood he had seen and the decay he had smelled and the daily horrors he had survived, why should he have to answer to someone who had never served a day in uniform, much less in combat? Yes, the lack bothered him.

On the other hand, Simmons was privy to dangerous secrets and shadowy doings that Kinnear, a straightforward soldier, had no desire to know. He had seen how visitors from Washington deferred to the Old Man, even if only verbally. Simmons not only knew where a lot of the skeletons were buried—but also knew how they had become skeletonized. The repercussions manifested themselves in small but important ways. Alone among those individuals assigned to Sector Seven, only Simmons could conjure up equipment, personnel, cash, and whatever else happened to be needed at the moment just by dialing a number. A useful man to know, to have on your side. Also a little bit scary.

Simmons and his family had been involved in Sector Seven work from its inception. Kinnear snorted. It wouldn't surprise him a bit if someday the Old Man's son was running the show. Or—given the way things were going these days—his daughter.

The voice on the other end of the line omitted any pleasantries. The brusqueness did not bother Kinnear. He knew Simmons well enough to expect it. The Old Man was not deliberately rude—just businesslike.

"Colonel, I keep hearing . . . things. When I try to

inquire as to the details, the people in question mutter their responses. I don't like mutterers. Doesn't look good in the reports. 'We're ten percent over budget, the supplier muttered.' It's bad news. I want a status update on everything that's going on there. Don't leave anything out. And Tom?"

"Yes, sir?"

"Don't mutter."

Might as well start with the good news, Kinnear decided. "Operation Ice Man is on schedule, sir. Transport to the coast will begin in—" He glanced at the wall clock. "—thirty-eight minutes. Everything is online and on timetable. The freeze-transfer methods the tech boys put together are functioning as all the models predicted."

"Very good." Simmons paused briefly. "And?"

Kinnear swallowed. He had considered several possible approaches to breaking the news and had discarded them all. There was no way to sugarcoat what had happened.

"There is—we are facing the possibility of an operational difficulty with *Ghost One*, sir." There, he decided. That was direct but minimal. He wondered if he would be allowed to get away with it.

He was not.

"'Possibility'? Don't dance with me, Colonel. I have a tendency to kick. Explain."

That was that, Kinnear realized. He dumped everything he had held back. "We're currently having difficulties locating the ship, sir. Everyone available has been put to work on it since the breakdown. Engineering believes it may be nothing more than a straightforward communications glitch." *Or,* he thought, *it could be something worse. Something a lot worse.* But Kinnear saw no advantage in pointing that out to the Old Man unless he was pressed for a further opinion.

Simmons sounded simultaneously angry and irritated. "Oh, for God's sake! Why wasn't I informed immediately?"

Kinnear took a deep breath. "That was my decision, sir. We're still working on trying to determine the ship's exact status. I didn't want to forward a hasty report that might have been not only in error, but also unnecessarily distressing."

"I see." Kinnear could almost hear the wheels in the Old Man's head grinding against one another at the other end of the line. "And if it's not a communications glitch?"

"Anything is possible, sir. You know that as well as anyone. Nothing like this has ever been tried before. Hell, nothing like *Ghost One* and its journey have ever been *contemplated* before. Utilizing reverse-engineered alien technology, attempting a solar cometary . . ." He let his voice trail away before finishing, "As soon as I have something more definitive, I'll inform you immediately."

"No, you won't," Simmons informed him. "Someone else will inform. *You* have something else to do."

"Sir?" Kinnear held the phone close. What charming excursion did Sector Seven have in mind for him this time? He had a feeling it would not involve the relaxing weekend in New York that had been promised to him a month ago.

"You're going with the Ice Man," Simmons explained tersely. "I want you to personally oversee his transfer from the base all the way down to the newly completed station site."

Swallowing past the sudden tightness in his throat, Kinnear asked uncertainly, "Are you relieving me of my command, sir?"

There was a weary sigh from the other end of the phone. "No, Colonel—Tom. I'm not. It's just that we have a new—you're not the only one who has to deal with unexpected problems, you know. One of our field operatives hanging around a bar close to Lubyanka recently acquired some interesting intelligence. It's as sketchy as a two-year-old's drawing, but the gist of it is that somehow the Soviets have infiltrated us up there We don't know how deep it goes or for how long it has been going on, but the short version is that your situation may have been compromised. I've seen the report. It could be nothing more than a disruptive KGB plant, it could be incorrectly decoded—or it could be something real. But until I and the rest of the palm readers down here determine exactly what's going on, I want my best man handling oversight."

Not a demotion; a compliment. Kinnear was visibly relieved, though there was no one present to share his satisfaction. "I understand, sir. Personally, I've seen nothing to justify that kind of suspicion. Personnel have been unchanged for some time, and my people on watch haven't reported anything out of the ordinary. How good is this intel?"

"Like I said, it's hazy at best. But we can't chance knowledge of the Ice Man falling into Soviet hands—much less the Ice Man himself. We've got problems enough in the world without adding that to the mix. Is Lieutenant Colonel Nolan still running the day-to-day on *Ghost One*?"

"Yes, sir."

"Glad to hear it. Good man. Tell him I want an update on *Ghost One*'s status in no more than two hours, even if the situation remains static between now and then. It's possible that if we are dealing with an infiltration, it may be focused on the mission rather than the Ice Man. Fill him in on the situation, Tom. In the meantime, I want you assuming direct command of Operation Ice Man until completion. Understood?"

"Yes, sir." Well, at least he would soon be working in

warmer weather. That would go a long way toward making up for the long, tense hours that now lay ahead of him. He wouldn't get much rest until the Ice Man had been safely delivered to his new home in the lower forty-eight. "I understand, sir."

"I knew that you would, Tom. In addition to what will go into the official follow-up, you also have my personal thanks. Keep me posted along the way." A startled Kinnear wondered, *Was that a hint of a chuckle at the other end of the line?* "You're going on the mother of all road trips."

"I'll see to it, sir," Kinnear replied. "I'll make sure we get where we need to when we need to." He hesitated uncertainly, then decided to risk it. "If we run into trouble, we can always stop and buy a few bags of ice along the way."

"That's the spirit, Colonel! That's why I keep making sure you get your promotions."

Tom winced at the implied paternalism. "Thank you, sir."

"I'll be in touch." There was a click as Simmons terminated the conversation.

The Old Man was as subtle as a punch in the nose. Kinnear recalled one of his first meetings with Simmons. Subordinates and colleagues were calling him the Old Man even then. Both men had found themselves in a briefing on Southeast Asia, which was just beginning to heat up before exploding into a full-fledged conflagration. During the briefing Simmons had directly and bluntly addressed the vice president of the United States, calling him a barely literate peasant who was going to get a lot of men killed for no discernible reason. At the end of the deposition he had stood up, dropped a couple of dominoes on the table in front of him, snapped, "There's the sum of your theory—all plastic and no substance," and walked out of the room. The congressional chamber that was being used for the briefing had not seen the kind of silence that followed Simmons's rant since it had been necessary to close it off while it was decontaminated for vermin.

The intervening years had not changed the Old Man a bit. Meanwhile vice presidents had come and gone. Lately rumor had it that Sector Seven was going to be shut down as a separate, autonomous entity, and that everything was going to be put under the control of the military and the office of the president himself. That might loosen things up, Kinnear mused. Or it might be the end of Sector Seven's unique project altogether.

He yawned, stood up and stretched, then walked over to the rack and grabbed his parka. It was usually colder down in the Research Division, and he had a lot of work to do.

Well concealed within the twists and turns of a dark igneous formation, Bumblebee peered carefully around the black rocks at the alien ship. He was more than close enough to get an up-close view of the strange craft. It made no sense. Why would anyone attempting to emulate Cybertronian design downgrade the numerous advanced systems? The material that had been used in fabrication was but a pale imitation of Decepticon body armor. Even a casual evaluation was sufficient to prove to Bumblebee that this strange visitor was far inferior to anything originating on Cybertron.

In addition, there was this curious and unsettling matter of the organic life-forms it contained.

A more detailed scan of the vessel showed that they were still inside and, in their own soft, pulpy way, very much alive. They did appear to have some primitive scanning technology of their own. Though they had given no sign, it was possible they were aware of his presence.

He brooded over the situation. Now that he could

confirm that the visitor seemed innocuous enough, he could simply leave. That would be the sensible thing to do: there was the impending skirmish to think of. On the other hand, while he and Optimus and the other Autobots were battling Decepticons, the bizarre visitors might take the opportunity to leave, making it impossible to learn anything more about them.

While they had readied their weapons out in space, they had not attacked. Given the chance, they had elected to flee rather than fight. Whatever else the aliens might be, this strongly implied they were not inherently aggressive. Though that did not tell him what they were, it did tell him one thing they were not. Confronted by Autobots, rarely would a Decepticon or Decepticon ally ever pass up a chance for battle.

Therefore, it stood to reason that whatever he was looking at was not an enemy. Since the Decepticons barely managed to get along with one another, it was hardly likely one of them would be able to do so with a cluster of tiny internalized organic symbionts. Given their size and primitive weapons systems, they certainly did not present a very serious threat. Not even to a smaller Autobot like himself.

Stepping out from among the rocks and deliberately exposing himself, he started walking toward the ship. He kept his weapons concealed and his hands visible and open. If they were intelligent and also curious, it might be possible to establish communication with them. Learning why their vessel so closely imitated Cybertronian designs might be as easy as asking directly. Optimus often said that the best scouts were the ones who took the initiative. Though he was not as large or as powerful as some of his brethren, initiative was a characteristic Bumblebee could boast of in quantity.

He called out as he moved closer. Would they be able to understand a digital greeting? Did they have access to translators, or to broadcast direct cerebral input?

A horribly familiar shape suddenly appeared from above. Bumblebee whirled, just in time to see the massive form of Starscream plummeting out of the sky directly toward him.

All thoughts of interspecies contact were forgotten as Bumblebee instantaneously ranked his options. He had little hope of defeating the much larger Decepticon, who was also faster and mounted much more powerful weapons. Under such circumstances flight was the best, and maybe the only, choice. Regrettably, given his surroundings and his physical situation, it was not a very promising one.

"Perish, Autobot!" Starscream screeched. His pulse cannons fired as he closed in on Bumblebee's exposed position.

Maybe next time! Retreating at speed, Bumblebee darted back into the cover of the tortured volcanic formation from which he had emerged earlier and unleashed his own weaponry at the diving Decepticon.

Forced to evade, Starscream let out an electronic snarl along with another heavy barrage. Energy blasts ripped glowing furrows into the ground. Rock that had long ago been molten turned white hot and liquid once again.

Threatened with entombment, Bumblebee drew upon his personal data to transform hastily into a four-wheeled vehicle capable of astonishing speed and agility over the most difficult terrain. Aloft, he could not hope to evade the much faster Starscream. The ground offered opportunities for concealment and cover that the open sky did not. He would take his chances on the surface.

Every time Starscream's sensors ranged the fleeing Autobot, Bumblebee would pivot or reverse course. When the Decepticon slowed down to try to match his ground-bound target's speed, his quarry would speed up. Bumblebee's weapons systems might not be the equal of his pursuer's, but his processors were just as fast. The hunt became a deadly game of speed-up, slow-down, and reposition, with each fighting mechanoid trying to outguess the other and anticipate his adversary's next move. Throughout it all Starscream maintained a steady if futile fire.

Below, Bumblebee kept darting and dashing, making maximum use of whatever cover the tectonically tormented planetary surface provided. If he could hold out long enough, Starscream might make a mistake. He might over- or undershoot badly. That would give Bumblebee time enough to transform back to his primary shape and flee the planet's gravity. Once clear of the atmosphere and depending on the lead time available to him, he could conceivably make it back to the *Ark* before the trailing Decepticon blew him out of the ether.

As he continued to race and run for his life, it occurred to him to wonder what had brought Starscream to this empty, uninhabited world in the first place. Had he tracked Bumblebee's descent—or were the Decepticons also aware of and interested in the alien visitor? Given that peculiar craft's uncanny resemblance to Decepticon designs, such interest would hardly be surprising. There was, Bumblebee decided as he took a sharp turn to the right, a good deal more of interest here than making contact with a sentient organic species. Certainly it warranted further investigation.

None of which he would be alive to participate in if he didn't keep moving.

"Lieutenant Jensen!"

As he passed through the last of the three climate locks and entered the research zone, Kinnear's breath became visible in front of his face. Similar puffs of condensation marked the location of individual technicians, engineers, members of the science team, and specialized contract workers, giving the spacious enclosed area the look of Yellowstone in winter.

"Here, sir!" Jensen's voice called back. Waving his hands to clear the air in front of him as he advanced, the junior officer stepped around the corner of the massive, multiwheeled, custom-built transporter.

"Sorry to interrupt your work. I know how busy you must be." Kinnear nodded to where personnel were racing to finish the final preparations for the move. "How busy everyone is."

"Not a problem, sir." Jensen halted in front of his superior. "What can I do for you?"

"I'm coming with you," Kinnear told him. "I've been ordered to personally oversee the transport of the Ice Man from here all the way to the new facility in the States."

Jensen's brows lifted slightly. "Ordered, sir?"

"Even I report to someone else, Lieutenant." Looking past the younger man, Kinnear studied the transporter. Similar vehicles had been constructed and customized to move missile stages and entire buildings. They were slow but sturdy. That suited Operation Ice Man. Having to try to explain the Ice Man if they had an accident was not a scenario he wanted to deal with. "What's our current status?"

Before answering, Jensen pursed his lips in thought. "Are you sure this is a good idea, sir? With all due respect, you're not a field man anymore, and while I don't anticipate trouble, it would bother me if anything did go wrong and your—retirement—was to be jeopardized."

Incredulous, Kinnear silently counted to ten, doing his best when he spoke to keep his voice level. "I may have been a desk jockey for a while now, but I've been in the 'field' longer than you've been alive." He straightened. "Your concern for my future well-being is commendable,

Lieutenant, but misplaced. I've been given my orders and you've got yours. Once again: what's our status?"

Jensen nodded once, sharply, then announced, "We're good to go, sir." He glanced at his watch. "The Ice Man is secure, and all relevant systems are up and running. The escort vehicles are waiting for us outside. Once the final checks are done, we can load up the last of our technicians and head out."

"That's what I wanted to hear." Kinnear forced a smile. The two of them were going to share some long, anxious days ahead, and it would not do to start out with any awkward feelings—real or perceived. "Lieutenant, er, there's something I need to mention to you."

"Sir?" Jensen queried.

"I've just been made aware of some possible security concerns. Nothing for certain, but serious enough to warrant taking a little extra care. There is an outside chance that we may have a foreign operative in our midst." A pair of techs approached, and he waited for them to pass on by before continuing. "Sector HQ received some intelligence that suggests our base here may have been infiltrated."

Jensen's eyes went wide. "That's hard to believe, sir, given the rigorousness of our security procedures."

"I'd like to think we both know our people here very well, Lieutenant," Kinnear replied, "but it's impossible to follow everyone closely. Security level is upped two stages as of now. If anyone asks about the change, press them on why they're inquiring. If you're convinced they're as reliable as we hope everyone here is, tell them the upgrade is part of a preprogrammed drill." His expression was somber. "Hopefully that'll be the extent of it.

"Moving along: let's get the various team leaders in here for a quick briefing. There are a couple of items I want to run by all of you before we set out. Oh, and tell 'em to bring their maps. We're going to make a last-minute change to our original route."

"That's going to add time and trou . . . " Jensen stopped midprotest, took a step back, and saluted quickly at someone approaching from behind the colonel. "Sir."

Kinnear turned to see Phil Nolan headed his way, hurriedly dodging the tangles of cables and stacks of crates and containers that littered the floor of the hangar like an undersized tailback with half the defensive line of the Chicago Bears close on his tail.

"Tom!" Nolan called out. "Hold on a minute!"

Kinnear turned. "What's up, Phil? You look like you just hit the lottery."

The other officer was nearly out of breath. "You're not gonna believe it. *I* don't believe it. We got a transmission from Walker!"

Glancing around and noticing that a small crowd was starting to gather, Kinnear stepped forward and put a restraining hand on his friend's shoulder. "Let's go upstairs. There's something you need to know, anyway."

"All right, sure, but this will only take—"

"A minute, I know." Kinnear gazed meaningfully into the other officer's eyes. "But not out here, okay?" He looked back at the silent but attentive Jensen. "Lieutenant, get your team leaders and their supplements together. Have everyone in my office in ten minutes."

"Yes, *sir.*" Pivoting on his heel, Jensen moved off smartly to gather the requested specialists.

"Come on, Phil." Kinnear led the way toward the stairs leading up to his second-floor office. "We need to talk." The other officer's enthusiasm could not excuse his lack of discretion in the transport chamber. Kinnear ground his teeth. The man had been driving a desk for too long. He had stopped thinking like a soldier and started thinking like a damn civilian.

No one intercepted them as they climbed the prefab

staircase, their boots clanging on the metal steps. Once inside his office, Kinnear shut the door behind them and gestured toward a seat. "Sit down." Moving behind the desk, he settled expectantly into his own chair. "You said we received a transmission? That's terrific, wonderful. Terrific, and unbelievable. What did it say?"

Nolan pulled his chair close and removed a slip of paper from his breast pocket.

"It reads, 'This is Captain Samuel Walker, commanding *Ghost One*, calling SSAB Command. Our current position is unknown; crew are safe. Request position assistance using alien-derived locator beacon. Postsolar acceleration propelled ship well beyond database. Transit wormhole or other unknown astrophysical distortion probable. Present location extrasolar. I repeat, extrasolar. Subsequent visual-only contact made with multiple alien artifacts that, while different, possess marked resemblance to Ice Man. Visual indication of possible hostile reaction to our presence. Please advise as to course of preferred action. Meanwhile will react and respond as circumstances dictate. Walker out.' " Nolan tossed the printout onto the desk. "That's all of it."

Kinnear paused for a moment to ponder the fantastic contents of the message. "'Present location extrasolar'? 'Alien artifacts'? 'Hostile reaction to our presence'?" He gaped at the other officer. "Where the hell are they? They're supposed to be on their way out to the edge of the solar system, and then back toward Jupiter for slingshot back to Earth. And what's all this about wormholes and distortions?"

Nolan pursed his lips. "Well, at this point we really don't know what to make of a lot of it. But the scientists and the techs have been able to agree on a few things. I was on my way to update you when the transmission came through."

"At this point, I'm happy to live with 'a few things,'" Kinnear told him. "Let's hear them."

Nolan tapped the printout. "We were finally able to trace back the alien locator beacon. The transmission didn't come through normal space. That's in keeping with what the techs predicted when they put the design together." He swallowed. "We don't know where *Ghost One* is on its way to, except that it's somewhere outside the solar system." Kinnear's eyes widened. "Way outside the solar system. Could be twenty light-years, could be twenty thousand."

"What?" Kinnear almost yelled. "Don't throw distances like that at me, Phil. We know what kind of speed *Ghost* is capable of, and it's not even a middling *fraction* of a light-year. How'd they get that far? That's not even conceivable."

"I know, I know," Nolan acknowledged. "Our best engineering people are working on the models now, but the fundamental element is right there in Walker's transmission. Maybe wormholes or similar distortions in the continuum are more common than we suspected when you get closer to the sun. We haven't sent enough probes there to know one way or the other. Whatever kind of dimensional deformation the *Ghost* encountered, the bottom line is that the ship went into it and came out—somewhere else."

Kinnear knew Nolan was expecting some kind of response from him, but what could he say? He was a soldier and an administrator in Sector Seven. He knew a lot about people and just enough about physics. He looked past the hopeful officer. Einstein didn't walk through the door to bail him out, and neither did Planck. Too bad.

"If you're looking for ideas from me, Phil, I'm afraid you're waiting on the wrong brain," he finally responded. "So now what? We got a transmission from them. Can you send a reply? What do the techs say about getting them home?"

Nolan shook his head slowly. "We're going to try to transmit back to them, but Tom . . ." His voice faded to a whisper before trailing off completely.

Though he feared he knew what was coming, Kinnear had to ask. "What is it?"

"They . . . Well, it's extremely unlikely that they can make it home. Even if they could retrace their precise course without an iota of deviation, it might not matter."

"Why not?"

"A wormhole, if that is indeed what they went through, is theoretically unstable at best. It can move around, it can collapse under its own gravitational forces at any time. Or vanish and reappear somewhere else—like halfway across the galaxy, or even outside it. In addition, just because a particular time–space distortion allows travel one way, that doesn't mean it wouldn't annihilate a solid object attempting to travel in the opposite direction." His finger traced aimless designs on the tabletop. "It's not like the daily commute over the Verrazano, Tom."

"Oh, hell."

"More or less." Nolan looked away. "I'm afraid that we're going to lose them. According to some of the science guys, there's nothing left to do but write the post-mortems."

"Damn," Kinnear murmured tightly. "So you're telling me that there's no other options? No other way for them to get back?"

"Not as we understand the physics of it right now," Nolan replied. "We're working on it, obviously, and if we can come up with something, we will. But we're dealing with a situation where our best people aren't even sure they understand the physical models involved."

Kinnear nodded. "All right, but no matter what, if you do manage to get a transmission through to the *Ghost*, you don't tell them the odds, okay? At least not yet. We don't want them to lose hope out there until we've lost it here. Do the techs have any idea how long this wormhole or distortion is likely to remain open?"

Nolan leaned back in his seat. "A minute. An hour. A week." He shrugged. "We can't call up the wormhole forecast for the immediate galactic vicinity. We just don't know, Tom. How can you ask someone to give a probability for something we weren't even sure existed until this happened?"

"Okay, I understand." *Forget the physics,* Kinnear told himself. *Stick to something you do know, like how men and women react under stress.* "They know that they're in trouble—and I still don't understand this business about alien artifacts and such—but they also need to be told there's a chance they can make it home. Give them the best advice you can, but like I said, keep it optimistic."

"Understood." Nolan's expression twisted. "I wish I had better news."

"Me, too. And it only gets worse."

"Worse? How could this get worse?"

"The Old Man thinks we've got an infiltrator," Tom informed him.

Nolan stared. "A spy? Industrial?"

Kinnear smiled humorlessly. "Any of your people manifested a serious desire lately for vodka or borscht?"

VI

It was not so much that Starscream gave up the chase as that he found himself distracted. Neither the alien vessel nor the puny organic creatures onboard had made a move to intervene in his ongoing skirmish with Bumblebee. Indeed, they had shown no interest in it at all. Hovering high above, he made a choice. Eradication of the infuriatingly nimble Autobot could wait until later. At the moment he found himself more and more drawn to the inexplicable alien visitor.

A quick but thorough transcan confirmed that the rough design was in fact somewhat derived from Cybertronian sources. But the technology that had been used to build it was extremely primitive. The alloy that was the principal component of the vessel's hull was insubstantial. A single blast from his pulse cannons would in all likelihood reduce it to blackened scrap.

Still, his curiosity was piqued. Considering its unashamedly crude origins, how had it come to be here in this distant and uninhabited place? Plainly these lifeforms understood little about the basics of advanced mechanoid technology. Reviewing the details of his scan, Starscream realized that he could interface with their laughable computer systems, though he would have to carefully moderate the speed at which he transmitted data or risk overloading their entire system.

Knowledge was one of the pillars of power. How was it that these frail organics may have possibly encountered Megatron and survived long enough to not only study his design, but actually adapt it to their ends? What did they know about the long-missing leader of the Decepticons? And most important, how could he turn any such information to his own advantage?

As he scanned inside the ship, it was apparent that the organic life-forms were in a panic at his presence. They had weapons. Not that he believed they could seriously harm him with them, but one could never be certain. Lower life-forms could be surprisingly devious. So far, they had not attacked. It was possible that they realized how overmatched they were and had no desire to provoke a fight. On that basis alone he was willing to credit them for minimal intelligence.

Of course, lower life-forms did not have a monopoly on deviousness.

Getting information from them, for example, would be faster, easier, and more efficient if he could convince them to share it willingly. While he could extract what he wished from their tiny onboard data bank, drawing information from sometimes recalcitrant living beings could be slow and—messy.

A plan began to take shape in his mind, and Starscream allowed himself a moment of amusement. Touching down nearby, he scanned the ship's unprotected internal communications until he isolated the unbelievably simple programming. A moment or two was all that was required for him to download all the data in the onboard storage. It required several moments for him to process, analyze, and translate the basics of their unsophisticated language. He reviewed the first message he intended to display on their internal visual monitors, and then sent it.

"Greetings. It is fortunate that I arrived when I did.

The other creature you encountered would surely have destroyed you and your ship otherwise."

That should do it, he decided. Straight to the point and not too complex for their simple protein-based brains. It had been a long time since he'd had the opportunity to apply time-honored Decepticon strategy to a nonmechanoidal life-form.

It felt good.

Optimus stared out at the dark shapes that were making their way toward the *Ark* from the far side of the nearby moon. Silently he cursed himself for not trusting his earlier hesitation. It should have been obvious from the initial sighting that the unusual alien ship was a Decepticon trap of not-so-subtle design. How else to explain its obvious yet distorted Cybertronian resemblance? When directness failed, enemies often resorted to trickery. Usually he could see it coming and unravel the ruse well in advance. This time he had dismissed his suspicions. Now a battle, with the *Ark* and his friends once again at risk, seemed inevitable.

How many times had he already faced the Decepticons and survived with his Spark intact? Too many to count. But every clash exacted a price. In energy, in patience—or worse still, in colleagues forever lost. Each battle made the Allspark seem more and more a distant goal, the likelihood of finding it and restoring Cybertron to what it had once been was a dream that was slowly fading into the distance of time. They had spent so long searching for it that sometimes the search seemed to have become an end unto itself.

Moments like this made Optimus think that it was time for them to put the quest aside. Time for them to find a new home where they could live out a peaceful existence. The galaxy in all its endless possibilities was simply too vast—the places the Allspark could have fetched up too many—to make continuing the search for it a realistic endeavor.

Drifting next to him beneath the looming bulk of the *Ark*, a watchful Jazz gave his leader a gentle nudge. "At least when Megatron was in charge he had some restraint. He knew when to pick and choose the time and place for a fight. I'm starting to think that Starscream would destroy the Allspark itself if it meant finishing us off."

"You must be reading my thoughts." Optimus turned to his friend. "The notion of having to engage in battle every time we exit back into normal space exhausts my patience. Ratchet, what do your scans show?"

With Jazz having insisted on leaving the ship to face the Decepticons, Ratchet was now in sole command of the *Ark*. With Ironhide covering his other flank, Optimus felt that the three of them were as ready as they could be to face the coming onslaught. He was restless but not afraid. They had survived worse.

"No report back yet from Bumblebee," Ratchet was telling them. "You've got three Decepticons headed in your direction. Analyzing their energy signatures, I'd say it's most likely Blackout, Bonecrusher, and Frenzy. I've also got a lock on the *Nemesis,* but it's holding position at the moment." He paused, then added, "Not that I expect it to stay that way."

"Optimus," Ironhide rumbled, "we should attack now. For once, let's strike the first blow rather than waiting for it to fall. The defensive strategies we have used repeatedly in the past are becoming too familiar to our enemies. One day they will find a means to overcome them."

"I know how you feel, Ironhide," Optimus conceded. "But you know that's not our way—and never can be. Once we succumb to the temptation of first strike, we mark ourselves as no better than the Decepticons."

"I'm just as familiar with the old principles as you, Optimus," Ironhide responded. "It's not that I disagree with them, or with you." His attention was directed outward, at the ominous oncoming shapes. "I'm just asking you to consider that we won't be any better than the Decepticons if we're annihilated, either."

"In a moment neither of you will have to worry about the viability of your position," Ratchet interjected. "Here they come."

Scrutinizing the approaching Decepticons as they approached soundlessly across the void, Optimus plotted strategy. "Jazz, I want you to take Frenzy. Ironhide, you've got Blackout. I'll deal with Bonecrusher."

Everyone quietly voiced their understanding. Jazz mumbled something about always having to fight the little ones. Optimus smiled inwardly. His companions were dedicated and supportive, and he was proud to be their leader. Proud to be one of them, conscious of the trust they had placed in him. Although he had been Prime for many centuries he could see that their confidence in him was still strong, even when on occasion they were beset by doubts as to the likelihood of their mission's success. They had all suffered injury and loss, he reminded himself. They had the right to question him, as Ironhide had just done, even though it was rare that a significant failure had occurred through any fault of his.

The seemingly endless quest was taking its toll on them all, mentally as well as physically. Perhaps Ironhide was right. Maybe it *was* time to alter tactics. He glanced up at the *Ark*.

"Change of plans," he announced abruptly. "Ironhide, you and Jazz go back to the ship. I know it doesn't carry the kind of firepower that we do individually—it's a transport, after all—but ready everything that you can."

"Ahh, you *were* listening!" There was a teasing note

in Ironhide's voice. "And while we're secured on the *Ark* what will you be doing?" He gestured toward the oncoming Decepticons. "Keeping all the excitement for yourself, is that it?"

Optimus laughed. "I'll be going out to teach our impulsive friends a lesson, if that's what you mean."

"Not without me." Jazz was insistent. "I won't let you go out there alone."

Optimus turned to his combative smaller companion. "Ironhide is right, Jazz. It's time we approached things a little differently. Let me handle it this time. I'm tired of seeing my friends get hurt."

"You're not having all the fun without me," Jazz protested.

"Yes I am." Optimus pointed up at their ship. "Now get moving. If what I have in mind pans out, I'm going to need both of you on the *Ark*."

Grabbing Jazz by the arm, Ironhide started toward the hangar bay. "Come on, Jazz. Optimus knows what he's doing—so let's let him do it."

"All right," Jazz muttered unhappily. "A command's a command—but I don't have to like it."

"No, you don't," Ironhide agreed as he continued to haul his friend toward the ship.

Optimus smiled to himself. The younger Autobot continued to argue even as he was half guided, half dragged into the *Ark*. For all his impulsiveness and flair, Jazz was a good soldier and boon companion. Someday he would make a fine administrator. Someday—if there was ever again anything to administrate.

He turned away from the *Ark* and launched himself out into space. Noting his change of position, the Decepticons immediately swerved to intercept. They also unloaded their combined weaponry, but at this extreme range it was easy for him to evade incoming fire as he led them away from the ship.

"Keep moving!" That was Ratchet transmitting, Optimus knew. "We'll swing into position to cover you!"

The *Ark* was in motion, maneuvering for the best possible advantage while keeping clear of the fighting. It was vital to give Optimus a chance to return fire while not compromising his room to evade. The weapons on the *Ark* opened up, and he heard Ratchet broadcast his personal battle cry. When the Decepticons adjusted to confront the new threat, Optimus unexpectedly whirled and shot directly at his attackers.

As the massive figure of Bonecrusher closed the space between them, a small metal shape shot away from Blackout's body. Extending forward, metal pincers reached for Optimus's chest plate. The much smaller Decepticon slammed into the Autobot leader.

Scorponok! The vicious little mechanoid must have been fully repaired since their last encounter, Optimus realized with a start.

The frenetic Decepticon's multiple limbs were a frenzied blur as they fought to penetrate Optimus's ventral plating. If Scorponok could cut his way past the armor to the systems below, Optimus knew he would be in real trouble.

Grabbing at his chest while continuing to elude his pursuers, he tried to work his hands beneath the feral metallic monstrosity. He managed to grasp one of the pincers and shove it away, twisting until the composite tendons within the metal began to fail. Pressing his advantage, he plunged his other hand into his attacker's far less heavily armored chest cavity and tore furiously at the instrumentation and electronics within.

Scorponok scrambled madly as he tried to escape. Optimus was happy to assist, flinging the Decepticon away from him as hard as he could. His instrumentation damaged, Scorponok went spinning through space, barely recovering enough to adjust his altitude so that he would swing in a disturbed arc away from the massive Autobot. In the distance, the *Nemesis* had finally begun to move, and the damaged Decepticon was struggling to head in its direction.

Convinced the smaller mechanoid was no longer a threat, Optimus turned in time to see Frenzy and Blackout closing in on him. Having separated from the others, Bonecrusher was accelerating toward the *Ark*.

"Time to extinguish, Optimus Prime!" Blackout transmitted. The charging Decepticon's sense of anticipation was almost palpable.

While Optimus knew that his adversary was not as large or powerful as he was, Blackout was hardly an opponent to be taken lightly. He was an experienced and clever fighter. Nor would it do to let the much smaller Frenzy get behind him, where the other Decepticon could latch onto his back and cause uninterrupted havoc. Optimus readied himself.

Such a waste, he thought. So much energy, so much effort, so much life abandoned to the service of hatred.

When the pair of Decepticons closed in, he feinted toward Blackout. As expected, Frenzy immediately tried to circle behind him.

Instead of finishing the strike he had begun, Optimus spun at the last possible second. His timing was perfect. A massive metal fist slammed into the side of Frenzy's head, sending him reeling away. Making use of the Autobot's distraction, Blackout instantly backed his drive and brought his integrated weaponry to bear.

In the distance Bonecrusher had reached the *Ark*. Avoiding its external armament, he forced his way into the hangar. More than occupied, Optimus had no choice but to concentrate on the battle at hand. Those he had left behind would have to deal with Bonecrusher's assault.

A barrage of plasma erupted toward him, concentrated

enough to do plenty of damage. The series of blasts struck him twice. Optimus felt the temperature of his armor rise alarmingly. In places it began to buckle. Instead of turning away and trying to flee, he launched himself directly at Blackout, bringing his own weaponry online. Ironhide would have been pleased.

Expecting his prey to defend, not attack, Blackout retreated, trying to keep a consistent distance between them. While a complex evasive maneuver allowed him to avoid the incoming fire, it also forced him within his target's physical reach. Optimus slammed into Blackout full-force and at speed. At the same time as they grappled furiously, Optimus knew that Frenzy might well have recovered by now. If so, the other Decepticon could be expected to throw himself into the fight at any moment.

"Get off me!" Blackout snarled, trying to find enough room to fire at Optimus.

"As you wish." Activating his drive, Optimus whirled and, utilizing their calculated common center of gravity, succeeded in hurling Blackout directly into the path of the hard-driving Frenzy. The two Decepticons smashed into each other with satisfying force.

Risking a quick glance away, Optimus's sensors picked up a sight that for the moment, at least, eased his fears. Emerging from the dark, gaping maw that was the *Ark*'s hangar, Bonecrusher came flying out into space. Ironhide and Jazz were close behind and firing away with becoming enthusiasm. Optimus could almost sense the larger Decepticon's frustration as he was compelled to focus his efforts on evasion and defense instead of continuing his attack.

Turning back to his two dazed and damaged opponents, Optimus was preparing to engage them afresh when a blanket transmission from Blackout brought an end to the battle that was as sudden as it was unexpected.

"Decepticons, fall back! Retreat!"

More than any tactic his adversaries had employed in the course of the fight, Optimus was bemused by the abrupt announcement. They still had him two on one, and though Ironhide and Jazz were both seasoned warriors, he knew from experience that Bonecrusher rarely backed down from a battle. He was tempted to press the apparent advantage and continue the fight. Just as he had decided to order pursuit, Ratchet reached him over the secure battle frequency.

"Optimus, you should probably get back here."

"Why? I think we've gained the strategic advantage," he responded.

"Bumblebee just reported in. Starscream was on the planet below, but in light of what's transpired it's reasonable to assume that he is now headed our way. Bumblebee barely managed to survive his attack, and he is not out of trouble quite yet. Let the others go. We need to regroup and reconsider."

Starscream, Optimus thought. Disclosure that he was at hand was no surprise. But why was he down on the surface of the uninhabited planet instead of in the middle of the fight? Certainly his participation could have had a huge impact on the outcome. "Understood," he informed Ratchet. "I'm on my way."

It made no sense for Starscream to avoid the clash for any reason Optimus could envisage. What could he and the Decepticons be up to? Something shrewd, no doubt. For all of Megatron's monumental maliciousness, he was very direct, rarely deviating from his single-minded goal of the Autobots' destruction. In contrast, Starscream was cunning and insidious. Optimus knew that he and his friends would have to prepare for any number of possible surprises.

He gave the thwarted Bonecrusher a wide berth, approaching the *Ark* at an angle that would allow him to keep a sensor on the other retreating Decepticons as well.

"Your day will come, Optimus!" Blackout transmitted openly. "I will be there to celebrate your destruction."

Across the space that separated them, the Autobot leader regarded his foe. "You may be right, Blackout," he broadcast back. "But if it's in my power, I'll rip your Spark from your chest before I switch off." He pointed at the *Nemesis* drifting in the distance. "Tell your master the Autobots are done running."

The war was going to end here, he decided there and then. Ironhide was right. They'd had enough of fleeing and retreating, of always absorbing the first blows so they would be sure of being able to escape and continue the search for the Allspark. This place, this time, this obscure corner of the cosmos was as good as any for a final reckoning. One way or another, it was time to finish this.

The Autobots were going to stand and fight.

Ironhide and Jazz were waiting for him inside the hangar, having already repaired the damage Bonecrusher had done to the portal in the course of his initial assault.

"That was an interesting ploy you utilized out there," Ironhide observed with obvious satisfaction. "Maybe not quite what I had in mind, but a variation deserving of admiration."

"Ironhide, my old friend, you were right when you said we needed to change tactics. I understand that it is difficult to be patient when you're losing. The line between breaching our ancient principles and acting no different than a Decepticon is a fine one. We must continue to find new and creative ways of dealing with them—and we will."

"Then we should do it fast," Jazz argued. "Starscream isn't likely to wait around for us to come up with a carefully thought-out response."

"You're right, of course, Jazz," Optimus admitted. "I

have an idea or two. Before we respond directly or in kind, though, there's something we need to do first."

"What might that be?" the younger Autobot inquired.

"We must ensure that Bumblebee returns safely." Optimus turned to gaze out a port at the empty world floating nearby. "That accomplished, I promise the both of you that before we leave this place you'll each have all the opportunity for combat you can handle."

Another geologically tormented section of the barren plateau provided Bumblebee with a reasonably safe place to pause and take stock of his situation. Whipping around a particularly impressive pillar of twisted stone, he hastily transformed back into his normal bipedal mode. Once the familiar form had been fully reconstituted, he peered out to run a scan in the direction from which he'd come.

There was no sign of Starscream—a fact for which Bumblebee was profoundly grateful. In the course of his desperate flight from the far more robust Decepticon he had managed to send a brief report back to the *Ark* informing them of their powerful adversary's presence. He knew it had been received: he was not surprised that it had yet to be acted upon. At the moment he was pretty sure that his friends were dealing with more immediate Decepticon problems.

As for the odd alien vessel that had originally drawn him down to the surface of this inhospitable world, whatever its true significance and whatever it meant to the Decepticons, it was apparently enough to keep Starscream from pursuing him indefinitely. While not afraid of a fight, Bumblebee was intelligent and experienced enough to know that considered flight was the wiser alternative to valiant suicide. While he could more than hold his own against an equally matched opponent, he knew that his design did not include the fully developed fighting capabilities of someone like Optimus Prime or Ironhide—nor was it intended to. He better served the cause as a scout, relaying information as opposed to acting on it. Going up against Starscream alone would not have helped anything.

Knowledge of one's limitations and the ability to operate effectively within them are also strengths, he reminded himself reassuringly.

He found himself contemplating the nearby stone pillar. Directly in front of him stood a second stone tower that was a near duplicate of the first. As he allowed his perception to roam he saw that there were a number of such structures. Not only were they remarkably similar in shape, but on closer inspection he realized that they formed an almost perfect semicircle. *The natural world,* he mused, *can play tricks with one's sensory input.* The better to resolve the apparent contradiction, he took a closer look.

Natural or artificial? he found himself wondering. In Starscream's continued absence he took a few moments to examine the pillars and their immediate surroundings. Wind, and nothing else, howled and eddied around him. If synthetic, what could have been the function of the pillars and the reason for arranging them in such a fashion? Were they simply markers of some kind left behind by a long-vanished race, or did they hint at some deeper purpose? Ironhide would not have cared, and Jazz would have quickly grown bored by the enigmatic, inanimate spires. Bumblebee's curiosity was another mark of his difference. Unlike his companions, preoccupied with recovering the Allspark, he had always found other lesser species and their individual habits fascinating. It was one of the qualities that made him such a good scout.

While he wanted to investigate further, he knew he needed to get back to the *Ark* as soon as possible—and before Starscream thought to return to finish him off. Perhaps once the Decepticons had been dealt with and the mystery of the alien ship solved, time could be allotted to explore this world in greater depth. Until then, such questions would have to give way to matters of greater urgency. In war, the accumulation of knowledge for its own sake was always one of the first casualties.

Taking a new and more direct line, he started back in the direction of his original landing site. As he did so he reopened digital communications on what he hoped was still a secure channel. "Jazz, Ratchet, are you . . . ?"

Without warning or precursor of any kind, the ground suddenly swirled and dropped away beneath his feet. He broke off the transmission as he realized that he was waist-deep in thick, clinging grit and descending fast. It would have been an easy matter for him to break free of something as simple and straightforward as a pit full of quicksand. But this new geological phenomenon was sufficiently different from anything in his data banks to hold his attention. The sand and rock not only slid away sharply beneath him, but also whirled like a cyclone. The speed with which they were swallowing him was breathtaking: they were up over his shoulders in seconds. As his head sank out of sight, he sent off a last transmission identifying his position. There would be time enough to go into details later, when he had gained a better understanding of the phenomenon. Absent an emergency call for help from the *Ark*, he fully intended to follow the experience through to its conclusion. It might be the only piece of solid scientific information he had time to take away with him from his sojourn on the unnamed planet.

As the sand closed in over his head and darkness descended all around him, he switched reflexively to perceptive sonics in order to make sense of his surroundings. He could hear the hiss and rattle of grit against his epidermis as he continued to sink and could feel it circulating around him.

More seconds passed before he felt his legs break free. The distance to the ground below did not allow enough time or need for him to engage propulsion. There was no one present to hear him slam feetfirst into the stone floor. Straightening, he mulled over a multitude of perceptive options before settling on the one that offered the best vision in surroundings that to a human would have constituted impenetrable darkness.

He was standing in a natural cavern. The usual speleotherms decorated ceiling and floor, walls and channels. The place was dead now, devoid of the running water that had formed and decorated it. A number of tunnels led off in several directions. As far as providing an easy route back to the surface, one was probably as good as another. He would check for airflow and use it to guide him upward. Walking out instead of flying would give him time to consider the unique geological forces that had initiated this harmless and fascinating subterranean diversion.

As he started off, he attempted to reopen communications. Might as well let his friends know what had happened and that he was still all right. Only when he initialized did he realize that his communicator must have been damage during the plunge.

A quick diagnostic confirmed that everything else was intact. *Perfect,* he thought disgustedly. He had to settle for sending out a compressed electronic transmission as he began walking.

It did not take long to locate the direction of maximum atmospheric inflow. He was advancing in its direction when he heard the first sounds. Initially he mistook the whispering, hissing noise for air moving through hollow formations. When it stopped, resumed, paused, and started up again he knew the source was not a constant airflow.

It was coming from the part of the cavern he had just left.

He had decided this was a dead planet, devoid of life. Apparently this was to be his day for making interesting mistakes.

VII

Lieutenant Colonel Philip Nolan sat behind the desk bearing the customized MISSION DIRECTOR sign that had been a gift from the engineering team and brooded over the problems facing him. The short version was that. . .

He didn't like the short version.

Tough. There was no avoiding it, no dodging it, no getting around it. *Ghost 1* was effectively lost, and its crew were as good as dead. He could not avoid the facts, much as he wanted to. He had never been the kind of man who could. A catastrophe for Sector Seven and its once untouchable agenda, the loss would haunt him for the rest of his days despite the fact that he had known—they had all known, hadn't they?—that the mission the unique ship had embarked upon verged on the suicidal.

Still, no matter how extreme, a risk is not the same thing as a certainty. Nolan remained unsure how he was going to break the news to the crew of *Ghost 1* that the chances of them coming back were virtually nil. Assuming that the techs in charge of communications managed to make the jury-rigged alien transmission system work well enough and long enough for him to say even that much.

He sighed. There was nothing to be done about it, and the best he could probably forward to *Ghost* for now was the old *We know there's a problem and we're working on it*. As encouragement, it was pretty insipid.

Looking up, he found himself caught in the long-suffering gaze of Christolph Smythe. Bespectacled and balding, the director of communications was waiting patiently for Nolan's input.

"We're ready with the alien transmitter, Phil. As ready as we'll ever be, I expect. What do you want to say?"

No more time to stall, Nolan realized. No place to run and hide. He indicated the console that dominated one side of his desk. "I can monitor everything from here. Can you also route my response?" He did not have to add that he preferred to compose the transmission away from the intent eyes of the communications staff and anyone else who might be hanging around at that especially solemn moment.

Smythe nodded as he adjusted his glasses. They looked thick enough, Nolan reflected, to stop a shot from an M1. Or an ill-considered inquiry. Coming around the desk, the engineer adjusted a small portion of the console's elaborate instrumentation, then stepped back.

"Whenever you're ready, sir. Just remember, this is the first time we'll be utilizing the alien system in this fashion. We have no idea if it will work, far less if anything we send will actually reach the *Ghost*—wherever it is."

"Understood." Nolan picked up the mike, hesitated, and nodded up at the engineer. "I know you and your gang have done the best you can."

"We all have, sir." Civilian or not, Nolan thought that at that moment Smythe looked very military. Turning back to the console, he depressed the pertinent button. "*Ghost One, Ghost One,* this is SSAB Command. Do you read?"

His voice went out, echoing and strange, through a kind of space–time that was still more theory than reality. The notion of instantaneous intergalactic communication on any level was so fanciful that Smythe kept the three fat volumes of schematics his team had developed from working on that portion of the Ghost project sandwiched between hardback copies of *Alice's Adventures in Wonderland* and *Through the Looking-Glass*.

There was no response. He repeated the query. Both he and Smythe were about to call it a valiant try and return to their routine when something came crackling through the console speaker.

A voice. Human, almost recognizable. Practically throwing himself at another mike, Smythe exchanged frantic words with other members of his team. The voice from the speaker cleared, became intelligible.

"SSAB Command, this is *Ghost One*." Over another speaker set in the console Nolan could hear wild sounds of celebration from the communications team. "And we are very glad to hear from you."

Unable to help it, Nolan caught himself grinning. The crew of that lost, distant spacecraft deserved better news than he was going to have to give them. He bent back toward the pickup.

"*Ghost One,* we've received your transmission and we're aware of your situation. Do you have a status update?"

"We're alive," the voice replied after an expected repeat of the longish delay. "Since we don't know how well or for how long this contact will last, let's get the basics out of the way. Where are we, and how do we get home? From here it looks like we've come through some kind of continuum anomaly into another star system."

The sounds of celebration vanished. Throughout the complex, everyone who was privy to the ongoing exchange waited with bated breath to hear how the mission commander intended to respond.

Nolan coughed slightly. "Ahh—*Ghost One,* we're working on those details right now. We—uh—we concur with your assessment of your present location. You could be a few light-years away or—" He swallowed. "—you could be on the other side of the galaxy."

"The what?" Walker shot back after the delay. "That's impossible!"

"*Ghost One*, all of this is 'impossible.' Us having this conversation right now is impossible. However, unless we are all of us—you there and us back here—operating under the effects of a mass delusion, that is the situation as we presently understand it. It's remarkable enough that we are able to communicate across even the slightest of interstellar distances, let alone from here to where you may actually find yourselves. As to your exact location, however, we are currently as much in the dark as you are."

"If that's the case, then how do we get home?" Walker demanded. "Should we try to reenter the anomaly, or wormhole, or whatever it is that threw us here?"

Nolan took a deep breath and plunged on. He had no choice. "*Ghost One,* we're working on all of that. Right now what we need is for you to stay calm. Unfortunately, we don't have too many more answers than you do at the moment."

"Grade A marvelous" was Walker's eventual reply. There followed a long silence that had nothing to do with the vagaries of interstellar communication and everything to do with the reality of unpleasant facts taking hold and sinking in. "Speaking from a purely scientific point of view—we're screwed, aren't we?"

Nolan knew what the odds were, but he forced himself to say the lie anyway. Walker could berate him for the prevarication when—he got back. "Speaking from a purely scientific point of view—not quite yet, *Ghost One*. Hang in there. Let's have that status update. The more we know, the better our chances of figuring out a way we can help."

There was another lengthy pause, then Walker replied coolly, "SSAB Command, stand by for status update."

"*Ghost One*, go ahead with your status report."

This time the delay seemed longer than any that had preceded it. Staring at the silent console, Nolan feared that contact had finally been lost.

"SSAB Command," Walker finally resumed, "*Ghost One* has successfully set down on an unknown and apparently uninhabited planet with a breathable atmosphere. As regards our earlier reference to possibly hostile alien artifacts, we have taken the precaution of assuming a defensive posture. The ship has been adjusted to allow for defensive . . . "

Static crashed through the end of the transmission.

Quietly frantic, Nolan thumbed the relevant controls. "*Ghost One*, this is SSAB Command. The last part of your transmission failed to come through. Please repeat."

The muted, indifferent howl of distant stars hissed over the speakers, and then, " . . . we are not alone, SSAB Command. Repeat—*Ghost One* is not alone. The Ice Man has a family."

Nolan felt a cold shiver track down his spine and his arms broke out in goose bumps. The silence throughout the complex was total and unbroken.

The Ice Man has a family, he repeated to himself. That was not something he or anyone else on Earth would rejoice at hearing. He tried to convince himself he had heard wrongly.

"Please advise, SSAB Command." Walker was not finished. "Repeat—please advise."

Now, this is interesting. Nolan observed that his hands were shaking. "Stand by, *Ghost One*."

Mission Control erupted with sound as everyone started talking at once.

Now what do we do? he asked himself. "*Please advise?*" What could he say. What could they do? The answer that came back to him was the same one he had started out with.

Nothing.

The creatures inhabiting the alien ship, Starscream had learned, had a name for themselves: humans. They repeatedly referred to their homeworld as "Earth." Nomenclature that was simple, straightforward, and self-centered. Additional detailed scanning led him to the conclusion that they were little more than animals who had somehow unlocked a few basic secrets of technology. Just enough, it would seem, to propel their primitive vessel sufficiently far from their homeworld that they could die. From the first scan, it was evident they were lost and very frightened. They had only the barest conception of how they had actually managed to reach the location in space where they presently found themselves. Starscream found this extraordinary as well as disgusting.

Though their presence here was nothing more than an accident, he knew that when skillfully exploited, even the accidental actions of primitives could prove useful.

Ignorance and fear were a combination that left those subject to their influences open to manipulation. Still, there was more he needed to know before he felt comfortable proceeding with his intentions. He proceeded to communicate with them anew via their anachronistic computation system.

"Your ship is a design I am familiar with. How did you come to acquire it?"

Unbeknownst to the humans, he could overhear his question being discussed within the ship. There was some argument against revealing anything. It was his claim to have driven off their "attacker" that finally persuaded them to respond positively. When it finally came, it sent an undampened surge through every circuit of his being.

"An alien being or machine—or machine being—reached our world long ago. The theory is that it lost control and crashed near our northern polar cap, subsequent to which it became frozen in the ice. Since finding it—him—it has become common to call the alien the Ice Man. Our scientists and engineers have worked hard to replicate as much of his integrated instrumentation as possible, a good deal of which has so far defeated our best efforts. This ship represents one of the more successful efforts at this ongoing process of reverse-engineering."

Starscream absorbed every detail of the response before replying. "And what of the alien now?"

"He remains frozen and inert. Too many imponderables are attached to releasing him from stasis." There was a pause, then, "It may be only a species-specific reaction on our part, but his appearance does not engender confidence."

"You are wise in your assessment." Starscream could hardly contain himself. It was too much to be believed! The great Megatron—held captive by these incredibly primitive organic life-forms. *Truly the universe favors those who persist,* he told himself with satisfaction. "However, there is a much more significant threat to your world," he continued. "To all worlds. It should be of concern to you and yours as well."

"Threat?"

"Indeed. A plague of noxious creatures who call themselves 'Autobots.' The alien who fled when I raced here to protect you is one of them."

"Why would they be a threat to us?"

Starscream was thoroughly enjoying himself. "Thousands of years ago the Autobots and my own people lived in peace, far from here, on our mutual homeworld of Cybertron. We shared available resources with each other, including a source of energy that held tremendous importance to all of us. This is known as the Allspark. The Allspark is literally the source of life for our people. Then there came a day so deceitful that the very memory of it darkens my thought processes and makes it difficult for me to speak. A day when their deceitful leader, Optimus Prime, decided to no longer share the Allspark."

It was plain that the humans were waiting for him to continue. Much as he was enjoying spinning the story, Starscream purposely stopped. It would be more effective if they drew their own conclusion. Primitive or not, they did not disappoint.

"War?" came the eventual response.

"Just so," he replied. "A war horrific beyond your imaginations. Merely to think of it sends pain coursing through my system. Those of us peace-loving ones who survived the initial duplicitous attacks had no choice but to adjust our forms for defense. Many perished before we could adapt. The Autobots showed no mercy, even to those who begged."

This time there was a longer delay before the humans responded. It was not unexpected. "We are sorry to hear this. Unfortunately, we are also all-too-familiar with the nature of war. What was the result of yours?"

With a facility born of much practice, Starscream had no trouble embellishing the lie. "In the course of the biggest battle to date, at a place called Tyger Pax, there was an explosion of unprecedented magnitude. The Allspark was blown into space and disappeared through a distortion. My people have been looking for it ever since. The large alien who crashed into your world was probably an Autobot scout, searching for it."

"We are confused," the humans told him. "Much of

what we know of the cosmos around us is conveyed to us through our eyes. By this measure, the being who landed on our world does indeed appear threatening. The entity you chased off—did not."

"That," Starscream replied smoothly, "is what makes them so dangerous. During the war the Autobots often employed deception as a means of getting close to us. Adopting a benign appearance was but one of their many cunning subterfuges." He paused, adding, "And even now, even as we speak here on the surface of this unknown world, the war rages on."

The humans took a moment to digest this. "But you have already said that this world is not yours. Not your 'Cybertron.' Please explain."

Starscream knew that in order to make good use of the situation he would have to manage it with caution. He chose his next words carefully.

"The ship that brought me here suffered a malfunction at approximately the same time that your ship was exiting the wormhole." Let them think the two incidents were related, he mused. "Ordinarily, we would have repaired our vessel immediately and continued with our search. Unfortunately, at nearly the same time our enemies the Autobots also arrived—quite possibly attracted to these coordinates when you utilized the wormhole as a passage for your vessel." He paused to let that sink in.

"Unsure of your intentions, we began to back away. While we were concentrating on your ship, the Autobots caught us unawares and fired on us. Our vessel was disabled. It was only through good fortune that we were able to survive at all. The defense we mounted has allowed us to withdraw to a safe distance and consider our options."

"Then that was their ship we saw when we emerged here?"

"Yes, and activating your defensive capabilities was

certainly the right decision," Starscream assured them. "It was the Cybertronian resemblance of your vessel that gave them pause long enough for you to escape to the surface of this world."

"Will they come after us again?" the human speaker inquired quickly.

Starscream paused long enough to give them the impression that he was giving serious thought to their question. "The individual whom you saw here was only a scout. They are certain to come after you in greater strength. The Autobots will slaughter members of any species they encounter."

Based on the increased volume of modulated sound waves within the ship, the humans were understandably upset at this news. "But why come after us? We fled immediately. Surely a ship our size poses no threat to them."

"They are a vicious race," Starscream growled. "Although you could have not possibly realized that the design of your ship would put you in greater danger, they do not know this, and to be sure, they will not listen to reason. They have not listened to reason in centuries. All they are concerned with is the destruction of my people and the recovery of the Allspark."

"What can we do? Are you saying that you are willing to help us?"

"As I told you, my ship is disabled," Starscream murmured. "But—I may be able to help you, yes."

The response was immediate. "How?"

"I have a plan," he told them. "If you are willing to help me, if we work together, I am confident that we can destroy the Autobots *and* their ship. Once this section of space has been made safe, I and my friends can devote our resources—which are considerable—to helping you return to your own world."

The humans' excitement was inclusive and unrestrained. *Why shouldn't it be?* Starscream mused. It was not as if they had been presented with any other options. Of course, there was no way he was going to let the pitiful, deluded creatures anywhere near the other Decepticons. But he fully intended to introduce them to the Autobots.

If he managed the situation right—and there was no reason to believe he could not—the gullible humans and their harmless ship would be annihilated. A result he had looked forward to from the moment of first contact—except that now it would be Optimus Prime who would carry out the extermination on behalf of the Decepticons. The effect that would have on the nauseatingly altruistic leader of the Autobots once the truth was revealed to him would be delicious. With luck, it might even lead to a crippling demoralization.

The universe helps those who are ready and alert to warp it to their own ends, he reflected.

Ratchet looked up from his instrumentation. "Optimus, I think we've got a problem."

"When don't we?" Jazz quipped. "I tend to short circuit when we *don't* have a problem."

"Funny," Ratchet responded. "But I'm serious."

Optimus had a feeling that he knew what was coming. Taking precedence into account, he should have expected it. "Let me guess. It's Bumblebee, isn't it?"

Ratchet nodded. "He checked in not long ago, as I reported, but then . . ." He stopped, only continuing when Optimus encouraged him to do so. "Then I received another transmission just moments ago. He initialized contact, and then he simply cut off."

"Jazz, did you hear all this?" Optimus asked.

The smaller mechanoid shook his head. "No, but I was preoccupied with our defensive efforts and neglected constant monitoring of the relevant communications."

"We'll deal with that later," the leader of the Autobots replied. "Did you get anything else, Ratchet?"

"Just a carrier wave," he explained. "It is possible that the shutdown was intentional, as if he was closing off all outside communications to temporarily concentrate on something within his immediate vicinity. A sudden threat, perhaps? Or it is conceivable that the Decepticons have managed to place a communications block between the *Ark* and the germane portion of the planetary surface."

Optimus considered the possibilities. Starscream had recently been down on the surface—and could be there still—but the other Decepticons and their ship were up here. Leaving the *Ark* unprotected was not an option, but neither was ignoring the risk that Bumblebee might be in serious difficulty and in need of assistance. The decision he came to was obvious, but not easy.

"Ironhide, you, Jazz, and Ratchet will stay here to protect the *Ark*. If the Decepticon threat increases to the point that it poses a danger to the ship itself, you are to withdraw from this sector and return only when it's safe to do so. Engage in extensive evasive maneuvering, if that is what is required. I will go down to the surface and find Bumblebee."

"Don't go by yourself, Optimus," Jazz protested. "Take one of us along, if only to watch your back."

Optimus shook his head. "No," he declared firmly. "If the Decepticons return in strength to resume the fight, you'll need everyone here. If the only one of them down on the planet is Starscream, I can handle him by myself. I won't risk any of you or the *Ark* on a rescue mission designed to aid only one of us."

"Maybe Jazz is right, Optimus," Ironhide argued. "Starscream can be a handful, even for you. He's big and quick and clever. And we still haven't determined what that other ship was or what it is doing here. You could be heading into serious trouble." An arm gestured broadly. "This entire confrontation—the *Nemesis,* the Decepticons, the 'alien' vessel—could all be part of an elaborate ploy to lure you into a trap."

"If you're suggesting that Megatron is down there, I must disagree." Optimus remained convinced that his initial analysis of the alien craft was still correct. "If he was, he certainly would have attacked by now. I admit that this is only speculation, but based on what we've observed so far I still consider my analysis feasible."

"Out of communication or not, if he'd run into old Megs down there, Bumblebee would have found a way to let us know," Jazz admitted. "He would have gotten that kind of information to us if it had taken his last iota of energy."

"Yes, he would have," Optimus agreed readily. "So we are decided. While I am gone, Ironhide is in charge. I'd like to have a ship to come back to. If in my absence you can avoid an all-out engagement with the Decepticons, then, so much the better."

"We'll do our best," Ironhide told him somberly. "Just make sure you and Bumblebee get back in two pieces. We're eventually going to have to deal with those Decepticons, and I don't want to have to fight them alone while Ratchet is occupied with the need to replace your damaged components."

"I am in complete agreement with that sentiment." Optimus chuckled. "Stay safe, my friend."

"I will."

"Keep us informed, okay?" Jazz requested. "Regular updates."

"Better to maintain communicative silence until I've located Bumblebee," Optimus replied sensibly. "As soon as I've done that I'll resume contact. I reiterate with emphasis: if you run into serious difficulty, don't wait around for us. Get out of here, run the *Nemesis* in circles, and come back when the sector is clear."

"Affirmative, Optimus." Ratchet spoke calmly but firmly. "Just don't expect us to run out on you unless we are left with absolutely no choice."

Optimus laughed again. "The notion would never enter my cerebral processors." Turning, he headed once more for the hangar bay.

Given Bumblebee's continuing lack of transmission, there was a real possibility that he had run into serious trouble down on the planet's surface. Decepticon trouble, in the form of Starscream or someone else who might be down there whose presence was still unknown. What worried Optimus more was the realization that Bumblebee would willingly place himself in a dangerous situation or territory, risking his Spark, if he thought it would be of assistance to others. Despite his comparatively modest size, he was a fearless warrior who would take chances that even more battle-ready Autobots would elect to avoid. He was braver than many soldiers Optimus had known in the course of his long life, but that did not mean the leader of the Autobots wanted him to take risks that he could otherwise evade.

Still, he knew that repeatedly holding Bumblebee back was not a good idea, either. The younger Autobot idolized the bigger, stronger warriors who were his friends, and wanted to make sure that he was consistently a useful part of the team. He could never fulfill himself if orders kept him always stuck on board the *Ark*, forever doing nothing but routine maintenance. It was not fair to keep him from making an equal contribution to the effort, even if Optimus did worry about him constantly.

Launching himself from the hangar and swiftly transforming into his cometary protoform, Optimus hoped that Bumblebee had not run into trouble bigger than he could handle on his own.

Or worse still, that he had not run into Megatron.

* * *

Kinnear looked up from the map and peered through the blowing snow. No sooner had the convoy left the base than the storm had given the weather forecasters a meteorological finger. Altering direction with the indifference of a capricious breeze, it had turned south to slam straight across their carefully planned new route. When it came to the weather, the Arctic was more dangerous and unpredictable than a junior government tax auditor with a bad hangover.

"It's really coming down out there," he observed worriedly.

Next to him, Lieutenant Jensen nodded from the driver's seat as he kept his eyes fixed firmly on the narrow roadbed ahead. "It's good news, in a way," he countered. "Sir."

Kinnear looked over at the junior officer. "Good? How so?"

Jensen chuckled softly. "No sane infiltrator would be out in this weather, sir. With all due respect, no sane human being would be out in this."

He activated the heavy-duty, triple-bladed arctic wipers and they whirred to life, smushing the accumulating snow into a slushy gray mass at the bottom of the window. Their vehicle was the second in line behind the lead convoy truck. Behind them was another truck carrying a squad of well-trained guards, and behind that, the extended tractor-hauler carrying the Ice Man. This was followed by still another truck packed with soldiers. The remainder of the convoy carrying the technical support team was strung out behind, their slow-moving vehicles concealed by the blizzard.

"That's true enough," Kinnear agreed. "But we've got a job to do, good weather or bad. It could be a lot worse." Leaning forward, he did his best to make out the road ahead. This wasn't going well. From the passenger seat, he could feel the truck's chained tires slipping and sliding on the icy road. Suspected infiltrator or not, maybe changing routes at the last minute hadn't been such a good idea.

"For example," he explained, "if we had gone ahead and canceled we would have had to redraft, reissue, and refile every one of the relevant forms."

"Sir?"

Kinnear continued. "Paperwork. The soldier's worst enemy." He tried to see outside again. "Along with the weather. This is cold, but it still beats Southeast Asia. There it rained nonstop for months and the damn bugs would eat a man alive—sometimes from the inside out. At least here we don't have to deal with any parasites."

"Give me toes that are freezing over toes that are being gnawed on any day, sir." Jensen tried to peer out his side window. "Better snow than rain. Rain would turn this road into an ice rink."

Kinnear's attention had turned to the lead vehicle in front of them. "Speaking of ice . . . "

The truck on point swerved sharply to the left and its brake lights flashed on, then off, then back on. They stayed on as the truck started to slide. "Don't do that," Kinnear heard himself whispering. "Tap the brakes . . ." If they had taken the station's tracked vehicles, the nightmarish scenario that was developing would not now be playing out in front of him. But once they hit a normal civilian road, the snow machines would have become too slow and too conspicuous.

Of course, if the weather report had been accurate, they wouldn't be having any difficulties at all.

The lead driver could not hear him, and was clearly starting to panic. His vehicle continued to lose traction. Even through the blowing snow Kinnear could see that his brakes were completely locked up. "Oh, hell," he muttered. "Slow down, Jensen, or we're going to end up . . ."

Jensen did not hit the brakes hard. Kinnear was sure of that. It didn't matter. The truck's wheels locked, sending it into a skid from which there would be no recovery until something else stopped it.

Tom felt the truck slide sideways. For the briefest of seconds he saw the wide-eyed and openmouthed faces of the guards in the back of the lead vehicle through his passenger window rather than the windshield. "Steer through it!" he started to yell, when a quick flash of light from the headlamps of the first truck temporarily blinded him.

A frantic Jensen worked the wheel, trying to regain control, but it was already too late.

Their truck did a complete 360 just as the vehicle they were following slowed from doing the same. The two slammed together with a horrible, grinding *crunch*. Glass shattered, and a sudden wash of icy-cold air flooded the truck's forward compartment. The impact sent the lead vehicle sliding away in the opposite direction from Kinnear and Jensen's. Demonstrating the kind of skilled winter driving Kinnear could only wish Jensen had shown, the next truck in line behind them managed to slip to its left and avoid rear-ending them. Still sliding, Kinnear felt time slow down, the images flashing by with strobe-light precision. Looming directly behind them as they continued to skate backward was the extended heavy-load tractor-trailer carrying the Ice Man.

Ignore us, Kinnear thought wildly as the much bigger vehicle filled his field of view. *Hold your line. Whatever you do, hold your line.*

Jensen gave a shout and one more desperate spin of the wheel. Their truck hit a ridge in the poorly maintained road, slipped partway into the paralleling drainage ditch, overbalanced, and rolled. Kinnear felt the darkness coming and heard the sharp crack of his leg breaking as the vehicle began to crumple around him. Just before the world went black, he had time to wonder how bad the chain-reaction crash was.

Then there was nothing.

VIII

The last thing Bumblebee wanted was to be caught in a narrow tunnel with whatever was on his trail. Whirling, he moved quickly back to the nearest large chamber. Putting the nearest wall against his back, he waited. The sounds of something moving were louder now. Moments later his receptors were able to make out the rough outlines of at least two creatures. Judging from the echoes he was picking up, there might be more.

If he kept still—and depending on the senses that were available to them—they might not even see him. That thought was followed by another: his luck just had not been that good today.

Adjusting his perceptual acuity, he obtained a better look at his pursuers. Large and limbless, their most notable feature was a set of thick, triangular teeth in a rounded mouth. Their formidable jaws looked capable of chewing through rock as easily as prey, and it struck him that the tunnel he had just vacated might not have been as natural in origin as the speleotherm-decorated cavern. Given their size and wormlike bodies, it was possible that the creatures bored their way from cavern to cavern in search of food, water, or a place to breed. If not presently preoccupied with the particulars of survival, he no doubt would have found the biological study captivating.

Though wholly organic and lacking his seamless body armor, they were significantly larger than him. Their sinuous, humping forms seemed to comprise one continuous stretch of muscle. If one of them managed to wrap itself around him, he knew that his armor would not crack under the resulting constriction. Which would be small consolation if he was crushed like a cheap piece of cast-off metal. Nor was constriction the only threat the creatures presented. Teeth that could gnaw through solid rock might well be strong enough to pierce metal plating. As to what that impressive dentition could do if it reached his vulnerable internal components, he preferred not to speculate.

His best defense might well be one that would not give a raging Decepticon a moment's pause: he doubted that any organic life-form would regard him as an enticing meal. On the other hand, primitive carnivores such as the ones that were on the verge of confronting him could reasonably be expected to attack first and taste later.

His lack of movement did not prevent them from noting his presence. As they turned in his direction he activated his integral weapons systems.

Once they had decided on a target, they attacked with unexpected speed. Their muscular bodies shoved small boulders out of the way and snapped intervening stalagmites as if they were made of thin plastic instead of solid limestone. Thicker obstacles were slithered around or over.

I'm not edible, you mindless protein converters, he thought in frustration as he tensed in readiness for the coming assault. It was bad enough that he had to worry about Starscream and the other Decepticons. Now it appeared that he was going to have to do battle with inimical local life-forms as well.

When the first strike finally came, the nature of the attack surprised him. Instead of continuing to accelerate toward him across the broken ground, the nearer monster retracted in on itself and leaped like a coiled spring. As it launched itself in Bumblebee's direction, he hurriedly opened fire. Due to the unexpected nature of the assault his aim was slightly off, but the limited plasma blast he unleashed seared a long black streak down the side of the creature's body. It made an odd noise as its flesh carbonized: something between a hiss and a screech. Flying through the black air of the cavern, it opened its fearsome jaws wide as it struck. Raising his right arm, Bumblebee caught the creature just behind the gaping, snapping maw. It took all his strength to hold that writhing, uncontrolled, serpentine ferocity away from his head.

With his attention occupied by the first attacker, the second monster was free to strike. It launched itself and clamped its teeth onto his right arm. The pressure the powerful, muscular jaws brought to bear was astounding. Feeling metal beginning to buckle, Bumblebee had no choice but to release the creature he was struggling to keep at arm's length. Shoving it to one side as forcefully as he could, he brought his left arm across in an attempt to pull the second creature off. Though he yanked at it with all his strength, the mindless carnivore refused to release its grasp. In another surprise, the rear half of the creature's elongated body showed surprising flexibility and muscular control as it suddenly whipped around.

Bumblebee felt his legs go out from beneath him. He hit the rock floor hard, still clinging to his adversary. Realizing that if he stayed prone, he risked being swarmed by the whole hissing pack, he forced himself erect, keeping the squirming length of toothy meat eater in front of him. No sooner had he regained his footing than another of the creatures slammed into him from behind and wrapped its coils around his waist.

He felt fangs scraping madly against the back of his

head and was thankful that—so far—they had not been able to break through any of his external plating. Given their persistence, though, he felt that it was only a matter of time until one of them found and succeeded in piercing a vulnerable spot. He had to end the fight before that happened.

Letting go of the monster he had been trying to pull off him, Bumblebee spun to his right as fast as his servos could manage and slammed his right arm as hard as he could into the rock wall behind him. The creature attached to his extended limb made a sickening squishing sound and released its grip. As soon as his arm was free, Bumblebee reached back over his head. Grasping the other monster's skull with both hands, he wrenched forward. When the creature came free, he threw it halfway across the cavern.

Taking advantage of the brief lull in the assault, he jumped up onto the top of a large boulder that had fallen from the ceiling. They'd be on him again in a moment. He could hear them hissing to each other as they searched for their momentarily missing prey. Lowering himself into a crouch, he readied for their next assault when a new sound caused him to turn toward the tunnel he had only recently vacated. Full of motion and movement, it was now blocked.

More of the creatures were coming. A lot more.

Of all the Autobots no one reveled in the study of other species more than he did—but this was carrying individual interaction a little too far.

Optimus had been able to pinpoint the location of Bumblebee's last transmission without difficulty. As he dropped toward the unnamed world's surface, all of his external sensors were on high alert. Starscream was somewhere about, and they had yet to uncover the true nature of the mysterious alien ship. Unless one or the other was involved in Bumblebee's ongoing silence, he did not want to have to deal with either of them until he located his friend. As a precaution he descended indirectly, approaching the indicated locality low and slow in the hope that both Starscream and the aliens' attention was directed elsewhere.

As Bumblebee had reported, the planet itself was an interminable wasteland of broken rock and twisted scrub. There was no sign of any sapient life. If intelligent beings had at any time inhabited this world, they were long since dead or gone.

Setting down effortlessly, he transformed back into bipedal mode and quickly made his way toward a cluster of oddly regular rock pillars. According to Ratchet, Bumblebee's last communication had been transmitted from here. As Optimus advanced he scanned the area for trouble. There was no sign of impending danger. Still, with so many unknowns in the vicinity, he moved with caution.

In contrast with everything he had observed in the course of his descent, the homogeneous placement of the tall pillars suggested the involvement of a higher intelligence. Momentarily diverting his attention to them, he made a careful inspection of the closest one, which confirmed his suspicion. Still visible despite the ravages of untold centuries of erosion, runes had been scored into the surface of each column. Many were on the verge of being completely worn away by the wind and blowing sand. Studying them, Optimus had no idea what they might signify. Given the semicircular arrangement of the pillars, perhaps this had once been a primitive shrine of some sort.

The tall structures formed a perimeter around a sandy, slightly depressed central area. Three had been toppled. Had they remained standing they would have completed a circle around the central homogeneous ground.

Working his way around the shallow depression, Optimus saw that it had been recently disturbed. Adjusting his sensors, he began to scan not just his immediate surface surroundings, but downward as well.

As he looked on, the center of the depression seemed to eddy and flow slightly. Some kind of sinkhole, he surmised. Maybe the pillars were not a shrine. Maybe they had been erected as a warning. Or they could be both—if this had once been a place of sacrifice.

As he was examining his surrounds, his sensors recorded the muted rumble of an Autobot weapon being discharged somewhere below the surface. Assuming that Bumblebee was not engaging in gratuitous target practice, that could not be a good sign. Optimus's first reaction was simply to lower his own guns and blow a hole in the ground to reach the source of the verified detonation. The trouble was that Bumblebee might be moving around. There was a risk that he could unknowingly find himself in Optimus's line of fire from above.

In addition to the echoes from a new flurry of shots, Optimus's sensors began to isolate from the subterranean chaos a distinctive massed hissing sound. Bumblebee clearly needed help, and he needed it now. Further analysis could follow once the little Autobot was safe. Safety concerns aside, Optimus decided he could not wait any longer. Inclining his weaponry downward, he took careful aim at the center of the shifting sand and let fly.

The burst from his pulse cannon produced a small volcano of sand, soil, and shattered stone. He kept firing until the last of the swirling grit had been blown away. Then, without another thought, he leaped into the exposed cavity, adjusting his receptors as he dropped.

Landing feetfirst on the cavern floor below, he was greeted by the sight of Bumblebee backed into a corner.

Half a dozen or so indigenous monstrosities were closing in around him. Without hesitation Optimus advanced, unleashing a salvo at the three creatures closest to his friend. If by some extreme stretch of the imagination they turned out to be sentient, he would offer up any necessary apologies later. Their actions, however, left him convinced that any such provisional recriminations would not be required. Noting with gratitude the arrival of his leader, Bumblebee promptly counterattacked.

The relentless carnivores were enormous, massing almost as much as Optimus himself. Reacting to his intrusion, several of them twisted around and launched themselves in his direction. He tried to dodge them while continuing to shoot. Their skin was so thick and tough and their nervous systems of such a low order that they hardly seemed to feel the effects of his recurring blasts. One of them slammed into him full-force and actually managed to knock him backward several steps. The monster instantly wrapped itself around him and started to squeeze tightly.

Nearby, Bumblebee continued to fire away. Optimus looked on as one of the incredibly resilient creatures finally expired from multiple wounds. Another turned and slithered off, hissing at the numerous injuries Bumblebee had inflicted. Ignoring the individual wrapped around his torso, Optimus sighted in on the two that remained untouched and let loose another barrage. The head of the nearer exploded, splattering walls and floor with coils of organ and barrels of goo. Huge hunks of shredded flesh and muscle continued to jerk and spasm where they lay on the cavern floor, gruesomely reluctant to surrender their primeval life-force. The sole survivor of the attack turned and fled down the tunnel from which it had emerged.

Jumping over boulders and carcasses, Bumblebee came up behind Optimus and got a good grip on the anterior portion of the creature that still clung to the bigger bot's frame. Using a combination of strength and weight, the smaller Autobot finally succeeded in loosening the creature's grasp. That did not stop it, as it was wrenched free, from trying to whip its head up and around in an attempt to bury its teeth in Optimus's chest.

Bumblebee flung the writhing abomination aside. The head smashed into a limestone column as thick around as Optimus himself. Dazed but still defiant, the creature emitted a last furious hiss as it retreated back into the tunnel.

Extending his perception, Optimus could see that the surviving monsters had paused and were regrouping in the company of still more, fresh arrivals. From another direction new sounds suggested still more of the monstrosities were approaching. Optimus looked at Bumblebee and shook his head.

"No matter where we are, you always seem to find the most interesting ways to amuse yourself." More somberly, he conducted a rapid inspection of his friend. "You also managed to get yourself pretty banged up."

Bumblebee simply shrugged. His "amusing diversion," he knew, would provide ample fodder for the entertainment of his colleagues.

Optimus's tone grew more serious still. He carried out a second check of his friend, reassessing the damage. Yes, Ratchet would have plenty of repair work waiting for him when Bumblebee returned, but . . .

"I've seen worse," Optimus assured his companion. "Am I overlooking something?"

Bumblebee nodded tersely. Raising a hand, he gestured in the direction of his long-range communicator. At the same time, he silently and electronically communicated the basics of the state of affairs to his superior.

Optimus finally understood. "I see. Must have been damaged in your fall."

Confirmation was swift in forthcoming. The smaller

mechanoid looked downcast, most likely considering once again his inability to articulate through sound. While numerous other methods of communication were available to him and remained fully functional, there was something about the intimacy verbal communication offered that could not be replicated through perfectly efficient but far less expressive electronic transmission.

"I'm sorry, Bumblebee," Optimus told him. "Perhaps one day Ratchet will at last find a way to repair your vocalization module. In the meantime, we should remove ourselves from this place before those indigenous monsters, however scientifically interesting, arrive in greater numbers. Even I might have trouble with more than a dozen or so of them."

Bumblebee indicated his ready assent.

"Can you fly?" Optimus asked.

Shaking his head, his friend transmitted a summary of the damage he had sustained.

"No problem," Optimus rumbled. "Latch onto me and we'll be on our way."

Bumblebee was moving to comply when he heard the noise. The new sound was markedly different from those generated by the hissing creatures that dwelled in the tunnels. Optimus heard it also. Pausing in his preparations for liftoff, all sensors alert, he tilted his head back and peered out through the overhead gap he had made in the cavern ceiling.

"This really has been a day notable for the most disconcerting circumstances," he found himself murmuring.

Walker felt a sharp stab of pain directly behind his right eye: the beginnings of what he knew from experience was likely to turn into a pounding headache. Everyone was talking at once, either to one another or via the transmitter to the alien creature that called itself

Starscream. In the closed confines of the cabin emotions ran the gamut from exhilaration and expectation all the way through to a fear of the unknown that verged on panic. It continued until Walker, his extensive training notwithstanding, simply couldn't take it anymore.

"Shut up, the lot of you!"

The cabin fell silent. The pain that had started to swell behind his eye started to fade. He let out a sigh of relief. It was hard enough to keep control and figure out what to do next without also having to worry about his head exploding. His team was now staring at him with a mixture of surprise and expectation. Or maybe they thought he had finally lost it. He hurried to reassure them.

"I'm fine, it's okay." He deliberately kept his voice to just above a whisper so they would have to pay attention. "Everyone shouting at once isn't going to help resolve anything."

"Captain," Thompson started, but Walker held up a hand to stop him.

"Listen to me, all of you," he began determinedly. "Jake, you too. We need to *slow down* and analyze what we're dealing with here—and we need to do it one thing at a time. Before we start in on *anything*, I need a couple of aspirin and some water. Mike, can you oblige?"

The science officer dug into a small cabinet and pulled out a container of aspirin. Another storage compartment yielded water. He passed them both forward and added a slight smile.

"Sorry for the yelling, Captain." He looked around at his colleagues. "Obviously, none of us was ready for anything like what we've encountered so far. I've got a pretty good memory, and I swear I don't recall anything in the procedurals about the proper protocol for dealing with gigantic alien metal beings or what to do when one finds oneself dropped down into the middle of an interstellar war."

Walker stared back for a long second and then burst out laughing, along with everyone else in the cabin. As they regained control of their emotions, he flashed Avery a grateful thumbs-up. "Thanks, Mike. We needed that."

"I know," he replied. "So did I."

"Everyone better now? Good. Let's just stay calm and work through this one set of unforeseen impossible circumstances at a time." He uncapped the water and took a swallow, dropped the aspirin tabs into his mouth, then chased them with another hearty swig. Amazing, he thought, how beneficial and reassuring something as fundamental as a drink of cold water could be. It felt like a memory from home.

"The rest of you, get yourselves something to drink. Tea, coffee, anything. And eat, if you're hungry. The ship's not the only thing that needs fuel. We're going to need physical as well as mental strength if we're going to get through this."

Everyone suddenly realized that they were thirsty or hungry or both, and Walker waited patiently for them to sate themselves. Once the crew had helped themselves to the ship's supplies, he cleared his throat to get their attention.

"The way I see it," he started in, "we have more than one critical issue facing us. First and foremost, it doesn't sound to me like SSAB has the slightest idea how to get us home. They say they're working on it. Maybe they'll figure something out and maybe they won't, but it's something we should be working on ourselves. We might think of an approach that wouldn't occur to them. After all, we're the ones who are 'on site,' so to speak." He looked around the cabin. "As long as we're on the subject, anyone have any bright ideas?"

Clarkson spoke up first. "Actually, yes. It's been on my mind despite the advent of that chatty metallic monstrosity out on the plateau."

"Share it," Walker encouraged him.

Clarkson smacked his lips, and continued. "Well, if what SSAB said is true about us traveling through a created wormhole of some kind, then it's possible that it's still there. My feeling is that it must be, because that's the only way I can think of that we've been able to communicate with them. Unless the alien communicator operates on some level of physicality we're not even aware of, I would think that in order for our transmission to be reaching them and vice versa, the wormhole has to still exist."

"Craig's got a good point," Gonzalez agreed. "Even allowing for some kind of far-fetched alien functionality, the lack of any significant time delay in our communications with Earth suggests that our signal is going under space, or around it, or via something that, as Craig says, we don't understand."

"As long as it works," Walker declared. "We'll worry about the 'how' when we get home." He turned his attention back to Clarkson. "So the idea is that if we can relocate the wormhole, we could go back through it, right?"

Clarkson nodded slowly. "Theoretically, yes. Depending on how the applicable gravitational forces are structured, trying to go back through it might also reduce us to a cute molecular blob floating in space. Or something smaller. There's no knowing."

"Theory's what landed us out here in the first place." Thompson exhaled heavily. "We can't take that kind of a chance on theory. We need to *know* what will happen!"

"Fair enough," Avery agreed. "So what's our alternative?"

"'Scuse me?" Thompson asked.

"If we try to use the wormhole, or whatever the distortion is, to go back," Avery elaborated, "on the basis of a theory, one of two things is likely to result. We will live, or we will die. If we stay out here, we're going to die. Either the aliens will kill us or eventually we'll run out of food and water." He pointed to the alien world outside the viewport. "Air it looks like we've got, but I haven't seen much in the way of potential edibles since we landed. And," he finished, "nothing personal, but even if we could survive here I think I'd be sick of your face inside of a year."

"And vice versa," Thompson conceded. "Nothing personal, Mike."

"I'm with Craig." Gonzalez didn't hesitate. "It's try the wormhole or die."

Walker let them talk for another minute or two, running various protocols through his mind, then held up his hand for silence. "Something else is bothering me about the whole idea, and it has nothing to do with its viability. If we can figure out that going back through the wormhole is a possibility, and do it in less than a day, then it stands to reason that so can the specialists at SSAB. So—why haven't they said anything about it?"

When no one commented, he continued. "If we can go back through the wormhole, what's to say these alien creatures can't and won't follow us? Do we really want to lead them back to within a meteor's fall of our home planet? Envision a whole army of Ice Men and/or his relatives alive and kicking on Earth and ready to beat the composite metal stuffing out of one another and anything or anyone that gets in their way."

"Oh, crap," Thompson muttered unhappily. "Do I really want to know what you're implying, Sam?"

"I'm not implying: I'm saying. We can't go back." Walker let that sink in. No one said anything. "Not unless we can discover a way to get through the wormhole while closing it behind us." He looked over at his engineer. "Got any good ideas for *that* one, Craig?"

Clarkson didn't reply, and neither did anyone else.

"That's what I thought," Walker said into the resulting silence. "So we wait and see what develops. Maybe the immediate situation will change and we can look for a way to get home. But one thing we can't do under any circumstances is lead these destructive Autobots back to Earth."

"Not to put it too bluntly," Thompson muttered, "but you're saying we might just have to give up and die out here."

Walker met his copilot's gaze without flinching. "That's exactly what I'm saying, Jake. So we'd better work hard at making very good friends with this Starscream being. When all is said and done he might be our only way home."

"Starscream, this is Barricade on the *Nemesis*. Are you there?"

Annoyed at the interruption, Starscream paused in his ongoing communications with the humans. "What is it, Barricade?" he snapped. "I told you to wait to hear from me."

"Our scanners have picked up Optimus Prime heading down to the surface of the planet," Barricade explained. "Do you want assistance?"

Starscream considered and came to a decision quickly. "Negative. This is your chance. Don't throw it away. With Optimus out of the way, move the *Nemesis* into attack position—but don't attack. Feint and give the impression that you're going to do so, but use your approach to draw the remaining Autobots away from the protection of their vessel and then engage them. I expect their utter annihilation before I return. Is that understood?"

"As you command, Starscream." Barricade hesitated a moment. "What of the peculiar alien craft? Did you find it?"

"Oh, yes." Starscream could not conceal his satisfaction. "The creatures who infest it are very primitive organic life-forms. Their imitative ship malfunctioned during a short journey within their own star system. They are not even sure of the mathematics by which they traveled here, let alone the mechanisms. I will see to it that they are dealt with appropriately. You and the others devote your attention to the remaining Autobots."

"Of course." Barricade shut down the communications channel.

Starscream promptly resumed his conversation with the humans. "I apologize for the interruption. I was just in contact with my shipmates. They report that one of the Autobots, the monstrous creature called Optimus Prime, is on his way here even as we speak."

This information spawned an amusing chorus of childish babbling within the alien ship. Starscream allowed it to fester for a few moments before avowing, with profound nobleness of purpose, "I will, of course, do my best to protect you."

"Thank you," the human on the other end of the transmission replied. "What advice do you have for us? How should, how can we proceed to protect ourselves?"

"Wait," Starscream advised him. "While the Autobots are very deceitful, they are as susceptible to error as any sentient being. It may be that Optimus Prime will make a mistake and we will be able to destroy him quickly, with minimal risk to either you or myself."

They discussed options for several more minutes. Starscream paid only minimal attention to the infantile comments and suggestions. The majority of his concentration was devoted to a continuous and detailed scan of the surrounding region. He did not want Optimus Prime sneaking up on him the same way he himself had slipped in behind the hapless Bumblebee.

It was only a short time later that his sensors reported

the sound of advanced weapons fire. The source was underground and nearby, and he considered leaving the humans to investigate. Unnecessary for the moment, he decided. If one of his less subtle brethren or an unaccounted-for Autobot were to arrive here and take his place, all his hard work might come undone. The key to what he had concocted was making the humans believe in him—before he ensured their destruction.

"Is your ship capable of traveling a short distance?" he inquired.

"Yes. Why?" the human who was speaking asked.

"An advanced weapon was recently fired nearby. I believe it would be prudent of us to investigate."

The voice on the other end of the transmission sounded unsure. "You want us to come with you? Why?"

"If I leave you here alone and go to investigate, you will be more vulnerable than if you are with me."

There was some discussion of this inside the craft; then, "That makes sense. Yes, we will come."

"I am pleased," he replied with becoming humbleness. "I will travel at a velocity that will allow you to track me."

Rising from the rocky plain, Starscream headed off at an absurdly slow speed in the direction of the weapons' discharge. He almost winced at the sound of the alien ship as it lifted from the surface and commenced to follow in his wake. Compared with the inhabitants of Cybertron, with their integral propulsive systems, the humans' ship was a rattling, banging cacophony that sounded as if it might shake itself to pieces at any moment. Yet when he glanced back to make certain that they were indeed tracking him, he saw that the little vessel had reached altitude and was keeping up without difficulty. He accelerated slightly and was pleased to see that it promptly matched the increase. In flight the ship was nowhere near as graceful as a Decepticon or an Autobot, but in time perhaps their machines might develop into something better. Of course, if evolution proceeded down its natural path, their machines would eventually achieve consciousness on their own and assume control from their organic progenitors.

He sped quickly across the blasted landscape. Before long the reverberation of weapons fire grew louder. A transmission from the humans indicated that they wanted him to stop.

Irritated, he complied. Both fliers touched down on smooth rock. He had already decided that the primitive hardline communication was unnecessarily slow and uncertain. There had to be a better method of conversing.

"What is your concern?" he inquired impatiently.

"Are those the weapons you referred to, and are they still firing?"

"Yes," Starscream replied. "We will use caution until I can fully evaluate the situation. Knowing their irrational natures as well as I do, it is even possible the Autobots may be fighting among themselves. Believe it or not, they are reduced to that from time to time."

"And if that's the case here?"

"Then it would be an abdication of responsibility not to take advantage of the distraction to destroy them," he explained.

Giving the querulous organics no time to discuss the matter, he broke off communications and began walking toward the sound of combat. A series of rock pillars lay directly ahead, and his sensors told him that the noise of battle originated from somewhere in their immediate vicinity.

If all went according to plan, not only would the humans perish, but so would one or more of his ancient enemies . . .

IX

Kinnear struggled to swim up out of the blackness. Attempting to open his eyes felt like trying to lift a ten-ton boulder. He couldn't do it, didn't really want to do it. A part of him, the part that was conscious and trying to awaken him, yelled that if he did not wake up, did not face the icy cold and the excruciating pain in his left leg, he was going to expire. He would die frozen and bleeding to death in a foreign landscape of snow and ice and rock, and he would not have anyone to blame but himself.

Behind his eyes, he tried to think of something else. Anything else except waking up and dealing with the here and now. It was cold, cold—so what more natural than that he should flash back three years ago to the sweltering, stinking sauna that was Vietnam? He had been a lieutenant colonel then and Nolan had been a major. The whys and hows of that bizarre day, why two high-ranking officers had ended up running for their lives down a filthy backstreet in Saigon wondering as they ran how they were going to survive, did not really matter. What had mattered to him at that particular moment was the blood.

The blood that was dripping down the inside of his waistband and slowly soaking through his pants. The blood that was oozing like crimson honey from the gunshot wound in his lower left abdomen. The blood and the searing pain that shot through him every time he moved, took a breath, or even thought about taking one more step. He had wanted to quit then, maybe find somewhere to hole up until the pain went away of its own accord. Nolan had saved him. It had been Nolan's voice that he had followed through the haze of pain, Nolan's strong hand on his arm, pulling him forward, guiding him around the stalls of chattering merchants and the silently staring wide-eyed children clumped together in the streets.

"Come on, Tom," Nolan had kept saying. "Not much farther now."

"Where?" Kinnear remembered himself asking over and over, as if the query had come from somewhere else, from another person. "Where?"

"The embassy," Nolan repeatedly told him. "If we can get to the embassy, we'll be safe."

"Says who?" Kinnear remembered laughing and spitting blood—a combination of reactions to circumstances that most human beings, thankfully, would never have to experience. Who had shot him? Why? He remembered. Even the best assassins sometimes run into other assassins.

"Says me," Nolan had replied, dragging him on. "Keep moving."

And somehow, someway, Kinnear had. He'd put one booted foot in front of the other, his increasingly numb steps lubricated by his own blood, and Nolan had gotten him to the embassy. The last thing he remembered was the stunned look on the MP's face as they hit the gate, and then he had fainted. When he woke up, he was in an army hospital in the Philippines and Nolan was in the bed next to him.

"What happened to you?" he remembered asking, his mind still groggy.

"Same as you," Nolan told him. "Got shot."

Kinnear didn't remember that part. "Where?"

Nolan grinned across at him. "Right in the ass, Tom. That's where they usually shoot you when you're running away."

Both of them had laughed then, giddy with simply being alive. Happy to have completed their mission, even if they had both been shot doing it.

A gust of icy, decidedly untropical air tried to pull the skin off his face and Kinnear was hauled mercilessly back to the present. The wind also brought the sound of a familiar voice: Lieutenant Jensen.

"Sir! Sir! Come on, sir! You've got to wake up now!"

Kinnear groaned and forced his eyes open. Why couldn't they just leave him alone? It was not as if this were Phil, telling him to keep going. "All right," he mumbled, surprised at how weak his voice sounded. At how weak he felt. He tried to move. A bolt of pain shot through his leg, and he bit back a cry as his entire body locked up in an uncontrolled spasm. He was fully awake now, staring out into the darkness of a blinding, full-blown Arctic blizzard.

Jensen was kneeling in front of him. The expression on the junior officer's face was not encouraging. "Sir, are you with me now?"

Kinnear nodded. "Yeah," he muttered. "Why? Are we on a date?" Training took over. "Status?"

"Sir, your left leg is broken all to hell and the entire convoy is smashed up. Closed up like an accordion. Once the big rig lost it, everything went to hell. We've got a field tent set up, and we need to move you. You'll die of hypothermia otherwise."

Kinnear nodded again, knowing that no matter how much care his rescuers took while moving him it was still going to hurt like hell.

"There are morphine jabs in the medkit, sir," the solicitous Jensen continued. "I'll stick you and we'll give it a minute to work, then we'll get you moved to some shelter."

"No." Fully awake now, Kinnear's mind was working furiously. "No."

"Sir?"

"I can't think if I'm doped up on morphine, Lieutenant. I'm going to have to tough it out."

"Are you sure, sir?" Jensen sounded uncertain.

"I'm sure," Kinnear told him, even though it was a lie. Not the first he had told in his career, he reflected. Raising his head, he managed to look down at his leg, and grimaced. It was bad, all right. The femur had not punched through the skin, but he could see it pressing against the underside of the muscle. A makeshift splint had been applied while he was in the dark. Why couldn't it have been a nice, straightforward break? "Give me your belt," he muttered.

Jensen nodded and slid his belt out of its loops, doubled it over, and handed it to him. Kinnear took it and put it between his teeth. "Whenever you're ready, Lieutenant." He bit down hard on the cold fabric.

"Yes, sir." Looking around, Jensen signaled two men standing nearby, and they hurried over. "He declined the morphine. We'll move him as fast as we can. No stopping and don't drop him, for God's sake. Get him into the tent and on a cot, got it?"

"Yes, sir," the two men chorused.

In the dim light Kinnear could see they were enlisted men, a couple of privates. They looked scared. He nodded, trying to reassure them.

"Do what you need to do, men."

"I've got his leg splinted as best we can for now," Jensen exclaimed. "You each take a leg. Whoever's on the busted one, make sure you hold him above the break. Pull him gently out of the cab, then I'll grab his shoulders. We lift and go, got it?"

"Yes, sir," they chorused again.

"Good," Jensen muttered. "Let's do it."

And they did. As smooth as slipping a fresh diaper under a colicky baby. It didn't matter. Kinnear still screamed into the fabric of the belt. Screamed and bit down so hard that he damn near cut clean through the tough material. They were almost to the tent, a dark green shadow in the snow, when he passed out again.

Like the *Ark*, the *Nemesis* was more transport than warship, but Barricade acknowledged Starscream's orders and intended to obey as best he was able. His companions were in complete agreement with the strategy. Without Optimus Prime there to protect and guide them, the few remaining Autobots were vulnerable. It was a perfect time for an all-out assault.

"Everyone, you heard Starscream." Barricade activated the sublight drive. "We're going to move into attack position. Bonecrusher, I want you to lead the assault. I'll remain behind and employ the ship as a distraction."

A Decepticon of few words, Bonecrusher uttered a growl and gestured sharply as he whirled and led the others toward the hangar.

Barricade watched them leave the control room, then returned his attention to the ship's instruments. There was no point in trying to mask their intentions. The Autobots would see them coming, and Barricade was quietly pleased by this realization. Uncertainty and confusion might lead their foes to make a mistake.

As the *Nemesis* glided out of the moon's shadow he aimed it straight for the *Ark*. The limited weapons systems on the Decepticon transport were unlikely to destroy the Autobot vessel, but there was always the chance a well-placed blast might disable something critical.

"Autobots, foul Autobots, here we come," Barricade sang to himself. "Let our long war resume—and let it end here."

"Ratchet, Ironhide!" Jazz called out. "I think we've got company."

From the repair bay, Ratchet responded, "Company?"

"Decepticons," Jazz informed him. "The *Nemesis* just emerged from behind the near moon, and it's headed in this direction."

"We're on our way," Ironhide reported. "We'll go straight to the hangar bay."

"Ratchet, you need to come up here and take control," Jazz told his colleague. "You interface with the instrumentation better than I do."

Ratchet started to argue, but Ironhide intervened. "He's right. Besides, if you get killed, who's going to fix us?"

A reluctant Ratchet conceded the logic of the argument as Jazz completed a quick sensor sweep before stepping clear of the main console. "They're activating their weapons systems."

Ratchet chuckled. "Then they're in for a surprise. You and Ironhide head out to meet them. They'll want to fight hand to hand. Just remember that once you're out there I'll be powering up our new shields; you won't be able to get back on board until I lower them."

"We know." Jazz headed for the near portal, then stopped in confusion. "What do you mean we can't get back on board?"

"Over the years I've had a lot of time to tinker," Ratchet replied. "I've made a few modifications to our original defensive systems. They're much stronger now, and the shields function in perfect harmony with the similarly upgraded weapons."

"You've been a busy Ratchet, haven't you?" Jazz

commented. "What about Optimus and Bumblebee? We haven't heard back from them yet."

"I know, but remember that we're under orders not to risk the *Ark*. I'll keep monitoring for them. Meanwhile, you and Ironhide need to prepare for combat. If I give the signal, get back to the hangar. Remember Optimus's directive. If things don't go our way, we're to take off and return at a later date."

"I remember," Jazz murmured. "I remember and obey, but I don't have to like it."

"None of us does," Ratchet agreed quietly.

As he headed for the hangar bay Jazz found himself wondering what the next few hours would bring. Could they possibly end the war here and now, in this out-of-the-way, unfamiliar corner of space? If they could disable the *Nemesis*, any Decepticons who survived would find themselves stranded in this backwater corner of the galaxy for a long, long time. With luck, maybe forever.

He flashed acknowledgment at Ironhide as he stepped into the hangar. "I've got an idea."

"Oh, really?" Ironhide rumbled. "Since when are you a strategist?"

Jazz laughed. "I'm not, but this one just might work. Want to hear it?"

"I have a choice?" When Jazz had something to say, Ironhide reflected, everyone within range was subjected to it whether they were interested or not. Still, he nodded agreeably. "Go ahead. I'm open to anything that might help us get out of this in one piece."

"Good," Jazz replied. "Here's what I propose to do."

Kinnear came out of the dark once more and this time found himself on a cot. The dark green canvas of an army field tent snapped in the wind above his head. There were a couple of heavy blankets over him, and someone had set up space heaters and a generator. The tent had light and warmth.

He forced himself a bit more upright and saw Jensen standing near the opening, his face to the storm howling outside. He swallowed, hoping his voice would carry. "Jensen."

Apparently it was sufficient, because Jensen turned around. "Sir. Sorry about that. You turned down the morphine. It couldn't be helped."

"No, it couldn't," Kinnear agreed readily. "Listen, I know that everyone's working to get the convoy back on track, but if it hasn't been done already, I want you to get sentries out right now. I know the weather sucks, but put up a perimeter at one hundred yards and rotate the men at least every hour."

"Yes, sir." Jensen nodded understandingly. "I'll see to it."

"Next, if he's still alive and mobile, I want the driver of that lead truck in here right now."

"Sir?" Jensen eyed his commander doubtfully.

"This is lousy weather to drive in, and we implemented a last-minute route change," Kinnear said through clenched teeth, "but that's no excuse. You put a man on point because he's supposed to be the best. His slipup could cost us a lot more than probably even he knows. Get him in here."

Jensen nodded. The operation commander's leg might be broken, but it was clear that everything else was fully functional. "I'll be right back, sir."

Kinnear watched as the lieutenant headed out into the snow, barking orders as he went. His initial assessment of the man was further confirmed. Jensen had kept his head and had not panicked.

He returned a short time later, brushing snow and ice off his coat. "Sir, the perimeter has been established and a rotation is in place."

"And the driver?" Kinnear prompted.

The rising redness in Jensen's face was not entirely due to the effects of the weather. "We're, uh—looking for him, sir."

Kinnear blinked at the lieutenant. "Looking for him?"

"I know he survived the crash, sir," Jensen went on. "I saw him get out of the truck myself. But I'm having trouble locating him right now. We're kind of spread out. Things are improving by the minute, but there's still a lot of chaos out there."

"Uh-huh," Kinnear muttered. "All right, let's leave that for a moment and give me a sit rep."

Relieved, Jensen nodded. "Yes, sir. We've got six seriously injured and about a dozen banged up to a lesser degree or another. They're in the bigger tent next door, and the medics are already working on them. While you were out, one came in here and redid the splint on your leg. Said he'd be back in a little while to check on you."

"And the vehicles?" While not anticipating trouble, Kinnear prepared himself for the worst.

"Those that managed to avoid the chain reaction mostly did so by sliding off the road. Several are in the drainage ditch. Once we get some chains hooked up, I think we can pull most of them out, if not all." He hesitated. "The real problem is the Ice Man's special vehicle, sir."

Kinnear started to ask what was wrong there when a commotion outside stopped him. The tent flaps were thrown back and Jensen stepped out of the way as a sergeant and a specialist came in out of the snow. They were dragging an unconscious figure between them. The man's hands were bound behind his back. They threw him to the ground in a heap, sketched a quick salute, and the sergeant growled, "Caught this man trying to get past the perimeter, sir. Leaving the convoy, that is."

Clearly fighting to contain his anger, the burly noncom's expression and tone indicated that if his commanding officer would just give him permission, he would be more than happy to pick the offender up and dump him on the ground a few more times, just for exercise. "Had to knock him in the head pretty good to convince him to come back with us."

Kneeling beside the prone soldier, Jensen pulled back the hood of the man's parka. When he did, the soldier's helmet came off with it. "What the . . . ?" Startled, Jensen straightened and looked over at Kinnear. "A Corporal Hodgson was the driver of the lead truck. He hasn't been with us long, but I don't think this is Corporal Hodgson."

Standing by, the sergeant stared at the man on the ground, then nodded to the soldier who had accompanied him. Both men drew their service pistols and held them at the ready.

Kinnear gestured toward the prisoner. "Wake him up. We need some answers, and we need them fast."

Taking a medical carafe from the nearby field table, the lieutenant proceeded to upend it directly over the face of the sprawled figure. The man was lucky: the container held only cold water. He spluttered and coughed as his eyes came open, groaned, started to speak, and stopped himself.

"Who are you?" Jensen snapped.

The man blinked up at him. "Peter Hodgson, corporal, USA."

Jensen's gaze narrowed. "Bull." He nodded at the sergeant standing nearby. Raising his weapon, the noncom leveled its muzzle at the man's face.

"Let's try that again." Jensen wasn't smiling. "I'll count to three. One . . . "

"You can't do this." The man smiled knowingly.

"Two," Jensen said calmly. From the hospital cot,

Kinnear looked on without commenting. "Nobody will find your body. We're just doing our bit for the food chain. The polar bears and the wolves will be pleased. "Thr—"

Rapidly losing the smile, the man cried, "Stop."

Jensen nodded again at the sergeant. The noncom lowered his weapon. He looked disappointed.

"You Americans with your funny little games," the man told his audience.

"Help me sit up," Kinnear muttered.

Moving over to the cot, Jensen eased his commanding officer into an upright position. Adjusting to verticality, Kinnear waited impatiently while stars flickered before his eyes. Gradually the sparkling black and silver spots went away, and he was able to see the man on the ground clearly.

"I'm starting to pick up just a hint of an accent. Let me take a wild guess. Russian, *da*?"

"Corporal Peter Hodgson," the man corrected him. "Reporting for duty."

"Sure," Kinnear riposted. "And I'm President Nixon. I'd guess 'Pyotr' rather than Peter. Why don't you just spill it? You're not going anywhere. Unless it's to have lunch with the local wildlife." He nodded in the direction of the unabashedly eager sergeant. "I'm in no mood to play games, and neither are my men."

The man shrugged, relaxed. "It's not Pyotr—Peter. It's Sergei. Sergei Tasarov," he confessed. "Lieutenant Tasarov." The smile returned, albeit subdued. "Not reporting for duty, I'm afraid."

"I'm interested in your mission, not your rank," Kinnear told him.

"It matters not," Tasarov murmured. "I have done what I was sent to this miserable place to do."

"And what was that?" Kinnear asked. "You said you don't like our games. I don't think you'd like nude tag. It's a little chilly outside."

"The Ice Man," Tasarov explained. "My task was to stop him from getting into America." He sat up a little straighter. "I have done that. Even now my comrades are on their way here to take possession of this treasure."

"Your comrades?" Jensen's eyebrows rose.

Tasarov was enjoying himself now. "Soviet Arctic KGB special forces. Brought to this coast by submarines and waiting on my signal—which I was able to broadcast just before I crashed the truck." He looked back at Kinnear. "You'll find the miniature transmitter under its seat, if you care to look."

"How many?" A hard knot was forming in Kinnear's gut. The station itself had always been susceptible to attack. Obscurity and isolation had been its best defenses. Out here on the virtually nonexistent road he and his team were beyond vulnerable. "How many men?"

"Oh, but to tell you would be cheating." Tasarov was smiling again. "I will leave it as a little surprise for you. Just like my being here was a surprise, yes?" He gestured toward the tent's entrance. "Throw me outside if you will. I am from Irkutsk. This is like fall weather to me."

Jensen and Kinnear exchanged glances. "Do we have radio contact with SSAB?" he asked. "Or the coast?"

A grim-faced Jensen shook his head. "Very spotty, sir. The storm's been playing hell with our field units. Mostly all we're getting right now is static."

"Damn." Kinnear glanced back at the Russian. "So how'd he get a signal out?"

Tasarov laughed. "Americans think they are the only ones with technology. Satellite relay. You will be interested to know I was able to use the antenna on your lead vehicle."

Kinnear glared down at him. "In case you've forgotten, there's an Arctic blizzard raging outside. Your friends still have to find us in the storm."

"What do we do with him?" Jensen wondered.

Kinnear considered the infiltrator for a moment. He was not a cold-blooded killer, and if they could get him back to Washington there were others there who would eagerly embrace the opportunity to have a nice long, friendly chat with such a visitor. Meanwhile the man might get hungry or thirsty and decide he was willing to talk some more.

"Sergeant, take him over to the field hospital. Make sure he's well secured. I want a guard on him around the clock—assuming we're here that long. And—take all his clothes except for his underwear."

"I will freeze to death!" the Russian objected.

Kinnear's lips tightened. "Naw. You're from Irkutsk, remember? A little shivering won't kill you. Or maybe you'll just catch some simple pneumonia. As a tourist in these parts you should pick up a souvenir or two."

The Russian spit on the floor. "You cannot treat me like this! It is against the Geneva Convention!"

Kinnear stared hard at him. "You're not a prisoner of war, *tovarich*. The rules are a little different for spies. You know that." He gestured at Jensen. "Get him out of here."

Together with the other two soldiers, the lieutenant hauled the infiltrator to his feet and dragged him away. Jensen returned a short time later and gave his commander a sharp nod.

"It's done," he declared.

Kinnear nodded approvingly. "So now we've got another problem. Russians and—the Ice Man, right?"

Jensen nodded. "The hauler was damaged in the crash. Not severely, but with the weight it's carrying it doesn't take much to bring it to a halt. The mechanics are doing the best they can. The problem isn't the vehicle—it's the damage to the cargo. It's only a matter of time."

The chill that raced up Kinnear's spine had nothing to do with the local climate. "Until what?"

"Until he thaws out," Jensen explained. "I've double-checked with the techs. They say that even in this blizzard, the temperature isn't low enough to keep him in stasis if the special refrigeration equipment fails. Something to do with the endothermic properties of the metal composite he's made out of. Apparently it doesn't take much of a rise in ambient temperature. Once he starts to defrost, the reaction feeds on itself, accelerates exponentially, and is hypothetically impossible to reverse."

"How long do we have?" Tom asked.

"Three hours," Jensen told him. "Less if the weather starts to clear."

"If Ice Man wakes up, or reactivates in any way, we're going to have real trouble out here." Kinnear was shaking his head slowly. "What kind of trouble I can't predict, and neither can anyone else. I just have this feeling it will be—bad."

"I know." Jensen made an effort to find a bright side. "Maybe our luck will change."

Fighting through the pain, Kinnear sat up as straight on the cot as he could manage. "I personally don't find waiting for luck a viable strategy for dealing with a crisis situation. We're going to have to take the offensive. I'm ready to fight the Russians and the weather and do both on a busted leg, but I'm not ready to face a possibly rejuvenated Ice Man on top of the other two."

Jensen gave a slight shrug. "It could be worse."

"Worse?" Kinnear's gaze narrowed. "How could it get any worse?"

"He could be awake already," the lieutenant pointed out.

"Why don't I find that encouraging?" Kinnear made a rude noise. "Get the chief tech in here and let's explore our options."

"Yes, sir." Jensen turned to leave. Then he stopped and looked back. "I'm sorry, sir."

"For what?"

"For letting you down. Hodgson was one of my guys. I should've detected the switch."

"Given the breadth of your responsibilities, Jensen, and the rate of personnel churn at the base, it's not realistic to expect someone in your position to know every soldier at the station by sight. Forget it." Left unsaid was the question of what had happened to the real Peter Hodgson, corporal, USA. "Let's concentrate on the problems in front of us, rather than the ones behind us, okay?"

"Yes, sir. Thank you, sir." Jensen stiffened, snapped off a serious salute, pivoted smartly on his heel, and left the tent again.

Exhausted, Kinnear lay back down on the cot's hard pillow and pulled the blankets up higher around him. Despite the medication and treatment he had been given, his broken leg throbbed as if it were trying to snap clean at the joint and run off on its own.

Somehow, someway, he had to get both his team and his irreplaceable cargo out of here before the Russians showed up. Outside, the wind continued to howl.

For once, he welcomed the sound.

"Stay behind me," Optimus told Bumblebee. His head tilted back, the Autobot leader was gazing upward.

Bumblebee tried to peer around the much larger form of his leader to determine the problem.

The problem proceeded to announce itself. "Optimus Prime," Starscream sneered from above. "I see you have finally found a place where you belong: a suitably deep hole in the ground. I hope it is to your liking, since you will be spending the rest of eternity there."

Over Optimus's shoulder, Bumblebee could see the Decepticon hovering overhead in transformed mode. It looked eerily like Megatron in his aircraft shape.

Optimus replied in a controlled, even voice, "Starscream, I didn't come down here to fight you. Move on. There is no reason for those other, innocent lifeforms to get hurt."

"Why would you assume they are in danger?" the Decepticon leader replied. "Now I myself, well, if I departed could I really trust you not to sneak up on me from behind? Do you think I am naïve enough to believe you would simply head back to your ship without pouncing on this opportunity for a fight?"

"That's exactly what I intend," Optimus informed him. "I came down here to get Bumblebee, and now we'll go back to the *Ark*. If it's battle you want, that's fine. I accept. But let's finish it in free space where these other beings are not at risk."

Starscream chortled. He did not have a pleasant laugh. "Oh, there is going to be a battle. But I'm afraid you will be missing out on it." He turned away. "Good-bye, Optimus Prime."

Reaching down, Optimus scooped up Bumblebee under one arm. "Hang on!" Activating his propulsion system, he boosted skyward.

The instant he and Bumblebee started to emerge from the opening, Starscream opened fire. That was expected. What was not expected was that the alien vessel, positioned nearby, did so as well.

Demonstrating an agility and reaction time that were astounding even for one so advanced, Optimus spun 180 degrees in midair and disappeared back into the cavity. Rather than blowing his bipedal form to bits, the near-simultaneous blasts from Starscream and the missiles fired by the alien craft missed him entirely. Instead, they brought down hundreds of tons of rock.

Landing on the cavern floor, Optimus sprinted for the nearest side tunnel. Above, the roar of weapons fire continued. An avalanche of smoking stone and shattered pillars proceeded to plug the cavern and the overhead gap behind him.

Now the only quick way out was through one of the tunnels. Once safely clear of Starscream and the unexpectedly belligerent aliens, he would have to find a weak place where he could blast a path through to the surface. Sensors indicated that the nearly fatal bombardment from above had finally ceased. A tap on his arm caused him to turn.

Bumblebee gestured meaningfully up the tunnel they had taken. Until now, the hissing of the worm-things had not been all that noticeable. As the two Autobots stood there, however, it began to rise rapidly in volume.

Scanning their immediate surroundings, Optimus noted a number of smaller branches leading off the main tunnel. As near as he could tell at the moment, one was as close to the surface as another. If they kept moving, hopefully they would avoid another encounter with the persistent and mindlessly aggressive creatures. Starscream's taunt that there was soon to be a battle involving the *Ark* was preying heavily on his thoughts.

"Come on, Bumblebee. Let's get away from this place."

The smaller Autobot nodded and followed as Optimus started down the tunnel he had chosen. Opening up, the passage was soon nearly as large as the one they had left behind. For that, Optimus was grateful.

Even though Starscream was not a witness to their flight, he did not like the idea of having to crawl.

Nolan stared out at the Mission Control center, but his gaze was turned inward. He was remembering when he had first finished Officer Candidate School and been assigned a duty station he had never imagined existed except in cheap paperback novels and action films.

He was to take command of an elite unit of soldiers that traveled the world doing black ops missions for the CIA. Missions that required more attention to espionage than regular special forces units could handle. His men and women were soldiers, yes, but they were also much more. Each was a trained assassin, most spoke at least three languages, and any one of them would be comfortable everywhere from a back alley in Shanghai to a ballroom in London. No wonder those who were in the know at the Pentagon referred to them as "the Bond Squad."

At the time, Phil had not even been sure he wanted the command. He ended up taking it and spending another six months training with the new force before everyone agreed that the team was ready. Their first mission turned out to be the hardest. Afterward all the others seemed, if not easy, at least less bloody and complicated.

The mission's parameters were simple enough, at least on the surface. Go into Moscow and come back with a dissident who wanted to defect to America in exchange for supplying the CIA with a list of valuable aliases. The boys at Langley had salivated over the prospect. The list promised to compromise half the Soviet agents in Eastern Europe. Despite the difficult location the operation had been laid out as a straightforward snatch-and-go. It ended up a running firefight on a grass airstrip where he lost one man and had to haul out several more who had been seriously injured. But they got their target out safely, and the list.

Afterward, he found himself wondering if it had been worth it.

Nolan remembered the man he had lost and had to leave behind. In the aftermath he had sworn to never again leave behind a member of any team that was his responsibility.

He had kept that private, personal promise throughout all his subsequent years of service. He'd carried Tom Kinnear to safety practically on his back when an assassination op in Saigon had gone wrong. And while he knew that his days of field duty were long since over and done with, the idea of leaving someone, anyone, behind was not in his nature.

Which meant that there had to be a way to get *Ghost 1* back through the wormhole.

Rising from his seat, he signaled his director of communications. Smythe moved at a speed that belied his appearance.

"Phil?" Smythe inquired. "What've you got?"

"I want the senior staff in the secure conference room in ten minutes."

"We're going to try to get them back, aren't we?" Behind the thick glasses, a smile creased the other man's face.

Nolan nodded. "Damn right we are. There's got to be a way. We sent them out there. We'll get them back."

"I'll get the staff together," Smythe told him.

"I'll meet all of you there in a few minutes. I want to check in with the Ice Man convoy and make sure that everything is on schedule."

Smythe flashed him a thumbs-up, then turned and headed out to collect the senior staff.

Nolan had just turned away from his desk when one of the several phones rang. The red phone.

That phone never rings, he reminded himself. It was not supposed to.

Reaching down, he picked up the handset and slowly brought it to his ear. "Nolan," he said.

Faint with distance, the voice on the other end declared, "Lieutenant Colonel Nolan, this is Simmons."

Nolan tensed immediately. He had only met the Old Man twice, and they had barely exchanged a few polite words. The Old Man spoke to Kinnear, not him. "Sir?" he managed. "How can I help you?"

"You've got a problem out there," Simmons informed him unemotionally. "I just spoke with the captain of the ship waiting to transfer Ice Man to the mainland. He hasn't heard from the convoy in over an hour. Nor are they answering radio calls, not even on the emergency frequencies."

Nolan's thoughts sped. "Colonel Kinnear is—"

"A very capable leader," Simmons finished for him. "I know. Which is why I'm worried. You know that they're supposed to radio in status reports periodically en route and they haven't. No one has been able to reach them. I refuse to put that down just to the local weather, no matter how bad. Kinnear bring you up to speed on our intel before he left?"

"Yes, sir," Nolan replied. "I agree with you on the weather. It's terrible here right now. Even so, I can't imagine they've run into anything more serious than icy roads and slower-than-anticipated travel times. On top of the blizzard conditions, we've been experiencing heavy auroras. As I'm sure you're aware, sir, that can play hell with communications."

"Maybe," Simmons conceded. "And maybe not. I want you to take a squad and go out after them. Ice Man is more important than anything else we're working on right now."

"But, sir—" Nolan began, *Ghost 1*'s situation uppermost in his mind.

"I know all about *Ghost One*'s status," Simmons responded, anticipating Nolan's incipient objections. "But they're God knows where. Kinnear and his people are here, on the ground, and maybe in some kind of trouble. Get a team together and go find them. I want a status report in no less than one hour. Understood?"

His heart sinking, Nolan caught himself nodding. "Yes, sir. I'll see to it, sir."

"I knew you would," the Old Man replied before breaking the connection.

"Great," Nolan muttered to himself. "So much for my time in the field being over." Looking up, he saw Smythe returning.

"I've got almost all the senior staff in the conference room," the communications director informed him, a little out of breath.

"Change of plans, Chris. You're going to chair the meeting. I've got to go after Colonel Kinnear and the convoy. It looks like they might have run into some trouble out there, and the Old Man himself has ordered me to take a look."

"Me?" Smythe balked. "Chair the meeting? Phil, I'm not qualified—"

"Yes, you are," Nolan told him. "As of right now. When I get back, I'll want a list of options on my desk. Right here." For emphasis, he jabbed a finger at the slick surface.

"What if *Ghost One* reports in while you're gone?" Smythe wondered aloud. "What do I tell them?"

"Ahh, come on, Chris." Nolan smiled encouragingly. "You know that drill better than I do. Tell them we're still working on it and stall, stall, stall until I get back."

"Okay." Smythe sounded unconvinced. "But don't fool around out there in the snow for too long. We don't know how much time we've got to work with."

Instead of replying, Nolan tossed the communications director a wave and headed for the hangar. Once more and quite unexpectedly, he was going to lead a squad into the field. It felt better than he'd imagined.

He'd been driving a desk too long.

Thompson flew *Ghost 1* over the barren landscape, trailing the alien that called itself Starscream. Through the foreport, Walker found himself frequently glancing down at massive rock formations and improbably clustered boulders. Occasional depressions boasted clusters of weirdly contorted scrub growth.

"Put us down here, Jake," Walker abruptly told his copilot.

Thompson looked over at him, then nodded forward, out the port. "What about our insistent alien friend?"

"He wants to talk, we'll talk." Walker shook his head. "Something doesn't feel right to me."

Behind him, Clarkson spoke up. "Excuse me for saying so, Captain, but that's a pretty feeble rationale for calling a halt."

Walker looked back him. "Right there is one reason why I'm in command and you're an engineer. Jake?"

"Setting down, sir." As he manipulated controls, *Ghost 1* settled to the ground in a gentle, effortless glide.

Realizing that the primitive organics were no longer following, Starscream swooped around in a tight arc and set down near the alien craft.

"Is there a problem, my friends?" he broadcast.

Walker listened to the cold voice from the speaker.

"Maria, tell him we . . . " He thought about it for a moment, then continued. "Tell him we need to run a diagnostic on our ship's systems."

She nodded, then typed out the message on a keyboard. The words appeared on the screen in front of her.

Receiving the broadcast, an irritated Starscream replied impatiently. The request was not surprising, really. He was astonished that the flimsy vessel had held together as long as it had. "Very well. I will wait. But you should make haste. There is no telling what mischief the remaining Autobots may be up to." Settling himself among the rocks nearby, he resolved to give the humans the time they had requested. Within reason, of course.

Within the *Ghost,* Thompson eyed his friend and superior curiously. "What's on your mind, Captain?"

"I've been wondering about those other aliens," he murmured. "The ones in the cavern."

"So have I." Avery swiveled around in his seat. "That was a pretty one-sided fight. Even though we joined in firing at them, as far as I could tell they never shot back. Kind of a peculiar response for a couple of supposedly bloodthirsty machine intelligences."

Walker nodded slowly. "That's what I've been thinking myself." Leaning forward, he stared out the port at the impressive form of Starscream waiting nearby. "While I can't come up with a *specific* reason to distrust this particular relative of the Ice Man, he keeps reminding me of something that happened to me back on Earth a few years ago."

"What was that?" Thompson inquired.

"My wife bought a car," he explained. "Or nearly did." He paused to gather the recollection. "She'd found this little convertible, a white Spitfire, on a lot not far from our place in San Diego. Just fell in love with it. Test-drove the thing two or three times before mentioning it to me, which was fine, and I agreed to go and have a look at it.

"The salesman was polite, smooth, all help and no hassle," he continued. "But there was something about him that reminded me of an oil spot on an ice-skating rink. You know—a pretty rainbow shimmer that'll send you ass over teakettle if you get too close to it?" Thompson nodded. The others listened knowingly.

"Still," Walker went on, "Julie wanted the car, so we went ahead and bought it. Three days later the head gasket blew and a mechanic friend of mine told me that they have ways of hiding that sort of thing for a short time even from knowledgeable buyers."

Thompson considered. "So what you're saying is that your head's about to blow, or else you think that this Starscream mechanoid is hiding something."

Walker didn't try to conceal his uncertainty. "I don't know what to think. Only that he reminds me of that used-car salesman. Everything's been too pat, too hurried. I get the feeling we're being led around. It might be to somewhere good—or maybe it's not." He looked helplessly at his crew. "Does any of this make any sense, or am I just being paranoid?"

"Paranoia is a constructive attribute in a captain," Gonzalez pointed out. "Since we're discussing it, one thing that's struck me about this Starscream is that he doesn't wait for questions. He just gives orders. Maybe they're only 'suggestions,' but they sure sound like orders to me." She eyed her shipmates. "Me, I like to know *why* I'm being given orders. I like background, I need reasons." She smiled. "Makes me a lousy soldier, but a good technician."

Clarkson was not smiling at all. "You think maybe he's lying to us, Captain? About what?"

Shaking his head, Walker replied, "I don't know. I just keep coming back to those other machine aliens down in the fissure. If they're supposed to be so aggressive, why didn't they ever return fire? The big one looked like it might have been trying to talk with Starscream. If they're as belligerent as he's been telling us, why make an effort to communicate instead of just going to guns? Damn it, something about this doesn't *feel* right!"

"I concur," Avery agreed. "There's no logic to it. It's been too easy."

"Easy?" Clarkson remarked. "You call all this easy?"

The science officer raised an eyebrow and replied in his deep voice. "Actually, yes. None of us is dead, and there's still hope we might find a way to get home. Then out of the blue, or more precisely out of the black, these aliens show up, and without any preliminary discussion or cautious conversation or careful exchange of how-do-you-dos, suddenly we've got one acting like he's our long-lost best friend. Why? Alien altruism? An irresistible compulsion to protect poor, feeble little *Homo sapiens* from the big bad Autobots? No, I think the captain is right. It's all just been too pat."

"I see your point," Thompson responded. "What *does* this Starscream creature gain by befriending us?"

"Let's suppose you're correct and we have reason to be suspicious," Clarkson commented. "Where does that leave us?"

"I don't know," Walker readily admitted. "But those two other aliens are dead or trapped in a collapsed cavern, and we helped bring that about. Maybe before we go blasting off into space with our big buddy Starscream to take part in some interstellar other-species war just because he says it's the right thing for us to do, we should consider all possible aspects of such a serious action."

"What do you want to do, Captain?" Thompson asked him. "We can't just sit here. As you pointed out earlier, it may be that Starscream and his friends represent our only hope of getting home."

"I remember," Walker acknowledged. "But for right now, we're going to try something else." He paused briefly. "We're going to lie."

"Lie?" Gonzalez stared at him. "Lie about what?"

Walker chuckled. "Well, it's not much of a lie. We're going to tell him we need to make some repairs before we can leave the planetary surface again."

"He'll believe that," Avery commented. "He has to know that our ship isn't his equal. It's an imitation, not an original."

Walker nodded, then changed the subject. "Here's a question to think about. What is it that makes them—alive? How are they more than just machines?"

"That's a heck of a good question. But one that will have to wait." Clarkson pointed through the viewport. "He's coming back."

Having exhausted his very limited patience, Starscream communicated with the alien craft. "Are you ready to depart?"

"Tell him no, Maria." As he gave the command, Walker wondered why he was whispering. "Explain that we need to rest as well as perform some essential work on our ship."

Gonzalez sent the message. The response was enlightening. "Rest? Are you experiencing malfunctions?"

Walker shook his head. "Explain to him that our systems function differently from his. In order to operate at full capacity we need to—minimize our functions for a period of time so we can recharge."

Once more she transmitted the message. Starscream's reply indicated that while he understood, he was still upset. "Very well. It is unfortunate you will not immediately be able to participate in the forthcoming noble conflict. I can linger here no longer and must return to my comrades. Rest assured that I will come back for you in a short time."

"Agreed," Gonzalez sent.

They waited a good fifteen minutes after Starscream left them before Thompson activated the drive again. The ship started forward on its landing skids. A moment later and long before it began to approach anything like liftoff velocity, it gave an unexpected shudder and started sliding to starboard.

"Uh-oh," Thompson muttered, suddenly fighting with the controls.

Along with everyone else's attention, Walker's was fixed forward. "Up, baby, get up. Up, damn it!"

"Hold on!" Thompson yelled.

As he cut the drive, the *Ghost* slid sharply sideways and came to a stop. Other than facing back the way they had come, there appeared to be no damage. Of course, appearances could be deceiving.

"Status report!" Walker snapped. One by one the crew reported. Communications, operational. Engineering, all normal. They had escaped disaster. In fact, insofar as he could tell, there was only one problem.

Thompson looked over at him. "We're stuck, Captain."

Walker considered. "We can dig out. Or maybe we'll have to put my paranoia aside and ask our oversized 'friend' for a hand."

"Better make up your mind fast, Captain." Clarkson looked up from his console. "We're sinking."

Walker gaped at him. "Sinking? What do you mean, we're sink—?"

Ghost 1 shuddered again. Outside, broken rock and loose sand were rising like pale mud around the mired ship. Despite the danger, Thompson tried to activate the drive. There was no response.

"I can't get us out, Captain!"

No one had any ideas. This, Walker thought frantically, might have been how the other aliens ended up underground in that deep cavity. Possibly this entire region was pockmarked with quicksands and sinkholes. The viewports were already covered, and they could feel the ship beginning to accelerate downward.

"Use the attitude thrusters and try to keep us upright, Jake," Walker cried. "If we land ventral-side down, at least we'll be in a position to try to work our way out. Even," he added, "if we have to dig."

Thompson readied the relevant controls. Sand and stone were replaced by blackness. Exhibiting the kind of reactions that had gotten him the assignment, he proceeded to fire and adjust the small thrusters. They hit the cavern floor with a resounding crash—but not a fatal one.

Then everything was still. And dark, Walker noted as he gazed out the still-intact foreport. Utterly dark.

"Everyone all right?"

A shaken chorus of affirmatives responded.

Before anyone could say much of anything else, the entire ship shook. Darkness was unexpectedly replaced by light. Peering up through the port, Walker and Thompson found they could see sky once more. Sky, and a by-now-familiar bulky figure gazing down at them.

Walker estimated that they were at least four or five hundred feet below the surface. Quite a sinkhole, he mused. If not for Thompson's skill with the thrusters, it was likely they would have found themselves stuck here permanently.

Gonzalez looked up from her station. "Captain, we have contact." Words appeared on the screen in front of her.

"It appears," Starscream was saying, "that you have run into difficulty."

Gonzalez did not wait for Walker. "Yes," she typed swiftly. "Thank goodness you came back. Can you help us?"

"I could, yes," the alien replied. "But while this accident of planetary geology changes my plans somewhat, I find that I can adapt to it. It turns out that your unexpected current location and situation suit my purposes."

"That," Walker muttered, "doesn't sound good. Ask him what he means."

Gonzalez obediently typed the message. The reply was immediate.

"I had planned on ensuring your destruction in space at the hands of my enemies, the Autobots. The intent was to shame them. But your unfortunate circumstances now preclude this outcome. Regrettable. Just as it is regrettable for you that you did not know what you had back on your homeworld."

A grim-faced Gonzalez once more requested clarification.

"Your Ice Man," Starscream explained, "is not one of our scouts, but rather is our long-lost leader, Megatron. A being who while powerful, is at base unworthy of leading us. I have since taken his place. If the other Decepticons knew he still existed, they would not rest until he was recovered. That, of course, would cost me my present position as their rightful leader."

Gonzalez looked over at Walker. "You were right, Captain. Our erstwhile 'friend' is something else entirely."

Echoing over the speakers, a discordant electronic screech filled the cabin. It might have been laughter. It certainly resembled nothing human.

"I wish I hadn't been," Walker declared. "Tell him we're willing to bargain."

She typed out the message.

"Bargain? Bargain for what, organic scum? In order to bargain, one must first have something to bargain *with*. Your usefulness to me has run its course, albeit prematurely. So be it. On reflection, I have decided to leave you to your grave."

The ground trembled around them. Clarkson inhaled sharply. Sand and rock began to spill into the cavern, slamming into the top of the ship, banging and bouncing off the curved metal.

"Move us, get us out of the way, Jake!" Walker yelped.

Everyone was shouting at once. Using the thrusters, Thompson managed to edge the *Ghost* forward. Broken rock and other debris continued to rain down, but behind them now as the ship slid forward on its skids into a side corridor that was just barely large enough to admit it.

Darkness once more descended around them—and this time it remained.

A long, drawn-out period of utter silence went unbroken until Avery finally murmured softly, "Now what do we do, Captain?"

At first Walker didn't respond. Then he swiveled his seat so that he was facing the science officer. "I don't have the first friggin' clue, Mike. I really don't."

Before anyone else could speak, Clarkson spoke up from his station. "Well, find one fast, Captain.

"We aren't alone down here."

Kinnear opened his eyes when Jensen, accompanied by a thrill of frigid air, reentered the tent. The colonel realized he had been drifting again. "Status, Lieutenant?" He tried to ignore the harsh croak of his own voice.

"Everyone else is accounted for, sir," Jensen told him. "We've got four tents set up: two for medical and two as shelters for the rest of the team."

"And the trucks?" Kinnear wanted to know.

The junior officer sighed. "Not doing as well as the men, I'm afraid. Right now we've only got one that's a hundred percent functional—the last truck in line managed to stop before sliding off the road. Everything else is at least dinged up or still in the ditch."

"Ah, hell," Kinnear muttered. "Where are we on supplies?"

Jensen perked up, relieved to be able to deliver some good news. "Fortunately, we've got enough G-rations to last several days. We've got plenty to drink; tea, coffee, and emergency bouillon, even if we have to melt the ice." He ran a hand through his hair, wiping away cold moisture. "You might as well know the rest. Nobody planned on this being a long-term trip. Deliver the Ice Man to the freighter and head back to the base. If we siphon the fuel from the most seriously disabled trucks, we can run the two portable generators for warmth and light for maybe a day and a half."

Kinnear's lips tightened. "We're not likely to have a day and a half, Lieutenant, so it's not as big a concern as you might think."

"Sir?" Jensen eyed him questioningly.

"My guess is that Tasarov's comrades will be on top of us long before then. If they can't get here in twenty-four hours, they know there'd be no point in them making the effort because despite this damn storm we'd have air cover by then. The last thing they'll risk is losing a sub or two in Canadian waters. I want you to strengthen the perimeter, one man every twenty-five yards, and pull them in to fifty yards. Have them dig foxholes in the snow. The digging will keep them warm, and the holes will get them out of the wind. Also, if you can find some rope, let's run some lines. I don't want anyone straying out beyond the perimeter. One light per tent, no more. Anyone needs more, they can use flashlights. With any luck at all—not that we've had any so far—our failure to report in has already been noticed and we'll soon have some help out here."

"Yes, sir," Jensen replied. "Can I bring you something to eat?"

Kinnear declined. The very idea of eating found him, already nauseous from the heavy medication he had received, on the verge of losing what little his stomach retained. "No, thanks." He nodded toward the nearby table. "Just some water, please."

Jensen passed him a half-full pitcher. Filling the glass at the side of his cot, Kinnear drank gratefully, setting the empty aside with a deep sigh of relief. "Better. Now, about the heavy hauler: what's its status?"

The other man shrugged. "Naturally, the mechanics have made it their top priority. I'm told that once they get it straightened out, as long as there's no serious structural damage, it'll run."

Kinnear let out a relieved sigh. "It'd better. The Ice Man and his special container are too big and too heavy to move with anything else—and we have to move him. If the techs are right and he emerges from stasis, then even based on what little we know about him, the Russians will be the least of our worries."

Jensen thought about it for a moment, then nodded. "I'll check on how it's coming right now."

"You do that," Kinnear replied. "I'll wait here."

The lieutenant cracked a smile, which was what Kinnear had hoped for. Sometimes breaking the tension was all one could do. A commanding officer had to act as psychologist and therapist as often as tactician.

"You all right?" he asked.

"I'm fine, sir," Jensen assured him. "Thank you. I'll be back as soon as possible." Turning, he strode through the tent opening and disappeared into the storm.

Kinnear lay down on the cot once more, feeling beads of cold sweat break out on his forehead. He had not said anything to Jensen, but he could feel a fever coming on and knew he was getting worse by the minute. His leg needed to be tended to by a surgeon, not a field medic trained to keep people alive for a short period of time until an evac chopper could come in and whisk them away. No chopper could find its way to them until the storm let up.

He began to drift again, thinking of Phil Nolan and the missions they had run together. Remembering his early days in the army and then later, when he had been recruited into Sector Seven. At the time he had thought it an honor, but now he knew better. It was a sentence to a life of secrecy that made even his days in black ops look like an open-book program. Sector Seven was an agency founded on secrets, lies, and convoluted deceptions designed solely to cover up those secrets and lies.

Maybe it was fitting that he should die out here. There were so many times in the past when he could have died, even should have died, and had not. Fleetingly, he thought of the crew of *Ghost 1,* lost somewhere in distant reaches of the galaxy, more alone than any humans had ever been, and forced to contend with the Ice Man's relations. They were doomed, he knew. It was a realization that pained him even more than the agonizing pulse in his broken femur.

He hated losing people. Hated it almost as much as failure. That was his hallmark: when Colonel Thomas Kinnear took on a mission, he delivered. Always.

Always, he corrected himself, *until now.*

He drifted some more until he heard the entrance open and Jensen came back in. Opening his eyes, Kinnear looked at the younger man hopefully. "Well?"

A doleful Jensen shook his head. "I'm sorry, sir. The mechanics are still working on it. Aside from trying to make the necessary repairs in the field and in bad weather when what they really need is a fully equipped motor pool garage, they're trying to fix the big rig with the Ice Man's housing still on top of it. They just don't have any room to maneuver." He started to spit, remembered where he was, and swallowed it. "Too much weight, wrong conditions—sir."

Kinnear nodded slowly. "I was afraid that would be the situation. Still, they need to keep at it. We can't just sit here hoping help shows up."

Jensen indicated his understanding. "We need to buy ourselves some time with the Ice Man, sir. And there's something else."

"Will it make me feel better?" Kinnear asked, afraid he already knew the answer.

Regretfully, Jensen did not disappoint him. "One of the techs reported that he saw a brief flicker in the alien's eyes, and another swears she saw one of his hands twitch. He might be reviving."

"Oh, good." Kinnear poured himself more water, wishing fervently as he did so that the pitcher contained something darker and stronger. His mind raced, and an idea struck him. "Get the fire suppression team together. Their gear has integrated heating for use in these conditions."

"Sir?"

"I want them to melt snow and spray the warm water over the Ice Man," Kinnear explained. "Inside his container, it'll freeze as soon as it hits him. We'll supplement it with the liquid nitrogen." He managed a smile. "We're going to turn his shipping container into one giant cube. Once the container is solid on the inside, keep the flow going until it's buried on the outside, too—except where the mechanics need to work. That's how they found him in the first place, right? Buried in the ice."

Jensen considered the idea, then grinned. "Sometimes simpler is better, sir. I'll see to it right away."

Kinnear was not finished. "And tell the troops on the perimeter to be ready for action. The Russians could show up at any minute."

Jensen nodded and hurried out of the tent.

Kinnear closed his eyes yet again. If they were lucky, hosing down the Ice Man's container and most of his vehicle would leave them with only one major problem to deal with at a time. He doubted it, though. Some days it just didn't pay to get out of bed. And on one of the few mornings when he desperately wanted to, he could not move.

XI

Optimus moved quickly down the new tunnel, then took the first branching to the left, away from the sounds of the pursuing carnivores. "We should keep moving," he told Bumblebee. "If there are enough of those monsters, they might be too much to handle." Bumblebee saw no reason to argue.

There was air flowing in these tunnels, which meant that somewhere there had to be an opening to the surface, or at least one they could more easily enlarge than the solid stone ceiling that was presently overhead. If they could avoid any further confrontations until they found such a location, there was a chance they could make it back to the *Ark* before full-blown bedlam enveloped their companions.

The collective hissing of the worm-creatures had begun to fade. Reaching yet another tunnel fork, Optimus paused. They had been on the move for some time without his sensors detecting any weakness in the solid rock overhead. Maybe it was time for another opinion.

"What do you think, Bumblebee?"

The smaller Autobot pointed toward the tunnel on the right. Optimus shrugged and nodded. "There's half a chance it's more promising than the one on the left. Let's have a look."

First sight was not encouraging. The corridor narrowed rapidly until there was barely room for Optimus to stand upright. Nevertheless, they continued onward. Very soon the tunnel opened into a new cavern. On the far side, the maze resumed. While the geology continued to fascinate, Optimus reflected that this was getting them nowhere nearer the surface. He had just settled on a new tunnel to try and had taken a step toward it when the mouth of the corridor suddenly vomited rock, sand, and gravel. The force of the unexpected eruption was stunning—strong enough to send both him and Bumblebee staggering backward. The shape that eventually materialized out of the settling dust and pulverized stone was one he recognized. It was not one he expected.

The alien ship.

Shoving Bumblebee behind him, he powered up his weapons systems. What the intruder was doing down here, he did not know. Nor did he care. What mattered was that he had seen it working side by side with Starscream. That was enough.

Advancing awkwardly into the mouth of the tunnel, the incongruous craft shuddered to a halt. Through its forward viewport and for the first time he could actually see the lifeforms that occupied the vessel. They were even smaller than he had envisioned. Sensors told him they were not true machines but some sort of higher animal life-form. Their visages were remarkably familiar. An interesting example of convergent evolution, he decided—if not some other unimaginable scientific distinction. Assuming the existence of a certain parallelity of meaning, he inferred that they looked more frightened than angry. The ship's maneuverable weapons slowly went down in a gesture that Optimus took for surrender, or at least an application for a truce.

He remained ready to respond, but unlike their previous encounter, this time the aliens held their fire. In fact, as he examined their craft he could see no indication that they intended to raise the weapons that had been unleashed against him earlier. Given their proximity, he could have easily annihilated them with a single blast. Instead he restrained himself while waiting for some sign, some indication that they proposed to resume mutual hostilities.

No such indication manifested itself.

Time ticked away. Eventually, he lowered his own weapons. If they intended to attack, they would already have done so. There was something strange going on here, and it had nothing to do with the appearance of their ship.

"Bumblebee, you're our best interspecies communicator. Do you think you can interface with them?"

By way of response, the smaller mechanoid offered an incredulous look that suggested his leader might be suffering from a serious cognitive malfunction.

"I think this is critical, Bumblebee." Using an open, weaponless hand, Optimus gestured toward the alien craft. "They don't want to fight this time. Surely you can see that. If they don't want to fight, one must assume they might like to talk. I can do this, but as we both know, this kind of interaction is one of your specialties."

For a long moment Bumblebee did nothing. But despite his personal feelings he had to admit to himself that he was tired of running nowhere and accomplishing nothing. Not that he thought treachery was so much more interesting than boredom, but it was evident that Optimus had made up his mind. They were not going to leave this place until Prime had satisfied himself as to the true nature of the small aliens—one way or the other.

As the smaller mechanoid crossed toward the peculiar vessel, Optimus observed with the aid of magnification how the lifeforms within reacted. While certainly eccentric, the expressions they flashed and the postures they struck appeared anything but aggressive.

Circling the ship, Bumblebee looked for a site where he might interface. Several external antennas offered a choice. Scanning the lot to divine their specific individual functions, he settled on the one he thought most likely and reached out. What he found were the most primitive computational devices he had ever encountered outside one of Cybertron's historical displays. Once he analyzed the operational codes and primordial programming, he indicated to Optimus that he was ready and able to attempt communication.

"Tell them we don't wish to fight with them," Optimus declared.

Bumblebee transmitted the message. Verification that it had been received took the form of a painfully slow but comprehensible response from the creatures inside the ship. In essence, it said exactly the same thing. They did not wish to fight, either.

"I thought as much, but it's good to have it confirmed," Optimus murmured. "Relay my words, Bumblebee." It took the smaller mechanoid a few seconds to finalize the necessary linkage.

Turning his full attention to the alien ship, the leader of the Autobots considered his next words with care before addressing the aliens within. "My name is Optimus Prime, and I am the leader of the Autobots, residents of a distant world called Cybertron. You should know first and foremost that we believe, above all else, that individual freedom of thought and movement is the right of all sentient beings regardless of shape, size, or evolutionary origin."

The response from the alien ship reassured him that his greeting had been well received.

"We are human beings, a sentient mammalian lifeform, from a planet we call Earth. We don't know exactly how we have come to be here. In our bewilderment, uncertainty, and yes, fear, we apparently allowed ourselves to be deceived by a metallic bipedal alien similar to you in structure and makeup who called himself Starscream. He said that the Autobots were evil. While your words are closer to our beliefs than anything he said to us, please understand our confusion. We mean no one any harm. The fight between your kind and his is not ours. We participated in the attack on you and your companion because this Starscream promised that if we did, he would help us find a way home. That's all we want: to find a way back to our own world. We do not want to fight with anyone."

Optimus caught himself chuckling. "All right, then. We won't engage in battle. And do not despair at having been overcome by the events that have overtaken you. It's not surprising you were deceived by Starscream. His people are called the Decepticons for a reason, and Starscream is often more manipulative than his absent leader: a Decepticon as evil as he was powerful. His name was Megatron. He has been missing and lost to our knowledge for ages."

There was a pause, then the humans replied, "We didn't know his name, but the mechanoid—the Decepticon—that you refer to is not lost. He is on our world, frozen in stasis."

The unexpected information shook Optimus to his core. If what the human creatures were telling him was true, it changed—everything. If somewhere out there among the stars, wherever these people hailed from, Megatron still existed intact and undamaged, and if he emerged from the stasis they said he was in, these humans would likely have no way to deal with him.

Simply to have something to occupy himself, simply for practice, and purely out of unrestrained hatred for everything and anything that was not Decepticon,

Megatron would destroy their world and every living creature on it.

Somehow, Optimus realized, he had to get these people back to their world. Not just because it was the right thing to do, but because they needed to warn their own leaders of the danger that threatened them.

Nolan watched the raging storm through triple-paned windows. Snow was howling in horizontally as the wind swirled it in all directions. On the ground outside it was accruing at a furious rate. Having been designed to look as if they led nowhere in particular, the roads away from the station would be extremely hazardous in these conditions. Normally that would not matter: a regular supply convoy would simply stop, sit tight, and wait for the blizzard to move on. But the convoy that had left earlier was anything but ordinary. He hated the idea of sending still more people out into this kind of weather, but the lack of communication from the trucks left him little choice.

"Sergeant Martin!" His voice carried over the bustle in the hanger.

Short black hair and brown eyes that peered out from beneath heavy lids accented Martin's sallow face as the sergeant crossed from the desk where he had been working since Nolan entered the hangar.

"Yes, sir!" he snapped as he approached.

It was more than a little ironic. Martin was exactly the man Nolan needed, and he should not have even been here. The sergeant's squad of Army Rangers had been granted special permission to visit the base to do some training under severe arctic conditions. Even though they had been kept well away from the Ice Man and those working directly with the alien, the relevant security clearances for the squad had filled half a briefcase.

Nolan met the man's gaze evenly. "I need your people

to perform a search and rescue. Have them get in their cold-weather gear and be ready to lock, rock, and roll fully armed in fifteen minutes."

Martin hesitated. He and his team were not technically under Nolan's command. On the other hand, the lieutenant colonel had gone beyond graciousness in seeing to it that the Rangers had been treated like honored guests. And a real S&R would only be a capper to the training they had already undergone, except . . .

He gestured outside. "Who was crazy enough to go out in that mess, sir?"

It was a fair question. Nolan explained even though he didn't have to.

"Base commander Colonel Thomas Kinnear is running a convoy to the coast. A convoy that's vital to national security. They've been out of touch for far too long. That's all you need to know for right now. You came up here for cold-weather training. You're about to get some."

"My thought also, sir. Will you be coming with us?" Unaware that he was doing so, the sergeant's gaze fell to Nolan's out-of-shape midsection.

Nolan noticed the direction of the Ranger's glance but bit back the words that sprang to mind. He needed this man's cooperation. "As a matter of fact, Sergeant, I will. Now are you going to stand here all day asking questions or are you going to get your people together?"

"Right away, sir." If Nolan's tone troubled the Ranger, he did not show it. Sketching a salute, he took off at a brisk trot across the hangar.

Breaking out a set of winter gear for himself, Nolan commenced the somewhat cumbersome process of putting it all on. Always start with the socks, he reminded himself. Then the special snowsuit and boots. This on top of his heavy underwear and light-duty shirt. Layers were more important than thickness. As he dressed he found himself thinking back to previous crises the program had suffered—and survived.

Early on, the Ice Man's ability to reanimate after having been frozen in the heavy pack ice had amazed everyone. It had been a near thing the first time he had started to revive, but the techs and the scientists had learned from the almost-catastrophe. It was the study of the ability of a lifeform, even a mechanical, non-carbon-based lifeform, to retain such a capability for revivification that had provided the first fruits of the reverse-engineering program.

The new snowsuits that had recently been supplied to the base were difficult to get into, being made of a single piece of white, metallic fabric, but they were very light and flexible once on. And they could withstand extremely cold temperatures, keeping the person inside comfortable even in severe arctic conditions. Their drawback was that they had yet to be put to a test like the mission he was about to lead, but he believed they would suffice. It was not as if he and the Rangers were going camping on the tundra for a month. With any luck at all they would be out and back and seeing the convoy on its way within a day or two.

By the time he had finally struggled into the suit, the Rangers were waiting.

"We're ready, sir." Martin jerked a thumb over a shoulder. "I've got a snowcat with a full tank warming up outside."

Nolan nodded, started to follow the sergeant out, and then returned to remove from a closet the rifle that he had been issued on arrival. It slipped over his shoulder as if it *wanted* to bang into his spine. It had been a long time since he'd worn any kind of field gear, and his back protested at the unexpected presence. He was more out of shape than he had thought.

On the hangar floor he scrutinized the squad: six, plus

the sergeant. Hard faces full of confidence, young bodies that reflected the results of serious training. None was less than an E-4, and according to their records all of them had combat experience.

Nolan remembered seeing the memo announcing their visit to SSAB because it was so unexpected. Almost all of the military's special forces units were serving somewhere in Southeast Asia. Having one request and receive permission to complete Arctic training had struck him at the time as something well out of the ordinary. Not that there wasn't a need for such training. Rangers had to be ready for anything. Still, it had left him wondering.

"Sergeant Martin," he asked sociably, "if you don't mind my inquiring—why are you and your men here?"

"Sir?" The noncom's expression was a blank.

"Every special forces unit we've got is off somewhere in the jungle, and you and your men are up here freezing your asses off. I never did quite buy the cold-weather training thing." He nodded toward the double doorway they were approaching. "This is liable to be a big deal coming up, and before we run into something more unexpected than bad weather I'd seriously appreciate knowing why you are really here."

Martin considered briefly, then gave a sharp nod. "We were sent here, sir, and told to keep ourselves ready to deal with any unforeseen problems. Our orders came straight from Washington."

"Washington?" Nolan pondered. "Who in Washington?"

"We aren't precisely sure, sir. The directive was prepared by someone referred to as the 'Old Man.'"

Nolan couldn't suppress a laugh. "Simmons?"

Martin looked surprised. "Sir? You know this man? He personally delivered our orders to our company commander. I overheard them talking."

"Then why the hell wouldn't he mention it to us?"

"We don't know, sir." Martin essayed a thin smile. "I'm just a staff sergeant. But we're here, and there's serious trouble or you wouldn't be standing there in full arctic gear a foot from my face asking me questions I can't answer. So let's go and do what we have to do. Personally I'd rather be slipping up behind Viet Cong in the jungle than playing soldier in the snow."

Nolan considered it all for a moment, then dismissed it. Now was not the time to add another mystery to his day. But Simmons continued to astound him. The man's resources were limitless.

"I understand, Sergeant. Believe it or not, I once used a weapon or two in combat myself. Let's move out." Stepping past Martin, he led the way toward the hangar exit.

It was pitch dark outside as the Rangers piled into the snowcat. Climbing into the passenger seat across from Martin, Nolan wondered how they would fare if they came up against something worse than the weather, and decided not to dwell on the possibility.

Out and back, he promised himself. *Reestablish communication, evaluate the situation, and return.* He still had a spaceship to save.

"Was this part of your plan?" Ironhide dodged a blast of plasma that had been unleashed by the streaking Blackout.

Jazz completed a vertical spin and took a quick shot at Frenzy before having to circle away from Bonecrusher. His shot went wide as Frenzy dodged. Just like the Autobots, the Decepticons made use of extraordinarily advanced predictive programming that rendered them extremely difficult to hit.

"Not precisely," he responded, having to execute a high-speed twirl as Bonecrusher tried to close in again.

He turned his full attention to the threatening behemoth. "You move pretty fast for a big bot," he quipped. "But not fast enough."

The huge Decepticon's attempt to engage physically failed as Jazz skipped nimbly out of his reach. "Stand and fight!"

"Not a chance." Adding a burst of speed, Jazz darted downward until he was hovering alongside Ironhide. "Are you ready?" he queried his bigger colleague.

"I predict that you're going to lose significant body parts out here." Ironhide was clearly unhappy with his friend's projected tactics. "This plan of yours isn't going to work."

"Too late to debate the fine points now." Jazz started forward again. "As soon as they're on me, get going."

"I'm sorry I agreed to this," Ironhide muttered. "If you get your Spark extinguished, I'll have to hear about it from Prime for the next couple of millennia."

Trailing laughter as well as the energetic particles that propelled him, Jazz shot forward. Though the Decepticons could not be sure whether this seemingly foolish move represented an attack or merely a taunt, it did draw the immediate attention of not just Bonecrusher, but Frenzy and Blackout as well.

Via coded transmission, the speeding Jazz contacted the *Ark*. "Ratchet, try to get Barricade's attention, will you?"

"Let's see if this attracts his interest." Ratchet proceeded to open fire with the *Ark*'s heavy weapons.

Free-space combat came to a sudden halt as the *Ark* unexpectedly opened up with its integrated plasma cannon. Exhibiting the same skill and precision he employed as a mechanic, Ratchet slammed a series of bursts square into the side of the *Nemesis*. The shields on the Decepticon transport held—just barely. Even at a distance, Jazz could see the defensive fields shimmer from the impact.

"Keep on them, Ratchet!" he transmitted encouragingly. "Don't let them relax."

He would have done better to pay attention to his own circumstances. Reveling in the potent assault on the *Nemesis*, he just did manage to dodge an unexpectedly swift grab by the hard-charging Bonecrusher. This nearly put him in Blackout's line of fire. Firing repeatedly, almost wildly, Jazz skipped and slowed, keeping just out of the reach of massive Decepticon hands and lambent streaks of destructive energy. Where others might have descended into panic, Jazz felt only exhilaration.

"Come on, come on," he goaded his opponents. "You pustulant inflammations on the fabric of space–time can do better than that, can't you?"

Beyond the massive frame of the furious and increasingly frustrated Bonecrusher, he could just make out, at the extreme limits of his detectors, Ironhide swooping around in a long, wide arc that should bring him back to the scene of battle within sensor shadow of the *Nemesis*. Jazz felt if he could stay intact and continue to occupy the Decepticons long enough for Ironhide to get inside their ship's shields, his companion would have the chance to wreak some serious damage to their engines. With luck, he might be able to disable them completely.

"Hold still, insect, and I will show you what I can do." Advancing with greater care this time, Bonecrusher closed in.

Jazz was thankful for the huge mechanoid's single-minded nature. Bonecrusher's anticipatory maneuvering and Jazz's skillful countermoves continued to keep the giant between Jazz and the other Decepticons. As a result, they could not shoot without risking a hit on one of their own.

"I'll hold still," Jazz teased his intimidating foe, "if you promise to be nice."

"Master of small words. Here is 'nice'!" Almost within reach, Bonecrusher accelerated and spun. His rear appendage struck forward as he tried to spear Jazz.

His nimbleness unaffected by the thrust, Jazz dodged cleanly to one side. The abrupt change of position, however, took him out of Bonecrusher's orbit. The instant their line of fire cleared, Frenzy and Blackout opened up with their assorted weaponry. Jazz avoided the blast from Frenzy, but it put him right in line to take a direct hit from Blackout's weapons. This well-aimed burst struck him dead center, sending him tumbling backward and out of control. Heat from the plasma surge threatened to penetrate his armor and melt vital components. He felt—pain.

Instead of expending energy on trying to stabilize his spin, he allowed himself to continue tumbling free in order to gain distance. Though uncontrolled, the spin did not prevent him from continuing to track Ironhide's position. His friend was now approaching the *Nemesis*, focusing on the vulnerable propulsion system of the Decepticon ship. He was so preoccupied, in fact, that he failed to react to the large metallic object that was closing rapidly behind him.

Starscream was returning to join the battle, and Ironhide didn't see him.

Frantically, Jazz shouted over all available channels. "Ironhide, abort! You've got company." He saw Ironhide turn to look behind him. Starscream was already nearly in range.

"Ratchet, fire! Give him space!"

On board the *Ark*, Ratchet had also detected Starscream's arrival. Once again he did his job and sent bursts streaking toward Starscream. Though the bigger, faster Decepticon kept coming, his angle of approach had been altered. It gave Ironhide enough maneuvering room to slip around the *Nemesis* and head at speed back toward the *Ark*.

So much for the brilliance of improvised strategy, Jazz concluded. He had not counted on Starscream showing up at precisely the wrong moment. He consoled himself with the knowledge that even Optimus could not have foreseen it.

What with Starscream's approach, Ironhide's dash for safety, and his own reflections, he neglected to sense Bonecrusher's proximity until it was too late.

"Told you I'd get you," the Decepticon growled. His armored, pointed tail flashed forward to spear completely through Jazz's right shoulder.

Circuits failed, internal alarms went off, and his body fought to erect workarounds to enable the seriously damaged area to continue to function without requiring a complete shutdown. Raising his other arm to defend himself, Jazz reversed his forward momentum and managed to slide off the piercing tail point. He was helped to fall backward as Bonecrusher's massive fist connected with his face. For the second time in not so many minutes he felt himself tumbling over and over through space, only this time the persistence of bodily rotation was not sustained by choice.

How badly, he found himself wondering as he spun, *am I hurt?*

The others were waiting for Walker to make a decision. With the *Ghost* having just survived a hard fall and now sitting well below the unknown planet's surface, and the roof of the tunnel they had dropped into having collapsed behind them, he did not need to consider for very long.

"We don't have a lot of options," he told his crew. "If this Optimus Prime decides to leave us here, it's likely we won't be able to get the *Ghost* out on our own. Or before we can somehow manage the necessary degree of excavation, one of the creatures he mentioned will get us.

We don't have much choice except to trust him—and his smaller companion."

Looks were exchanged, but no words. There was little anyone could say. Though they were far from happy with the captain's conclusions, his logic was unassailable. After the betrayal by Starscream, they had pretty much decided that none of the aliens could be trusted.

Walker, however, had a completely different feeling about Optimus Prime than he'd had toward Starscream. Where the first mechanoid had been evasive and self-centered, this Optimus creature evinced a simplicity and compassion that struck the captain as far more appealing—and far more believable. Even his choice of vocalization was more willfully empathetic.

Also significant had been his initial responses when he had first sighted the *Ghost*. Instead of seeking cover for himself, his first action had been to move in front of his smaller and weaker companion. Only when Optimus had analyzed the situation and felt it safe had he allowed his cohort to expose himself. The more Walker considered and compared the two separate and very different encounters, the more he found himself thinking that Starscream was the type of being who would shove a smaller underling in front of himself to ensure his own safety.

The most recent conversation with the two Autobots had been informative. Among other things, the one who called himself Optimus had indicated that he believed it was only a matter of time until their combined presence drew the attention of the indigenous serpentine monstrosities he and his companion had fought previously.

"Alien snake central," Thompson had taken to referring to the cavern in which they found themselves.

"Indeed." Though utterly unfamiliar with the term, Optimus was content to accept it as just as descriptive as any other.

While preparations were made to try to free the *Ghost* from its subterranean prison, the crew did their best to make ready for anything. Though conversation inside the ship had taken a decidedly nervous turn, there were no signs of panic. The crew were too well trained to give in to the emotions of the moment—even though their current situation was hardly one they had prepped to deal with. There was concern that in attempting to force a way to the surface, collapsing rock could damage the *Ghost* to the point that it would be unable to lift off. Once again Walker was comforted—if that was an appropriate description—by their lack of any choice. Ascending from the depths was going to require every bit of their knowledge and all of Thompson's redoubtable piloting skills. Even then, he knew there was a good chance the ship would not make it. There would be next to no margin for error.

On the bright side, he reminded himself, so far the cavern and the tunnels that led away from it into alien depths unknown remained devoid of worm-monsters.

This thought had just crossed Walker's mind when a polite *thunk* echoed through the hull. This was followed by a message from Optimus that materialized on Gonzalez's monitor.

"There is a small, almost imperceptible point of light in the ceiling of the cavern located directly in front of you," the mechanoid informed them. "I believe it represents a weak point. Because it is on the opposite side of the tunnel that constitutes your present semi-protected location, I am convinced I can enlarge the opening with minimal danger to your craft." Before anyone could applaud or cheer, the message continued. "Less encouragingly, I am afraid I have to point out that we have company."

Walker's gaze immediately shifted to the foreport. In the absence of light, he continued to rely on the *Ghost*'s infrared and sonic imagers to give him a picture of their pitch-dark surroundings. "Ask him if it's Starscream," Walker instructed Gonzalez. She sent the message.

While Optimus's reply was negative, neither was it encouraging. "No. My sensors indicate that Starscream has departed. We are faced instead with local difficulties. Many of them, in fact. One is larger than I am."

"Worms." Gonzalez looked over at Walker. "I never liked worms. Had to dissect too many of them in biology. Now what do we do?"

"Ask our new friend."

The response was terse, to the point, and pretty much what Walker had expected.

"We defend ourselves."

Optimus monitored the movements of the approaching creatures carefully. Given how much noise they were making and how much fighting they were doing among themselves—hissing, spitting, and snarling at one another—it was remarkable that they had managed to gather together long enough to locate himself, Bumblebee, and the alien craft. There were sixteen of them in immediate detection range, with potentially more crowded into the far reaches of the tunnel from which they were advancing. Tilting back his head, he rechecked the distance to the tiny opening he had detected in the roof of the adjacent cavern. On board the *Ghost,* Clarkson was doing the same. Several hundred feet, give or take an intervening stalactite.

Optimus determined that a couple of well-placed blasts with just one of his weapons should be sufficient to enlarge the opening such that all of them could escape. At the same time, he had to calibrate his bursts just so in order to ensure that pulverized stone did not fall so as to block or damage the humans' vessel. Nor was their safe emergence the only crisis weighing on his mind. He needed to get back to the *Ark* before Starscream and the other Decepticons could take full advantage of his and Bumblebee's absence. If the disparity in strength and numbers was not rectified soon, the outcome could be catastrophic.

And then there was the problem posed by the worm-creatures. In the absence of movement on his and his companions' part, they continued to mill about just beyond the entrance to their tunnel. Based on previous experience, any action or activity was likely to stimulate them to attack. He did not see how he could hold them off, help defend the humans, and still fire at the ceiling with the required precision. As he stood motionless and staring, the creatures showed no inclination to retreat the way they had come. There was no avoiding the most immediate problem. They would have to deal with the worm-snakes first. Without turning his head, he spoke to the equally immobile Bumblebee.

"Feeling up to a run?"

The younger Autobot nodded.

"Good. Here's what we're going to do. I want you to run across the cavern as fast as you can straight at our visitors. Fire as you go. As soon as they start after you, turn and retreat around the far side. I expect that the survivors, suitably enraged, will go after you. Meanwhile I will enlarge the opening overhead so that we can all get through. Your run should keep you clear of the fall area, but some of the debris should land on your pursuers, slowing them further. Once the gap is large enough, I'll direct the human vessel to depart. As soon as it has cleared the surface, I will attack and draw the worm-things to me. You go on up and I'll follow right behind you. With just a bit of luck we can all get out of here without having to engage in a prolonged fight."

He relayed the plan to the humans, who readily concurred with his strategy. Not that they realistically had any choice, but it was still heartening to know that they had not hesitated to place their trust in him. Once more without turning or moving, Optimus relayed instructions to Bumblebee. With a confident nod, the smaller mechanoid took off across the cavern floor, barreling straight toward the mass of writhing, twisting, waiting worm-beings.

Waving his arms and firing his secondary weapons systems, Bumblebee immediately acquired all of the worms' attention and then some. As the stink of singed snake-flesh began to fill the cavern, they charged swiftly in his direction, hissing and spitting in fury.

Stepping forward and inclining backward at a sharp angle, Optimus unleashed his weaponry on the roof. In the darkness of the cavern, the surge of concentrated fire would have blinded any human unlucky enough to have been looking in its direction. Those aboard the ship, having been warned what to expect, had turned away from the *Ghost*'s foreport and adjusted their monitors accordingly.

Cave formations and supporting rock were reduced to a cascade of gravel and dust as the roof of the cavern was collapsed. Sunlight poured into the depths. Permanently blind, the worm-things were not affected by the sudden intrusion of unhindered illumination. Exhibiting primeval, single-minded determination, they continued to pursue Bumblebee, chasing him around the perimeter of the cavity that was now exposed to light from above.

"Go!" Optimus broadcast to the humans. His urging was unnecessary. As soon as a sufficient gap had appeared overhead they'd had activated their secondary propulsion system. The clunky craft lurched into motion and commenced an awkward but swift ascent.

While the incursion of sunlight had not caused the worms to deviate from their pursuit of Bumblebee, the departure of the human vessel did create a momentary stir as their primitive nervous systems tried to determine the location of the possible new threat. Optimus proceeded to add to the confusion by turning his own weapons on the suddenly irresolute pack. First one, then a second coiled in upon itself as Prime's weapons seared gaping holes in their muscular bodies. Appearing to arrive simultaneously at a group decision, the survivors abruptly lurched in his direction.

"Now, Bumblebee!" he shouted as they closed on him.

Activating his propulsion, Bumblebee soared toward the opening in the wake of *Ghost 1*. A quick glance upward showed Optimus that both the humans and his friend had cleared the gap and were safely out in open air.

"My turn," he murmured, and activated his own drive.

He was about to emerge through the opening when something slammed into his right leg. Whether the worm had been lying in an unseen subsurface crevice or a concealed burrow, Optimus had no way of knowing. The pain that suddenly shot through him mitigated any immediate analysis. Enormous fangs comprising a composite of calcium and unknown metals pierced the plating on his lower limb. The creature's considerable weight threatened to send them both crashing to the cavern floor—where the rest of the pack waited in a coiling, expectant mass of tooth and muscle.

Applying maximum power to his secondary propulsion system, Optimus resumed his ascent. Still firmly fastened to his leg, the worm-snake came out along with him.

A quick glance to one side revealed that Bumblebee and the human ship had landed safely nearby. Below him, the worm-creature twisted and jerked, making atmospheric maneuvering dangerous as well as difficult. Its primal organic strength was impressive. Selecting a level section of worn rock, Optimus set down and prepared to deal with the unwanted guest.

No sooner had he done so than the creature whipped its body around him. Its mass alone was enough to send them both crashing to the ground. Stabilizing himself, Optimus rose and wrapped both hands around the entity, grabbing it just behind the ferocious head.

Within the *Ghost*, the crew crowded around the foreport to watch. Staring out at the alien landscape and the even more alien scuffle, Avery murmured thoughtfully to his equally enthralled companions, "I should be recording this and writing it all up—but I'm not quite sure how to frame it for the usual professional journals. 'Giant Sentient Mechanoid Battles Monster Worm on Alien Planet: A Scientific Abstract.'" He shook his head slowly at the wonder of it all.

A sympathetic Clarkson glanced over at him. "You might have better luck selling it to one of the networks—or *The National Enquirer*."

XII

Opening his eyes, Kinnear brought a hand up to pinch the nerve at the bridge of his nose. He could not keep drifting in and out of consciousness like this.

Jensen stuck his head in thc tent, and Kinnear motioned him over. "Get a medic in here," he muttered. "Now."

For once Jensen didn't even bother with a *yes, sir*, but simply turned and headed back out into the snowy night. Minutes later he returned practically dragging one of the field medics by the arm. The woman, a young sergeant whose name tag was unreadable due to the stains on her coat, looked almost as tired as Kinnear felt.

"Okay, soldier," he told her. "I need a stimulant. Something to mask the pain and keep me awake for a good while."

She looked unhappy. "Sir, in your condition and given the fragility of your leg—"

"I'm well aware of my condition." Kinnear cut her off more harshly than he had intended. "But that doesn't change the fact that if I'm half conscious, I can't command. Now do it. That's an order—and I'm not so 'fragile' that you can ignore it."

She gave a tired nod and dug around in her kit for a moment before extracting a prepackaged hypo. "This is something we offer for techs who are strung out after working under stress for an extended period of time but whose expertise can't be done without. It should keep you aware, maybe even hyperaware. For how long depends on your individual constitution and how your particular system reacts to the medication. But I've got to warn you that when it finally does wear off, you *will* sleep, sir. Deeply and for how many hours neither I nor anyone else can predict. The downside hits hard and fast."

"Understood," Kinnear replied. "I don't need days. The crisis we're facing will be resolved one way or another within twenty-four hours or so anyway."

The medic nodded once more, then pulled his arm out from under the blanket and pushed back his sleeve. She ripped open the package, did a quick swab with the included alcohol pad, plunged the needle into a vein, depressed it quickly, and pulled it out empty.

"No deposit, no return." She was not smiling. "You should start to feel it very soon, sir. I'll come back in a bit to check on you."

"Save your energy for the others," Kinnear told her. "Come look for me after everyone else is stable and not before."

"Yes, sir." Rising from his bedside, she favored him with a slight smile, saluted, and left.

Forcing himself to relax, concentrating on regulating his heartbeat, Kinnear lay back on the cot and waited for the potent chemical brew to begin its work. He felt the haze that had slowed his concentration start to fade, rolling away like fog on the San Francisco coast. Several moments passed. Then he blinked and sat up. Another couple of minutes and he was more awake than he had been in days. Every color and sound within the tent seemed to have taken on a preternatural sharpness. The constant pain in his leg, which had not left him for a minute since the accident, had receded to a barely perceptible throb. Nearby, Jensen studied his suddenly wide-eyed commanding officer warily.

Kinnear was just about to ask the attentive lieutenant to obtain an updated status report when the sharp reports of gunfire crackled through the night. Shouts echoed in counterpoint, followed by more gunfire. Turning sideways on the cot, Kinnear rose shakily. Jensen was at his side in an instant, helping to steady him.

"The Russians," Kinnear muttered. "Or their mercenaries. Tasarov wasn't lying."

"Orders, sir?" Jensen asked urgently.

"Send up every emergency flare we've got, regular intervals. If help is on the way, they need to know that we're here and that we're in trouble. Make sure the radio operators keep hammering every relevant frequency. *Somebody's* got to hear us."

His hand instinctively feeling for his pistol, Jensen nodded. "Anything else, sir?"

"Yeah, one other thing."

"Sir?"

"Pass it down that not one of the attackers is to get anywhere near the Ice Man. Understood? They are not to breach that perimeter under any circumstances. Operational secrecy must be preserved at all costs."

"Yes, sir." Jensen's eyes, like his tone, had turned hard.

Kinnear tried to straighten. As soon as he put any weight on his damaged leg, the pain overwhelmed the narcotizing effects of the customized opiate cocktail the medic had given him. Gritting his teeth in anguish and disappointment, he sat back down on the cot. He could evaluate the situation and issue comprehensible orders, but he personally was not going anywhere soon. Not under his own power, anyway. Stymied, he waved Jensen away. The lieutenant hesitated. Then he nodded understandingly, turned, and hurried out the entrance.

Lying back down on the cot and gingerly bringing his

bad leg up after the rest of him, Kinnear realized he was no longer tired. Just more frustrated than he had been in a long, long time.

The snowcat's heavy-duty wipers metronomed at high speed, trying to keep ahead of the swirling snow as it beat at the thick windshield. Nolan squinted into the blackness ahead, but even the special headlights barely illuminated the road for a few feet in front of them. They had been traveling slowly ever since leaving the base, and he felt his sense of urgency climb a notch higher with each passing minute.

They'd already tried using the radio to raise someone in the convoy. The lack of any response was ominous. From time to time the 'cat's treads slipped and skittered on the frozen secondary road that had been bladed out of the surrounding tundra. What must it be like trying to drive in such conditions in a truck? Every part of him wanted to go faster, but he knew that to do so would be to risk a crash, even in the 'cat. If they fetched up helpless somewhere, that would do neither them nor the convoy any good.

Where were Kinnear and the others? They might be fifty miles away—or the tail-end truck might swing into view around the next bend. Nolan's thoughts trailed off as the dark horizon lit up briefly with an eerie red glow that brightened and then quickly faded. Reaching over, he tapped Martin on the shoulder.

"Did you see that, Sergeant?" he asked tensely.

"Yes, sir," the Ranger replied immediately. "I saw it. For sure."

Leaning toward the glass, they both watched the sky carefully. A few moments later the flash was repeated. It was not an illusion, and it was not the aurora borealis.

It was a standard army-issue, self-igniting, high-intensity emergency flare.

"That's them," Nolan commented excitedly. "Note the color. They're in serious trouble."

"Maybe they've lost the track in this weather and they're using flares for extra illumination." Leaning forward, Martin stared at the road ahead. "They aren't regular combat troops."

Nolan nodded. "No, they're not," he acknowledged. "But Colonel Kinnear has served in more campaigns than you'll probably ever get to see. He wouldn't order the use of red emergency flares unless they needed more than extra light."

Martin nodded pensively "All right. Assuming that's the situation, how do you want to proceed?"

Nolan watched as a third flare temporarily banished the darkness. "Drive as fast as this thing will go," he ordered Martin without hesitation, "and try not to get us killed."

The sergeant floored the accelerator. "Noted, sir—especially that last part."

Jazz tried to lay down an arc of fire, hoping to buy himself time to make some rushed repairs, but when Bonecrusher had speared his shoulder the resulting damage had been more severe than expected. Only the weapon on Jazz's right arm still functioned. Firing as fast as he could and paying more attention to speed than accuracy, he barely managed to keep the eager Decepticons at bay.

Bonecrusher continued to try to get close again. A poor shot under the best of conditions, he was much more interested in fighting hand to hand. Besides, there was a definite satisfaction to be had from physically tearing one's opponent apart as opposed to simply reducing him to slag via repeated strikes with explosive or plasma weapons.

"Ironhide, let's get out of this!" Barely avoiding

another blast from Blackout, Jazz also had to keep a sharp eye on Frenzy, who was trying to circle to his left.

"I'm coming," the larger Autobot responded. "Hold your space!"

Cutting in behind Ironhide, the newly arrived Starscream now opened up with his own weapons. Bolts of plasma lit the darkness like splinters of nebulae. By the time Ironhide reached his friend and began offering covering fire, the two Autobots realized how badly they were outgunned, outnumbered, and overmatched.

"We can't keep up a continuous retreat," Ironhide transmitted. "Maybe we can surprise them if we make a run straight at them."

"I can't do it," Jazz explained apologetically. "I'm losing systems from neck to joints. What we need to do is get back to the ship and try to get it out of here before everything is lost. I'm down to one weapon. If we try a frontal, Starscream will obliterate both of us himself."

Ironhide continued to lay down a steady round of fire behind them as they fought to maneuver closer to the *Ark*. "Ratchet," he called, "be ready to lower the shields and let us in!"

Trying to maintain fire on the pursuing Decepticons, deal with the pain in his shoulder, pursue internal repairs, and fly a difficult evade-and-approach pattern did not allow for a nanosecond of analytical relaxation. Divert his attention from any of his tasks for more than a few seconds and Jazz knew he was likely to be reduced to globules of glowing, drifting metal and composite. As a consequence, he found himself moving in almost every direction but the right one. He tried to sustain a tighter flight pattern while Ironhide provided cover and Ratchet continued to blast away at everything in sight with the *Ark*'s guns. As they drew near the transport and its heavy weapons, the Decepticons seemed to hesitate a bit.

"Jazz, they're slowing slightly." Ironhide looked over

at his rapidly faltering friend. "If we're going to straight-line, the time is now."

Studying Starscream and the other Decepticons, Jazz saw that they had not only slowed down a little but were gathering together. It made sense. A massed attack was the only kind likely to have a chance of breaking through the *Ark*'s ship-mounted shields.

"I'm with you," he shouted.

Diverting full power away from their weapons and to propulsion, both Autobots stopped firing, dropped all pretense at maintaining mathematically complex evasion patterns, and headed straight for the *Ark* as fast as their drives would push them.

"Shields are down!" Ratchet informed them as they sped into the shadow of the ship and circled toward the hangar bay. With their attention devoted to preparing a full-scale frontal assault, the Decepticons did not notice the momentary change in energy levels surrounding the transport until it was too late. By the time Starscream realized what an opportunity they'd had, it was gone. His torrent of fire lit the darkness seconds late and dissipated itself harmlessly against the *Ark*'s invigorated defenses.

Jazz notified the mechanic once he and Ironhide were safely back aboard. "We're in! Raise the shields!"

"Already done!" Ratchet informed him calmly.

The bigger mechanoid glared down at his friend and companion. "So much for a change of tactics."

Jazz did not reply, knowing that what really bothered Ironhide was coming up short in a head-to-head fight. Favoring his damaged arm, the smaller mechanoid headed for the bridge as fast as his injuries would allow. Ironhide followed close behind.

The situation had turned bad and was getting worse. Even with the *Ark*'s weaponry and defenses, holding off Starscream and Bonecrusher, plus Blackout, Barricade, and Frenzy, was going to take all the skill and determination he and his companions could muster.

"We can't leave yet," Ratchet declared as they entered the control room. "Optimus and Bumblebee are still down on the surface."

Though Jazz did not find the current state of affairs any less depressing than did the mechanic, his resolve was stronger. "We have our orders. Take us out of here now, Ratchet."

The older mechanoid shook his head stubbornly. "We have to go after Prime. He wouldn't leave us behind and you know it."

"You're probably right," Jazz admitted, "but nevertheless we're going to do what he told us to do. We'll come back for him as soon as is practicable. That was the plan."

"I believe both of you are actually entitled to a tactical rethink, but in this case it doesn't matter. We're out of time." Ironhide gestured forward.

Visible via the main viewport, the cluster of tightly massed Decepticons was heading straight for the transport.

After seeing Jazz and Ironhide disappear into their redefended ship, Starscream had hailed his cohorts and gathered them around him. "Our opportunity to strike is now. Look how they are fleeing. If they had reinforcements available, we would have encountered them by this time. Barricade," he transmitted, "bring in the *Nemesis* and attack."

"They have made modifications to their shields, Starscream," Barricade replied. "Transcans indicate that our weapons will not penetrate them."

"I refuse to accept that analysis. Aim all your weapons in the vicinity of the hangar doors and maintain a continuous fire on that one area." He turned to his eager followers. "Bonecrusher, Blackout, Frenzy—come with me. Let us go and see if between our efforts and Barricade's fire we cannot break through and finish the Autobots once and for all." He led the way forward.

Paralleling his leader's course, Blackout wondered aloud, "What transpired while you were down on the planet? Did that craft we saw indeed know anything about Megatron?"

"Of course it didn't, you logic-shorted fool," Starscream retorted. "This is not the time for elaboration. We have Autobots to destroy."

"They are not going anywhere," Frenzy observed from Starscream's other flank. "It is plain that they fled to escape immediate destruction. Now we have them trapped together on their vessel, why don't you fully answer Blackout's query? Surely it could not take more than a moment or two?"

Starscream ignored them as the group drew within range of the *Ark*. If his companions continued to allow idiotic questions to divert their concentration, there was a chance the Autobots could escape.

"Optimus Prime and Bumblebee are dead," he explained hurriedly. "We have only these few remaining to eliminate. Focus! If we can catch them all here, the war is over."

A proximate burst from a plasma cannon brought him up short. Startled, he swapped forward motion for a rapid defensive spin, only to see one of Blackout's weapons pointed—at him.

"As Frenzy has pointed out, the Autobots are in retreat. They are not going anywhere, and we can finish them off at our leisure. Now tell us what happened on the planet's surface or my next burst will not be a warning shot."

Blackout's tone conveyed how serious he was. Fuming with impatience but facing the muzzle of a devastating weapon that was aimed directly at him from a distance of little more than arm's length, Starscream forced himself to reply calmly.

"Since you insist. But first you tell me something. Explain why you believe the Autobots are not going anywhere."

Blackout laughed knowingly. "First, they won't leave without Optimus Prime. Even if he *is* dead, they would not even leave his mangled and melted corpse behind. It is not in their nature."

"And second?" Starscream inquired. There had to be more to this minor mutiny than that. Blackout had always been the crafty one.

Laughing again, Blackout exclaimed jubilantly, "*Scorponok.*"

"What does he have to do with this?" Starscream did not try to conceal his bemusement.

"He is already on board their ship," a gleeful Blackout explained. "Did you think you were the only one of us adept at strategy? At this very moment, he is headed for their engine room." His tone turned celebratory. "As I said, they are not going anywhere."

Starscream uttered a silent curse. Events were not proceeding thc way he had planned. This was supposed to be *his* moment of triumph. But as well as knowing when to push, he also knew when it was important to give a little. "Well done, Blackout! Exceedingly well done."

"Save your thanks," the other Decepticon replied. "You can flatter me later. Right now I want answers—and so do the rest of us. What happened to the alien vessel? How did it acquire Cybertonian design?"

Cogitating rapidly, knowing that everything he said would be analyzed to the nth degree, Starscream replied carefully. "The alien vessel was destroyed when it fell into an underground chamber that collapsed on top of it. It broke like dry clay when it hit the stone floor of the cavern below. Clearly a poor imitation unable to complete even the most basic transformation. As to the actual design"—he offered an apologetic shrug—"who can say for certain? Maybe one day we will find out. Perhaps Megatron visited their world at some point and they managed a hasty and incomplete scan of his basic design without mastering any of the internals.

"I was unable to establish any kind of communication with the creatures.Their computational capability is absurdly archaic. My personal opinion is that they simply came up with the crude approximation on their own. Representing as we do the pinnacle of intelligent machine life design, it is only natural to expect all research in that field by lesser species to eventually produce schematics that resemble our various basic body types."

Blackout scoffed. "Came up with it on their own?"

"Blackout," an unrepentant Starscream replied, "there are billions of stars in this galaxy. We have visited many in our long search for the Allspark. On how many of those worlds have we seen intelligence give rise to the same technological developments over and over again? A hundred? A thousand? And you still think they could not have come up with it on their own?"

"He's right, Blackout," Barricade declared via tight-beam transmission. "Besides, the thing was hollow. It was nothing more complex than a transport shell for the organic carbon life-forms it carried inside it."

Thankful for the support, Starscream added, "There you have it. Are you satisfied yet?"

Blackout was shaken but still defiant. "Not quite. You said Optimus Prime and Bumblebee are dead. What happened to them?"

Starscream laughed. "That irritating idiot Bumblebee fell into a collapsed cavern, too. The planet's surface is riddled with them. Optimus went in after him, and they ran into the principal native carnivorous life-form. These are exceptionally powerful for organics, and some are as large as we are. I am sorry you could not have been with me to watch as the creatures overwhelmed them both."

"You expect me—us—to believe this?" Blackout exclaimed. "That *any* kind of mindless organic meat eater could overcome Optimus Prime? You must think we are as unintelligent as those insignificant organic life-forms that just 'happened' to create a ship that just happens to look Cybertronian."

Realizing that Blackout was spoiling for an attempt to assert his dominance, Starscream resigned himself to teaching the unremitting schemer a lesson. "No, Blackout," he murmured. "I do not expect you to believe it. I do not expect *you* to believe *anything*. So I am *ordering* you to believe it." He let that sink in. "Now are we going to fight each other, or are we going to finish the Autobots?"

"They will be here," Blackout shot back, "until we finish what is between us."

Activating his weapons, he opened fire.

This time anticipating the reaction, Starscream dodged out of the way. Missiles and plasma bursts shot past him. "Bonecrusher, Frenzy, Barricade!" he called. "He is disloyal. I command the Decepticons!"

"I think maybe we will just wait to see how this one plays out." Transmitted from the *Nemesis*, Barricade's words reached everyone simultaneously. "It has been a long time coming, and it will improve our operational functionality to have the matter appropriately resolved. One way or the other."

XIII

"*Ghost One*, this is SSAB Command, do you read? Over."

Walker breathed a sigh of relief and replied, praying that the outlandish, incomprehensible alien transmission system still functioned in both directions. "SSAB Command, this is *Ghost One*. We're still here—wherever 'here' is. Over."

"*Ghost One,* this is Communications Director Christolph Smythe—uh—Lieutenant Colonel Nolan asked me to step in while he went to address another issue here on the ground. We've been hailing you for a while now, *Ghost One*. Are you experiencing additional difficulties?"

Everyone on board laughed at once, Clarkson roaring so hard that he nearly fell out of his seat. Gonzalez had to wipe tears from her eyes.

Fighting to keep control of his own emotions, Walker managed to reply. "SSAB Command, you might say that. Details later. But we're five-by here right now. Do you have an update for us?"

"Affirmative, *Ghost One,* we do," Smythe informed him. "I'm afraid it's not exactly what you want to hear."

"SSAB Command, at this point what we'd like to hear is anything that references a way to come home," Walker responded. "Get us back to our own solar system and if we have to, we'll walk the rest of the way."

This time the eruption of laughter occurred at Mission Control. Things were probably pretty tense there, too, Walker reckoned. "All right, *Ghost One,*" Smythe continued, still chuckling. "Here's the situation as well as we can read it. The wormhole that you perhaps initiated and traveled through to get where you are is quite possibly still there. We can't scan your end of things, but the astrophysics boys insist it's still distorting space-time at this end. Furthermore, the location hasn't shifted relative to the sun or to Earth. The corollary, and I have to tell you that we're being more hopeful than certain here, is that the other terminus should still be exactly where it was when you emerged. Call it the apposite opposite. Think you can pinpoint that location again?"

Walker looked at his crew. One by one Clarkson, Avery, Thompson, and Gonzalez nodded. "My people say yes, SSAB Command."

"That's a good start," Smythe told him, "but it's just a start. There are other potential problems."

"Why am I not surprised? Go ahead," a solemn Walker replied.

"First," the communications director declared, "the wormhole or whatever kind of distortion we're talking about is not stable. If Avery and Clarkson haven't figured that out yet, I'd be stunned. Either way, assuming that it is still open on your side, it's possible that it could implode at any moment."

Walker could tell that Smythe was leading up to something. "Understood. Now give us the really bad news, Chris. I doubt it's any worse than what we've already discussed among ourselves."

Disturbingly, Smythe did not laugh or return the joke. If anything, his tone became even more formal. "Do you have your code book, Captain Walker?"

"Captain" Walker. The use of the honorific presaged no good, either. Walker opened a small console compartment in front of his seat, reached in, and removed a compact binder. It was sealed with a large red sticker strip, and the front cover read: CODE BOOK—CRYPTO CLEARANCE ONLY.

"I've got it," he announced. "I don't think I want to, but I've got it."

"Open it," Smythe directed him. "And turn to the third tab."

Still no joking around. Bad. Walker ran his finger through the seam to tear the sticker and opened the book, paging to the third tab. "Go ahead," he murmured.

"You're on the tab labeled ETC CONTINGENCY, right?"

"That's the one," Walker replied. "What am I looking for?"

"I'm going to give you a code," Smythe told him. "You're going to find the reply for it on your page. Give it to me, then turn to the next page for instructions. Do you follow?"

A feeling of dread twisted in Walker's gut. This book was not supposed to be opened except in the instance of last-case emergencies. Then again, he supposed that if the current situation did not qualify as a last-case emergency, nothing did. "Maria, write this down." Turning back to face the pickup once more, he murmured, "Go, Chris."

"Here's your code," Smythe responded. "Sierra, Echo, Lima, Foxtrot.Then there's a line break, followed by Sierra, Alpha, Charlie, Romeo, India, Foxtrot, India, Charlie, Echo." The communications director paused briefly, then, "Did you get all that?"

Walker glanced at Gonzalez, who nodded. "We've got it."

"Find it on the page," Smythe directed him, "and give me the reply."

"Read it back to me, Maria," Walker told her.

She complied, and he quickly found the code on the page. "Reply code is: Tango, Oscar, line break, Sierra, Alpha, Victor, Echo, line break, Tango, Hotel, Echo, line break, Whiskey, Oscar, Romeo, Lima, Delta."

Across the light-years Walker could hear Smythe sigh. "The code is authenticated. Turn the page and go to the line marked thirty-two."

Walker did so and found the line. He read it silently, then put the code book back in the console. His people were watching him intently. Unable to stand the silence any longer, Thompson voiced the anxiety that was hanging in everyone's mind. "Well, what the hell does all that mean?"

"*Ghost One,* are you still with us?" Smythe called. "*Ghost One,* do you copy?"

Slowly this time, Walker keyed the response. "Yeah, SSAB Command, we're still here. I understand."

"I'm sorry," Smythe murmured. "I'm so sorry, Captain."

"Not your call, Chris. But we're not out of the game yet."

Though he must have heard, Smythe offered no encouragement. "Keep us informed, *Ghost One*. And—good luck."

"Will do, SSAB Command," Walker responded. "Thank you for your help."

"It wasn't much," Smythe replied. "But you had to know."

Walker laughed—awkwardly this time. "It's all in the fine print, Chris. This is *Ghost One,* out." He closed the transmission.

"C'mon, Captain, *what did all that mean*?" Gonzalez repeated. "What did the code tell you to do?"

Walker looked back at them. Outside the viewport Optimus Prime waited patiently while the human communicated with his homeworld, even though time was inconceivably precious to them. They were amazing beings, Walker mused. He did not think he could have mustered that kind of patience had their situations been reversed.

"Captain?" Thompson prompted him.

"All right," Walker said. "Here's the deal. *ETC* is shorthand for 'extra terrestrial contact,' so the code is for what the crew should do in the event we encounter intelligent aliens. There are two subcodes: one detailing procedure in the event the aliens contacted prove to be friendly. The other is for—the other."

"I'd say that character Starscream qualifies as hostile," Avery commented. "And let's not forget the giant worm-things."

Clarkson was the only one who laughed—uneasily.

"You won't get any argument from me on either one." Though Walker forced a smile, everyone could tell that his heart wasn't in it. "Okay, here it is: the short version says that we can't even try to go back if there's any possibility of the aliens following us to Earth."

"What do they mean 'any'?" Thompson was fighting to stay calm. They had all been superbly trained to deal with every eventuality, including death. But the possibility that they might have a way to get home yet not be able to make use of it was one no one had foreseen. Except, apparently, the specialists who had put together the code book.

"How the hell are we expected to know what they can or can't, will or won't do?" Thompson was half yelling, half pleading. "I mean, come on, Captain! If there's a possibility of getting back, I say we take it and to hell with the code book. Probably put together by a bunch of egghead science-fiction writers working on an SSAB commission."

Before everyone else could chip in with their opinion,

Walker raised a hand for silence. "Yeah, Jake, I know you want to go home. So do I. So does everyone here. But unless we can hold off and survive until these Autobots and Decepticons either destroy each other or leave and we know they can't follow, we can't go home. Do you want to be responsible for leading these entities back to Earth? For giving them a new place to continue their war? Do you want a creature such as this Starscream circling our world wreaking havoc every place he decides to drop some plasma just to keep himself amused?"

"I just think . . . " Clarkson started to reply.

"*No!*" Walker shouted. "There is no 'thinking' here. These beings are so far ahead of us that our technology must be like—I don't know, cavemen's clubs to them. Our world wouldn't be safe with any of them around, much less a group of them. We can't try to go home. Not yet." His voice dropped, and he looked away. "Maybe not ever."

The cabin was quiet for several minutes. As usual, it was Avery who somehow managed to simultaneously change the subject while raising everyone's spirits.

"Well, I say if we can't go home, we may as well kick some alien butt. Nothing against that in the code book, is there? It strikes me that if nothing else, we owe this lying Starscream a good kick in whatever passes for his metal crotch."

The notion of doing battle with Starscream sent a shiver down Walker's spine, but Avery was right. If they were going to die out here, far from family, home, and anything remotely familiar, better to go down fighting than to sit around on the desolate world below waiting for their food and water to run out. Although the mechanoid called Optimus Prime seemed friendly enough, even honorable, there was just no way to know for certain. They had already been badly deceived once.

"Besides," a hopeful Thompson added, "if we can help

defeat or drive off these Decepticons soon enough, maybe the wormhole will still be there and we can try to get home afterward."

Thompson was refusing to acknowledge the reality into which they had been dropped. Knowing that they could not go home, not with the Decepticons *or* the Autobots in their vicinity, did not stop Walker from looking his copilot in the eye and fibbing with as much facility as he could muster.

"Mike's right, anyway. Let's tell Optimus that we're cocked, locked, and ready to rock. Even if we're not."

"Yes, *sir.*" Gonzalez sent the message. The reply came quickly.

"Optimus says that this is not our fight, but under the circumstances he is disposed to accept whatever help we think we may be able to provide."

"Swell." Walker realized how tired he was. How tired everyone on board must be. *Oh, well, what the hell,* he thought. *You only live once.* At least they would go out in a manner unprecedented in the history of human exploration. Pity no one back home would ever know about it. Sitting up a little straighter, he grinned encouragingly at his crew. "Let's go fight the bad guys."

"As long as they aren't snakes," Thompson put in. "I hate snakes!"

Walker had to smile. Turning, he indicated the desolate alien landscape outside. "Not a beach or a piña colada in sight. I say let's blow this dump, Jake."

"Aye-aye, Skipper. Har!" Rolling his eyes melodramatically, Thompson activated the ship's drive. "I guess I'm as ready for this as anyone can be. After all, I spent a good part of my adolescence fighting aliens—in comic books."

Walker found himself laughing. "I'll see you get your turn."

Through the foreport he could see Optimus and his

smaller companion rising. For a tiny experimental ship full of fragile humans, they had certainly come a long way. In every sense of the phrase. Would they have the courage to die well or, in the end, would they simply die?

Darkness greeted their emergence from atmosphere, and the stars began to appear around them. Mike had had the right idea for sure. They were explorers, space travelers, the first of their kind to step beyond the bounds of their home system. Better to die among the stars than on the dirt below. They were going to save the world—by not going back to it. They would be remembered as heroes who had given their lives in the cause of advancing human science and knowledge.

Humanity wouldn't know the half of it.

"Heroes," he whispered to himself.

"What's that?" Occupied with controlling the ship, Thompson spoke without taking his eyes from the instrumentation in front of him.

Walker started to say something, reconsidered, shook his head. "Nothing," he murmured by way of reply. "Nothing at all."

As they streaked out of the dead planet's grubby atmosphere and back into the cold clarity of empty space, Optimus found himself pondering the enigma posed by the humans and their singular vessel. The previous exchange of transmissions had left him with the distinct impression that something was seriously wrong, though they had said nothing to support such a supposition. Studying them through the foreport of their ship it was manifest that their expressions, so much more dynamic than those of his own kind, were virtual maps to their emotional states. Forced to guess, Optimus concluded that their present sensibilities resided somewhere between angry and sad. Hopefully, he and his friends would be able to help them once the Decepticons had been dealt with.

This thought was followed by another. If Megatron had indeed been to their planet, the question remained as to what would draw the malevolent leader of the Decepticons to such a backward, out-of-the-way world. Was the Allspark there, or had something else attracted him to that place? There were too many unanswered questions, and not enough time to delve into them now. What he did know was that compared with Transformers, the humans were a delicate organic species that was only beginning to learn how to make proper use of advanced technologies. They had come here by accident. Ensuring that they returned home safely would benefit their entire world.

In the distance he could see the *Nemesis* and the *Ark*. Each ship was keeping up a steady barrage at the other. In nearby free space Starscream was engaged in a one-on-one running battle with—and of all the things Optimus had seen that day, this made the least sense—Blackout.

Mystified, he transmitted on closed frequency to the *Ark*. "Ratchet, Optimus here. What's your status?"

There was a brief delay, then, "Thank the Allspark! Following your orders, we were preparing to leave. Jazz has sustained some serious damage, and if the Decepticons hadn't started fighting among themselves we would already be gone."

"For once I find myself relieved by a delay," Optimus replied. "Stand by."

Looking back, he transmitted to the human ship. "Bumblebee and I, together with the other Autobots, must deal with the Decepticons. While I appreciate and admire your offer of aid, I fear that your craft is too defenseless to engage in combat with our kind. In the absence of suitable shields, you would be quickly destroyed. I suggest that you set a roundabout course for our ship." He pointed to the *Ark*. "Wait there on the far side. As soon as we're able, we will make our very best attempt to help you get home."

There was some delay before a response was forthcoming. "Optimus, my name is Samuel Walker. I'm the captain of this ship and I command the crew. We have discussed the prevailing situation and despite your concerns we want to help."

Ahh, Optimus reflected. *They are not a communal life-form, as I first suspected. They do choose leaders, just like Autobots and Decepticons. The ship is only a tool.* "I understand. But I must repeat: it is not safe. You would be better served by staying out of harm's way until we can arrange for your return to your homeworld. I say again: this battle is not yours."

"Sorry to take issue with a superior life-form, Optimus Prime," Walker responded, "but we have a score to settle with Starscream. We don't run from a fight because it will be dangerous or because the odds are against us."

Optimus considered this for a moment, risking a quick glance at the ongoing Decepticon infighting. "Your bravery belies your size. Please recognize that Starscream is incredibly powerful, and the Decepticons have no scruples about killing. They take no prisoners. I am trying to keep you safe. The concept of vengeance is known to us. But home—to have and to know a real homeworld is more important. Ours is gone. Yours is not."

There was another long pause. "Your words only reinforce our decision, Optimus," Walker replied firmly. "Do what you must and so will we."

Finding this response oddly affecting, Optimus transmitted, "Very well. At least wait until you see an opportune moment to strike and allow us to take the brunt of the combat."

"We're brave but not stupid. We accept your tactical suggestion. Good luck, Optimus Prime."

"Fare well, humans," Optimus replied. He swiftly switched transmission from the smaller vessel back to the *Ark*. "Ratchet, I want you, Jazz, and Ironhide to leave the ship. It's time to end this. If we strike now, while they are distracted, we may have a chance to catch them at least momentarily off guard."

"We're on our way," the mechanic replied enthusiastically.

Signaling Bumblebee to follow, Optimus angled once more in the direction of the Decepticons. He was determined to win this fight. Not only to deal the Decepticons a severe blow, but also to give the humans a chance to return to their Earth. It would be pleasing to see someone benefit from all of this, knowing as he did that with each passing century the chances of the Autobots ever getting back to Cybertron grew less and less realistic. Destroying the Decepticons would at least render that unfeasibility a touch more palatable.

And make the universe a safer place for all sentient life.

Kinnear could not remember where he had heard the phrase that was running through his mind. Military history? Something from the Greeks or in Latin? Despite the cold, his brow was stained with perspiration.

The center must hold.

He said it aloud. "The center must hold."

In the near distance he could hear the *pop-pop-pop*ping of M16s and the distinct *phipthd-phipthd* of the AK-47s being used by the advancing Russian infiltrators. Interspersed with the gunfire was an occasional cry of pain or violent curse, sometimes in English, sometimes in Russian. He thanked the weather gods for the lingering blizzard. What with the cold, the icy wind, and the blowing snow, it would be hard for even the best marksman to get off a decent shot. It meant that fewer young men and women would die here.

Maybe no one would die. Maybe there would be only wounds to deal with; crimson stains sharp and brilliant against white snow and dark green uniforms. Maybe . . .

Flares continued to light up the sky outside the tent. He could see the glow, if not the exact location. Whether anyone else would see them—and if they did, would be in a position to respond positively—was dubious. But procedure called for unleashing the flares, and if nothing else the continuous cloudward barrage would give the advancing Russians something else to think about.

By now the operation had gone wrong so seriously and on so many levels that even beginning to address them would be a monumental chore. Things promised to get worse before they got better. *If* they could keep Ice Man frozen and *if* they could fight off the Russians and *if* they could somehow continue to keep everything under wraps . . . Kinnear listened intently as another round of automatic gunfire peppered the night. This time the sounds were closer and he could hear the hoarse yells of NCOs on the line.

Jensen stuck his head through the entrance to the tent. "Sir? I have to go to the perimeter, sir. We're going to need every gun we've got or they're going to break through."

"The center must hold," Kinnear mumbled. "There's a Latin translation, but I'll be damned if I can remember it."

"The NCOs have their own variation of Latin, sir." Jensen's face was pale, his breathing labored.

Kinnear thought back to his own first time in combat, remembering the sharp stink of cordite, the roadkill reek of death, the corruption that overwhelmed the festering human body after it had been left lying torn open and too long in the tropical heat. The fear.

"Easy, son," he murmured. "Remember to breathe easy. Is Ice Man still contained?"

"I believe so, sir," Jensen told him. "But I had to pull everybody except the civilian techs off him to defend the perimeter. One enemy at a time, right, sir?"

The lieutenant was treading perilously close to panic. He had stopped by only to check on his superior officer's condition, and Kinnear realized that the ongoing conversation was simply delaying and distracting the younger man. He should curl up in this bed and let the lieutenant do his job.

"One enemy at a time, Jensen," Kinnear agreed. "Don't worry about me. I'm still woozy and I've got to rest. Don't worry about me or what I think or any other damn thing. Just go out there and do what you were trained to do. Lead those soldiers and save our respective behinds."

The youthful lieutenant's eyes sparkled for a moment, and a grin flashed across his face. He was being cut loose. "Yes, sir!" he blurted. "Thank you, sir."

"You're welcome. Stay safe out there and listen to your NCOs. I saw combat patches on a couple of them, so they'll know the drill and how to adapt it. But don't let them—" He broke off and laughed. "I'm doing it again, aren't I?"

"Yes, sir." Jensen chuckled softly. "But thanks for the reminders."

"I don't think you need any. Now get going."

Jensen offered him a final smile and a quick salute before disappearing into the night. Kinnear heard one of the NCOs yelling the lieutenant's name. No greater compliment could experienced NCOs pay to a junior officer than *asking* for his advice. Yes, Jensen was going to make a hell of a leader someday, Kinnear reflected—if he managed to live through the night.

He settled back once more beneath the blankets. His heart was pounding as if he were running a long-distance race. He was sure he could feel the blood pulsing—too fast, way too fast—through his veins. Whatever had been in that stimulant the medic had given him, it had a kick like a drunken mule. The perspiration that had started on his face now coated his body in a layer of slimy, cold damp, and his broken leg was throbbing like an abscessed tooth.

The entrance to the tent parted again, and Kinnear kept his eyes closed. "Jensen, I thought I told you—"

"Apologies, Colonel Kinnear. It is not Jensen."

Kinnear's eyes snapped open. Sergei Tasarov stood inside his tent. There was evidence of developing frostbite on his cheeks and his nose, and his eyes were wild. Pushing back the pain, Kinnear forced himself to sit fully upright.

"Lieutenant," he replied evenly. "I figured you for dead by now. I hate it when I'm wrong."

The Russian laughed. "Dead, eh? We are the kind of men who are tougher to kill than that, yes?" His voice was unsteady as he answered his own question. "*Da,* I think so. I think you are the kind of man that would also be hard to kill." Half crazed from exposure, he scanned the interior of the tent. "I myself would kill right now for one glass of decent vodka."

Kinnear did not bother with a reply. The Russian had gone snow-mad. Wandering around insufficiently dressed in the cold and the dark, he had somehow found his way back. Still, assuming he had been turned out on the side of the temporary encampment opposite his recently arrived comrades, it was not surprising he had been able to make his way to Kinnear's tent unchallenged. As Jensen had just pointed out, everyone was either fighting the intruders or tending to the Ice Man.

"Under normal circumstances you would be hard to kill, yes, Colonel?" Tasarov was muttering. "But look at you now. I can see you are in pain. I am going to help you with that. I am going to release you from your pain."

Kinnear did not know where the Russian had acquired the knife that he now pulled from his belt, and he didn't much care. In the dim light of the tent the blade gleamed like an orca's tooth.

"It may, of course, take a while," the Russian growled. "An old soldier is like an old chicken—tough. But all we really have in this world is time." He held the blade up so that it would catch the light as he waved it methodically back and forth. "What does the Bible say? A time to sow and a time to reap. A time to live and—a time to die."

Gritting his teeth, Kinnear forgot all about the ache in his leg.

"I think your time is now." Knife gripped tightly in his right fist, eyes glittering, Tasarov crouched and moved toward the cot.

"My estimate is that we're about half a mile away." Sergeant Martin struggled to keep the snowcat on a wisp of a road whose boundaries were increasingly hard to make out under the steadily accumulating snow. "How do you want to proceed, sir?"

Nolan tried to see through the cascading whiteness. The wipers were having trouble keeping up with the ice. Finally he gave up and lowered his window. Shoving his head out into the bracing wind he squinted, trying to see if he could discern more than what they knew now—which was almost nothing.

"Do you see anything, Sergeant?" he yelled back into the snowcat's cab.

Following suit, Martin stuck his own head out the driver-side window. For several moments there was no response. Then, "There," he called out. "And again!"

"There what?" Nolan drew his head back in. Just a couple of minutes' exposure had left the skin of his face feeling like a slice of beef lifted fresh from a freezer.

"Listen," Martin advised him.

Cupping a hand to his left ear, Nolan tried to ignore the loud rattle of the 'cat's treads and the steady hiss of the between-seats heater. Very faintly, during lulls in the wind, he heard the *pop-pop* of rifle fire. "What the hell?"

"And look." Raising a hand from the wheel, Martin pointed. "Tracer rounds."

Sure enough, several streaks of hot yellow arced through the night sky, hugging the ground like miniature comets.

The Ranger NCO turned to Nolan. "Russians?"

Nolan nodded. "Unless we've misjudged the Canadians really badly, yes. We received word that there might be an infiltrator at the base, but we didn't know who it was or even if the intel was good or not." He gestured ahead. "Maybe they learned something about what we've been working on and decided to come have a look for themselves. Without bothering to get their passports stamped."

"In this weather?" Martin marveled. "That's gung-ho for sure."

"If they have half an idea what we've got," Nolan replied, "they'd want it. Real bad."

"Makes sense," Martin admitted. "Particularly when you consider that we beat them to the moon and that we're kicking their tails in atomics these days."

Nolan leaned forward as another volley of tracers lit the sky in front of them. "The question now is, how do we deal with this little invasion?"

"Stealth." As Nolam looked on, Martin began to shift out of driver and into Ranger mode. "If we leave the 'cat and walk from here, we can come up on their position virtually unseen." He lightly tapped his arctic white camouflage suit. "Especially in this weather."

Nolan did not hesitate. Plainly, there was no time to debate tactics. Up ahead, his friends were in trouble.

Maybe some of them were dying. "Sounds good. Take your people and double-time it. Don't wait for an invitation to join the party. Assess and respond. That's what Rangers do, isn't it?"

Martin grinned. "We don't always stop to assess, sir. Sometimes we skip right to the fun part."

"Don't let me keep you from it, then."

Pushing against the wind, the sergeant opened the door, hesitated, and looked back. "What about you, sir?"

Nolan bit down on his lower lip. "Much as I'd like to go with you, I'm too damn old and out of shape to go trudging through the snow. I'd just slow you down, get in your way. I'll drive the 'cat the rest of the way down the road—slowly. If any of our visitors have been pinned down in front of me, I'll stop, flash the lights, race the engine, and back up before they can figure out what to do. The distraction might be useful."

Martin nodded somberly. "Stay careful, sir. I'd feel bad if I drove you safely all this way only to have you end up in the ditch after I left."

Nolan laughed. "Hey, don't worry about it. I've driven in the snow in Manhattan and been cursed out by cabdrivers speaking a dozen languages. Now get going."

Martin saluted—smartly—and hopped out of the truck. Nolan could hear him out back gathering his men. After sliding over to the driver's side, Nolan peered out through the glass as the white-clad Rangers clustered together and the sergeant gave them their orders. All but invisible in their winter gear, they headed out into the swirling snow, disappearing like a line of ghosts.

Nolan watched until the last figure had been swallowed up by the storm. Then he turned his attention to the console in front of him. He was alone in the snowcat, the powerful forward heater warming his face.

"All right," he muttered to himself. "Let's see if I remember how to drive one of these."

He pushed in the clutch, shifted into first, and popped the clutch back out. The heavy 'cat groaned into motion once more. He could hear snow and ice crunching beneath the treads and feel the steering wheel jiggle and slip against his hands. The unpaved, unmarked roadway was slick and almost impossible to see beneath its wintry mantle.

"Hang on, Tom," he muttered to himself as he took a better grip on the wheel. "It may be slow, but the cavalry is on the way."

Starscream did not wait for Blackout to make his move. While the other Decepticon had been posturing and declaiming, Starscream had activated his own weapons systems. Unleashing everything he had in rapid sequence, he sent Blackout tumbling and retreating through space in a frantic attempt to escape the unrelenting salvos.

"Traitor!" Starscream snarled, firing again. "Megatron appointed me his second-in-command and you challenge me at every opportunity!"

Spinning wildly, Blackout managed to return fire, forcing Starscream to commence some evasive maneuvering of his own. "The need to eliminate incompetence supersedes any prehistoric directive!" he shot back.

Bonecrusher and Frenzy had both moved well out of the way of the fight. Like Barricade, neither appeared interested in taking sides. They held their positions in empty space and followed the struggle with interest, though both suspected what the likely outcome would be. It was the Decepticon way to fight for the role of leader, to ensure that the strongest and best among them was always in command. Blackout had been building up to this for some time.

"Incompetence!" Starscream howled. "For that insult alone, I will take you down."

"You can try," Blackout transmitted back. Abruptly changing tactics, he charged Starscream's position, weaving and dodging as he closed the distance between them.

Possessed of a far quicker reaction time, Starscream had no trouble avoiding his opponent's repeated attacks. His predictors prevented even the most concentrated bombardment from impacting his person.

Clearly a demonstration was in order, the Decepticon leader decided. It had been some time since any of his colleagues had sought to challenge him directly.

Adjusting his velocity while simultaneously accelerating forward, he spun a complete loop around his attacker. As Blackout whirled to compensate, Starscream slammed a fist into the other mechanoid's head and sent him tumbling.

"Time to repeat a lesson you seem to have forgotten," Starscream announced.

Blackout halted the spinning and regained control of himself just in time to catch a blast to the chest from one of Starscream's lesser weapons that sent him rotating out of control once more. He tried to return fire again, only to realize that in addition to being quicker, Starscream also had better aim. Amazingly precise, the most recent shot had shut down Blackout's weapons systems.

"A short memory can be fatal," Starscream sneered. Accelerating anew, he moved in close. As Blackout tried to get away, the bigger Decepticon slashed out with one hand and caught his opponent by the arm, pulling him close. "Here is lesson number two: pain hurts." At point-blank range, Starscream fired into Blackout's chest armor.

The immobilized Blackout let loose a metallic screech of anguish and tore madly at his chest as hot plasma melted through the outer armor and into the sensitive circuitry underneath.

Yanking him forward, Starscream slammed a fist into the other mechanoid's face. "Lesson number three: pain continues to hurt even when you wish for it to stop." Releasing his now badly battered rival, he took aim with his entire integral arsenal.

"Don't . . . ," Blackout mumbled. "You prevail. I concede utterly. You are the leader. I withdraw my challenge."

"We are not quite done yet," Starscream informed his cohort coldly. "Here is the last and most important lesson: pain is an excellent teaching tool that should be practiced by all leaders and recognized by all smart-mouthed soldiers." He fired two weapons, and Blackout's tattered defenses collapsed.

The other mechanoid was severely, but not mortally, damaged. Silent and nonreactive, he floated slowly away from Starscream. *It would take considerable effort to repair him and bring him back to what he had been,* Starscream thought. Hopefully the quartet of modest lessons would stick with the others for a while.

He turned to where they drifted, watching. "Any questions?"

"No, Starscream," Frenzy avowed unemotionally. "You are the leader."

"No questions." Bonecrusher nodded in the direction of the inert Blackout. "He got what he deserved."

Starscream contacted the *Nemesis*. "What about you, Barricade? Is there anything about today's instruction that finds you uncertain?"

"Nothing," Barricade replied. "I knew what the outcome would be before it began."

"Most gratifying." Starscream turned to his waiting colleagues. "Now that this time-wasting nonsense has been dealt with, I remind you that we still have some Autobots to finish off. Bonecrusher, haul Blackout over to the ship and leave him in the hangar bay. We'll deal with him later." He paused humorlessly. "Perhaps he will awaken from his 'rest' with a permanently reformed attitude."

Bonecrusher obediently moved forward and grasped Blackout by the arm, then turned toward the *Nemesis,* intending to rejoin his companions as rapidly as possible.

While awaiting his return, Starscream addressed the group. "Though Blackout was reckless to challenge me, his emplacement of Scorponok on the *Ark* may turn out to be most helpful. That is the only reason I did not take his Spark."

"Decepticons, behind you!" The warning call sounded from Barricade on the *Nemesis.*

Starscream had to turn a complete 180 before he was able to identify the source of Barricade's alert: Optimus Prime and Bumblebee headed straight for him. Circling in the distance was the troublesome alien ship that bore a resemblance to the Cybertronian. He had left it buried in the rock of the world below. Had he underestimated its builders' level of technology? Would his problems never end?

"I thought you said the alien vessel had been destroyed and that Optimus Prime and Bumblebee were dead," Barricade transmitted. "Did I misinterpret something?"

"It does not matter now anyway," an irritated Starscream growled. "We will finish them here once and for all. Barricade, leave the ship as soon as you can and rejoin us." He started forward. "Decepticons, attack!"

XIV

Kinnear waited until the Russian lunged and then rolled off the cot to his left, biting back a scream of agony as his shattered leg hit the hard, cold ground. If not for the stimulant he had been given, he would have been physically helpless.

The knife sliced through the canvas of the cot where Kinnear had been lying seconds earlier. Tasarov yanked it free and threw himself forward, striking downward a second time. The blade struck only frozen earth. On the floor, Kinnear rolled once more, stopping only when he came up against the side of the tent. He could feel the two broken ends of his femur rubbing together, and his splint was already coming loose. The stimulant had its limits. If he wanted to live, he would have to do something quickly.

Rather than leaping again, Tasarov crawled toward him on all fours, the knife clenched in his right fist. "Tough, *da,* but not indestructible. It is hard to run with a broken leg, yes?"

Kinnear felt oddly distanced, as if he were standing outside his own damaged body, watching it perform like a puppet in some obscure Kafkaesque play. Even the pain in his leg reminded him of a grafted-on special effect. He tried to move away, pushing at the side of the tent with the back of his head.

"Lieutenant Tasarov—don't do it. I have a family, children. Grandchildren. If our positions were reversed, you would have done the same as I did when you were discovered."

The Russian halted. "No, Colonel, I would not have done the same. I would not have had subordinates turn you out in the cold." He smiled thinly. "I would have killed you myself. Out of respect for a fellow officer, if nothing else."

"I didn't want your blood on my hands," Tom Kinnear mumbled. He was digging under the tent flap with both hands, as if searching for a way out.

"Then you are a coward undeserving of your rank." Tasarov resumed his doglike advance.

Kinnear's fingers closed around what he had been hunting for. "Or maybe just a grifter."

Tasarov eyed his prey uncertainly. While his knowledge of proper English was excellent, his command of the vernacular left a good deal to be desired.

His foe's moment of hesitation was all Kinnear needed. Yanking upward on the steel tent peg he had pulled free of its grommet, he lunged at the Russian officer. Chilled and weakened from exposure, Tasarov's reflexes were just a little slow. Before he could block the strike, Kinnear drove the tent peg halfway up to its steel head into the intruder's shoulder.

Tasarov howled in pain, gritted his teeth, and thrust the knife in his right hand deep into Kinnear's rib cage.

He felt it graze one of his ribs and then all his breath left him as the point of the blade penetrated his left lung. His throat immediately began to fill with blood and he coughed weakly, spitting red liquid into the Russian's face.

"You bastard," Kinnear wheezed, "you've killed me!" Forcing himself forward once more, he wrapped his left arm around Tasarov's neck and with the other yanked the tent peg free. "But I'll return the favor," he spat, "before I go."

Tasarov struggled in the other man's desperate grip, sawing away at his ribs, trying to get his knife free, but it was stuck. Each motion brought Kinnear a fresh wave of pain as agony blossomed in his chest like a flower petaled with razor blades.

He could feel himself weakening by the second. Modifying his grip on the tent peg, he grabbed the hair on the back of Tasarov's head and stabbed upward. The sharpened stake sliced through the flesh of the other man's neck as if it were veal, finally slowing to a stop at the base of his brain.

For a long second Tasarov's body continued to obey the final commands it had been given. The knife he still gripped jerked and twisted twice more before his arm realized he was dead. The infiltrator's blue eyes went sightless and his last breath, a meaningless groan, hissed out of him.

Releasing his grasp on the dead man, Kinnear shoved the body away. It hit the hard-frozen ground with a thump like a sack of potatoes. Ever so slowly, Kinnear lowered himself back down to the same unyielding surface, lying on his right side to keep the knife from penetrating any more than it already had.

He could hear his breath bubbling and hitching in his lung. His leg was full of fire. A wave of nausea and exhaustion swept over him. The stimulant he had been given had run the limits of its effectiveness. Now he only wanted to sleep.

If he fell asleep, Kinnear knew he would die. Since he was probably going to die even if he stayed awake, he decided that it didn't matter. He had spent most of his career putting his life on the line; now it had finally caught up to him. He was too old to absorb the kind of punishment his body had taken. His last mission would go down as a failure, but no one would be able to look back on it and say he had not tried.

And maybe that was enough, he thought, drifting once more. Was it? Was it enough? He mulled over the question, his mind blanking out the sounds of gunfire that were drawing slowly closer, the shouts of men fighting and dying. *Is it enough to go out this way? A ghost of the soldier you once were?*

Yes, he decided. If he was a shell of what he had been, then he was a shell who had performed his duties with honor. It *was* enough. Kinnear closed his eyes, feeling them burn beneath the lids.

It has to be enough, he thought. *I don't have anything left to give.*

A low, ominous noise reached him from outside his tent: the screeching sound of metal giving way and a machine coming inexorably to life. A very particular kind of machine. He had heard the same sounds only once before, but even in his present desperate condition he was unlikely to mistake them.

"Stop him, stop it!" a voice was shouting.

A grinding noise was followed by a heavy *thud,* as of a giant fist smashing into the ground.

Kinnear wanted to believe he was imagining all of this. He wanted to believe it was an aural hallucination, a fever dream brought on by the severity of his injuries. He wanted to rest, to sleep, to drift away into the pain-free embrace of death. He would not be allowed that release. As long as he clung to life he was still in command. Resignedly, he realized that his input would be essential.

The Ice Man had awakened.

Despite the snowcat's treads and weight, Nolan still had to fight the wheel to keep it on the increasingly icy roadway. Frozen pellets of snow pelted the windshield. More than once he had to fight the wheel to bring the heavy vehicle back onto the road. The sloping shoulder seemed to draw it like a magnet.

It didn't matter, he told himself. He just needed to get there. Off to his right he could see sporadic flashes of light from rifle muzzles and tracer rounds. It did not look as if the fight was lessening in intensity. He hoped that Sergeant Martin and his men would make the difference in the outcome.

Through the blowing snow he could now make out the faded glow of a couple of field lamps and the peaks of tents sticking up in the darkness. Whatever had happened, the convoy had stopped and tried to create a makeshift camp. As he stared forward the wind shifted, sending the capricious snow flying in another direction. The view ahead cleared. Suddenly he could see the jackknifed end of the modified heavy equipment hauler that had been carrying the Ice Man. The front end of the vehicle was smashed up pretty thoroughly, and the special insulated and refrigerated container looked as if it had been peeled open like a can of sardines. A few technicians could be seen running away from it, the reason for their precipitous flight outlined in the feeble light. He stared in shock.

His eyes went wide as snow exploded upward and a massive metallic hand appeared in front of him. He exhaled explosively.

The Ice Man was moving.

Maybe there was enough time to deliberate and to choose among assorted options, Nolan thought hurriedly. Maybe he had only seconds. What he did know, or at least what he felt, was that he had neither choice nor time. Pulling the survival knife from his belt, he leaned down and drove it through the accelerator pedal and into the floor. The snowcat's powerful engine roared and the vehicle surged ahead.

Emerging from the back of the hauler like a phantom

from another time and place, the Ice Man rose to his feet.

"Come on!" Nolan yelled. "Five more seconds!" Time unfolded in slow motion, like toothpaste from an old tube.

He fought to keep the swiftly accelerating 'cat in line as it skidded left and right, trying to go into a spin. Taking note of the noise and motion that were approaching out of the darkness, the massive alien head turned in Nolan's direction. He saw glowing red eyes narrow. The Ice Man had been in stasis for a long, long time, and God only knew what the massive alien machine was capable of doing. Those eyes—they looked like they could melt the front of the snowcat all by themselves. With him, the turkey, stuck in the oven.

Stepping clear of the damaged hauler, the Ice Man flung aside clinging scraps of torn steel as if it were so much aluminum foil. He took one stride, then another, before halting to scan the darkened landscape. Was he confused? Disoriented?

Fifty feet. "Stay there, you alien freak!" Nolan muttered as he leaned toward the wheel. "Hold still!"

He waited as long as he dared and a bit longer. Terrifying seconds stretched into nightmare hours. Then he shoved open the door and jumped free of the 'cat.

The hard ground came up incredibly fast. Nolan hit the surface rolling, but that did not stop his collarbones from snapping like the sticks of driftwood that piled up on the island's beaches.

He cried out as he bounced and rolled, the icy gravel of the roadway chewing up his face. Splinters of cold snuck down the neck of his parka. Sliding like an unaerodynamic, out-of-control sled, he did not stop until he slammed into the tire of one of the convoy trucks parked on the side of the road.

His breath left him with an ugly *whoosh*ing sound as

he came to a stop. More through luck than intent, he landed on his front. Lifting his head, he peered through tearing eyes as the speeding snowcat hit a bump in the road and flew the last three feet to slam into the back of the Ice Man's pillarlike legs. Though smaller than the alien, the burly 'cat was no lightweight. The impact collapsed him backward onto the hauler. Having survived skidding and jackknifing, the vehicle's reinforced fuel tanks buckled under the Ice Man's mass. There was friction.

The truck erupted.

A giant fireball rose as nearly full tanks ignited. The explosion was supplemented by the additional fuel on the snowcat. For an instant the freezing air around him was saturated with heat, and it was impossible to take a breath.

Stars danced in front of Nolan's eyes as he gasped for air. He had just enough time to fill his lungs before a second, even more powerful explosion followed the first. Arms and legs askew, the Ice Man was lifted into the air, only to fall back to earth with a reverberating crash. Fighting to get to his feet despite the pain in his shoulders, Nolan saw that the body of the fallen alien was straddling the drainage ditch that paralleled the roadbed.

"That's not going to do it," he groaned to himself as he straightened. He flinched as the flames from the inferno that had been the hauler set off the tank on the truck parked directly in front of it.

Gritting his teeth, struggling to focus, trying not to pass out, Nolan found himself staring at a tent that had been pitched near the road. The flaps fluttered dejectedly in the wind, and then his eyes dropped down.

Pulling himself across the frozen ground like a broken-down hound dog was Tom Kinnear. Blood darkened his chin; one leg stuck out behind him at an angle that would have looked unnatural on a department-store mannequin.

"Ah, hell, Tom," Nolan managed to gasp out as he limped toward the crawling figure. "You look like crap."

Kinnear tried to reply but could not. Their eyes met. The two men reached an agreement in the space of their gaze. Both were seriously injured, maybe dying, but it did not matter. The Russians did not matter.

All that mattered was stopping the Ice Man.

Staring out the foreport, Walker watched as Optimus Prime and the smaller Autobot were joined by two others from their ship while Starscream gathered his own forces nearby. From the looks of things, this small corner of space was about to become a kind of war zone never before observed by human beings.

"Perfect," he muttered. "And here we sit, doing nothing."

"Not exactly nothing," Clarkson called up to him.

Walker turned. "What have you got?"

The engineer's fingers flew over the keyboard in front of him as he repeated his calculations one final time. "It's there!" he announced. "The wormhole is still there."

Walker was careful to mute his emotions. This was not a time to start passing out funny hats and noisemakers. "How do you know?"

"Our long-range sensors are picking up emissions from it. We can't see it visually, but I know I'm right about this, Captain. I can give Jake the coordinates. True, sending the ship in might tear us apart, but it's our one chance to get back home and it's right where we left it." Unlike Walker, he made no attempt to hide the excitement he was feeling. For one thing, it helped to mask the fear.

Walker returned his attention to the view forward. All of the Autobots had come together now, and the final Decepticon was nearing Starscream's position. A battle the likes of which only the seriously addled could envision would soon be under way in the *Ghost*'s vicinity.

"Captain?" Clarkson was staring hard at Walker. "What are we waiting for, Captain? If we're going to make the attempt, the sooner the better. The hole could close up at any minute."

"What about them?" Walker gestured at the view out the port. "How do we know they won't follow? Do your calculations tell you how to close the wormhole behind us? Do they tell you what will happen to the Autobots if we leave them here?"

"No disrespect intended, Captain," Clarkson interjected, "but why the hell do we care? They can take care of themselves. So should we."

"Is that a fact?" Walker shot back. "And if Optimus Prime had shown that same attitude back on the planet, where would we be now?"

"It's not the same and you know it." Clarkson could not believe what he was hearing. "For God's sake, we're not even supposed to be here!"

"Craig has a point," Avery avowed. "But really, it's kind of moot if we adhere to the code directive. We aren't supposed to go back if there's any chance of *any* of the aliens following us."

"Who cares about a stupid code?" Clarkson's voice rose to a near shout.

"Captain, Optimus himself said to stay clear," Avery pointed out. "They don't want us involved, and while the whole idea of taking on the aliens and kicking nonhuman butt sounds great when you're watching a sci-fi movie, the reality is that compared with the least of them *Ghost One* is a hunk of space junk."

"What about you, Maria?" Walker suddenly asked. "What do you think?"

She shook her head. "I'm like Craig. I want to go home, too." Her voice went small and quiet. "But—they helped us down there. Without even being asked. If they hadn't, chances are we wouldn't be drifting here arguing about it. We can't just abandon them here until we know they're okay."

It was too much for the near-apoplectic Clarkson. "Vote! I say we vote."

Turning to stare at the engineer, Walker felt the muscles along his jawline clench. "I know you feel strongly about this, Craig, but in case you've forgotten, this isn't a democracy. I command *Ghost One.*"

"Then why'd you even ask for her opinion?" Clarkson riposted accusingly.

"Because everyone has a right to be heard before I make the decision," Walker told him, "and because despite what you may think, that decision will take everyone's feelings and opinion into account."

Before they could continue the conversation, the receiver crackled and the voice of Chris Smythe came on. "*Ghost One,* this is SSAB Command, do you read?"

Walker took a deep breath, let it out, then responded. Even in the far reaches of the galaxy, it seemed, everything happened at once. "SSAB Command, this is *Ghost One*. We read you. Go ahead."

"*Ghost One,* you need to be aware of something. Our instruments are telling us that the wormhole is starting to show evidence of destabilizing at our end. The math gang tells me it's not likely to last much longer. Gravitational instability and all that. If you're going to take a shot at using it to try to come home, you need to do so now. What's your status?"

"See?" Clarkson insisted. "It will close in front of us! The thing is too unstable to hold together." He tore a sheet of paper off his console and passed it forward to Thompson. "Here are the coordinates, Jake, so let's go!"

Thompson looked at Walker, the question in his eyes. *Stay or go?*

"SSAB Command, this is *Ghost One.* Stand by." Muting the transmit, Walker looked at the crew one by one. "I need a moment to think. Like it or not, this is my call. Please just give me a second, okay?"

No one said anything, and Walker closed his eyes. It was not simply a question of whether or not he wanted to go home. If that were the landscape, it would be easy to just tell Thompson to activate the drive and they'd go. But there was more to it than that. Circumstances had changed. Other entities were involved. Other intelligent, feeling beings. Other friends—and enemies.

For one thing, there was no telling how much Starscream—or even Optimus, for that matter—had been able to learn from their presumed scans of *Ghost 1*'s data storage. Had they obtained the star charts? Did they already know where Earth was? If he had to guess, he would have said that Starscream had acquired every bit and byte of data he could, while Optimus—well, Walker had a feeling that the leader of the Autobots would not have downloaded so much as a breakfast recipe without first asking permission. Such an invasion of privacy did not square with everything else the kindly and helpful mechanoid had said and done. Walker was experienced enough to know that nothing was ever purely black and white, good and evil. But these Autobots and Decepticons constituted about as clear a model of that state of affairs as he could imagine.

If *Ghost 1* reentered the wormhole, it was entirely possible the ship would not survive the journey back through, though both his science officer and engineer continued to believe in the possibility. Clarkson's urgency was now supported by data from Earth. Based on the combat he and his crew had already witnessed, it was probable that the wormhole would be gone by the time the mechanoids had finished battling each other.

But what was troubling him beyond what had already

been discussed was his belief that having once encountered and interacted with humans, sooner or later either Autobots or Decepticons or both would find Earth. Not through the wormhole, assuming that the math from back home was accurate and that it was indeed on the verge of collapsing, but through the simple process of searching and having endless years in which to do it. They were looking for the Allspark, and he knew where it was. That they would arrive eventually he did not doubt for a moment.

Knowing that posed a far more complex conundrum than simply deciding whether or not to try to return home. What was the best possible way he and the crew and *Ghost 1* itself could depart while leaving the best impression upon the Autobots and the most terrifying one on the Decepticons? Because if they were going to eventually come to his homeworld, he would rather the Autobots arrived as friends and the Decepticons thought twice about showing up at all.

Not that humankind in its current state represented any true threat to any of them. But in time—in time, the people of Earth would develop new technologies. New weapons and new defenses. Sector Seven would work to ensure that this came to pass no matter what else happened.

Time, then, was the key. The people of Earth needed time, and it was going to be up to him and his crew to make sure they received it. So that when these giant beings finally did show up, they would be confronted by humans far better able to take care of themselves and much better equipped to respond to any outside threat. For now, that would have to be enough.

He opened his eyes as the speakers came to life again. "*Ghost One,* this is SSAB Command. Please advise as to your status."

Walker turned once more to his crew. "The bottom line is that by going home we do a disservice not just to ourselves and to this mission, but to the rest of humankind as well. They aren't ready to deal with something like this, not by a long shot. In thirty or forty years, maybe—if we don't blow ourselves up or waste the planet in the interim. But right now, no. We have to make sure—absolutely sure—that if we make a run for it, the wormhole closes behind us. Furthermore, we have to leave the Autobots and the Decepticons certain about the kind of people we truly are."

A flicker of resentment flashed through Clarkson's eyes, but eventually he nodded. He didn't like it, but he realized that Walker was speaking the truth. Across from him, Gonzalez also nodded, her eyes bright.

Avery chuckled softly. "So we do what we've gotta do, Captain. That's all she wrote."

Walker's final look was reserved for Thompson. The copilot heaved a deep breath. "You've got a hero complex worse than mine, Captain—but I'm with you."

With difficulty, Walker managed to hide what he was feeling at that moment. It was not easy. "Thank all of you for doing the right thing, even when it's the hard thing." He flicked the transmitter before he or anyone could change their mind.

"SSAB Command, this is *Ghost One,* do you copy?"

Smythe's voice responded. "Go ahead, *Ghost One.*"

Walker thought for a moment about what to say and how to say it. He ended up going with his gut. It would be up to those back home to embellish his words, if any were so inclined. Some people always were, he knew resignedly.

"SSAB Command, be advised as to our status. As mentioned previously, we are not alone out here. Earth is in for a visit. Maybe today or tomorrow or in ten years, but it's inevitable. Prepare yourselves and prepare the world. Some of the beings with whom we have had contact are benign, some—aren't. Sooner or later, components of the Ice Man's extended family will find us. *Ghost One* is staying to make sure the door that's currently open gets closed and locked." He paused, then added almost diffidently, "This is *Ghost One*—signing off."

He turned off the transmitter for the final time. "Maria, shut down our communications with SSAB Command. We're done with that now and need to focus on the task at hand. We'll only get one shot at this."

Slowly but professionally, she did as he directed. Within the cabin, silence and contemplation now reigned.

"What've you got in mind, Captain?" Thompson finally asked.

"Activate our weapons, Jake." Walker managed a slight smile. "We want to be sure our future visitors get the right impression."

XV

Optimus kept his attention focused on the Decepticons as he waited for Jazz, Ratchet, and Ironhide to leave the *Ark* and join him and Bumblebee. The first thing he did when they arrived was to query Ratchet.

"Is the ship secure?"

"As secure as I can make it in our absence," the mechanic assured him.

"Good," Optimus murmured. "Let's make an end to this, then, right here and now."

"Sometimes," Ironhide murmured forlornly, "it feels like it will never end."

"I know," Optimus admitted. "And it never will so long as there are Decepticons left in the galaxy. Nonetheless, if we accomplish nothing else, we must try to ensure that this fraction of the war ends here. We cannot hope to find the Allspark and begin to restore Cybertron to what it once was if we're constantly fighting instead of searching."

"You won't get any argument out of me," Ratchet replied. "The sooner we can finally call an end to combat and go home, the better." He paused, looked at Bumblebee, and began assessing the damage to his colleague. "What happened to you?"

Optimus answered for the smaller mechanoid. "He suffered an uncontrolled fall into a sinkhole down on the planet. Do you think you can fix him up, along with Jazz?"

Ratchet considered. He put a reassuring hand on Bumblebee's shoulder. "Don't worry about it, my friend. Not a problem."

Bumblebee nodded understandingly, then pointed at the Decepticons and raised his weapon.

"Bumblebee is right. It's time," Optimus announced. "I will deal with Starscream. Jazz, you intercept Frenzy. Try to finish him quickly. We'll need your help elsewhere."

"So much for making it fun," Jazz quipped, as usual unable to take even the impending battle or his weakened state too seriously.

"Ironhide, Bonecrusher is your responsibility," Optimus continued. "Try to fight him at a distance. He's slow but very powerful. Which leaves Barricade for Bumblebee and Ratchet." He paused a moment before adding an essential reminder. "We can't afford to lose anyone, so be careful—all of you."

"I'm the king of careful," Jazz opined with a laugh.

Optimus shook his head ruefully. There was no Autobot like the irrepressible Jazz. "Just make sure you stay on your throne while you're handing down decrees." A glance in the direction of the Decepticons revealed that their position had changed. The enemies of all that was good and just were on the move. "Here they come. Spread out and ready yourselves."

He shifted to the left, placing himself between the Decepticons and the fragile ship of the humans. Whatever the final outcome of the coming conflict, the creative little creatures deserved the chance to go home. This was not their war, and Optimus was determined to give them that opportunity. *Everyone deserves to go home eventually—even pitiable organics.*

Starscream accelerated, and Optimus corrected himself. *Everyone, that is, except the Decepticons.* He activated his weapons systems. "Starscream," he transmitted, "I'm here for you!"

"Then come!" Starscream replied. "I've maintained a special file that is devoted to nothing but anticipation for this."

Despite many previous encounters, both sides knew it was a surety that new and different tactics would be employed. Usually an extended period of insults preceded opening maneuvers. This time Optimus didn't hesitate. Aligning his weapons, he opened fire.

"Your wait is over."

His first discharge was dead-on. It took the swiftly moving Starscream in the chest, hurling him backward. The Decepticon screeched in surprise. A moment later the rest of the Autobots opened fire, and the interminable war—yet again—was on.

Ironhide moved to engage Bonecrusher, firing and darting away, then repeating the sequence, careful not to allow the Decepticon behemoth to get close enough for physical interaction. In contrast, Jazz used his speed to close on a surprised Frenzy. Locking hold, he landed a series of rapid-fire blows to the small Decepticon's frame intended to end the encounter as quickly as possible. Bumblebee and Ratchet charged Barricade. At the last possible instant they executed an opposition in order to come at him from either side. Barricade could be as deadly as Starscream, and the two bots knew they would have their hands full.

Halting his tumble, Starscream spun and opened fire with his own weapons, missing badly. With a second volley, however, he succeeded in nicking Optimus's shoulder. The salvo did only cosmetic damage. Optimus promptly returned the volley, accelerating as he did so and forcing his opponent to dodge awkwardly in order to avoid the deadly discharge. At extreme velocities, the pursuit continued through uncaring emptiness. Speed and maneuverability were all that kept Starscream intact. Despite his skills, the Decepticon found himself hard-pressed to keep out of the grasp of his determined tracker.

I'll never get him like this, Optimus thought.

Abruptly and inexplicably, he stopped shooting. Without pausing to question why, Starscream took advantage of the lull to fire back, and Optimus found himself having to dodge as well. Risking a quick glance back at the others, he saw to his dismay that things were not going as well as he had hoped.

From the looks of it, Bonecrusher had managed to catch up with Ironhide at least once: the old warrior bore several deep gouges and at least one serious dent on his thick armor. Luckily, he had managed to stay clear. As Optimus looked on, Jazz sped to his aid. As per Optimus's instructions, the swift-moving Autobot had left Frenzy reeling and noncommunicative.

Bumblebee and Ratchet, however, were having a difficult time with Barricade. When the big Decepticon was not shooting, he was moving and working his position so that his frustrated attackers could not unleash their full firepower without the risk of hitting each other. Both of the Autobots appeared worse for wear. Already suffering from the injuries he had incurred on the world below, Bumblebee especially looked fatigued. Optimus realized that if he and his companions were going to have any chance of triumphing in this skirmish, he was going to have to end his personal combat with Starscream quickly.

Altering strategy once more, he accelerated straight at the Decepticon. Since he was still firing steadily, the blatant assault surprised his opponent. So much so that Starscream failed to take note of the tiny craft that was slowly working its way up behind him.

Having closed the gap with surprising speed, the only nonmechanoids in the immediate spatial vicinity were preparing to join the fight.

Optimus paid for his straightforwardness by taking a blast in the torso from Starscream's main batteries. He felt the blasts slam into his armor and hurl him backward. A moment later he noticed what his adversary had not: the human vessel slowly moving into position behind the Decepticon leader.

What were the humans thinking? he wondered. They didn't stand a chance in a clash on this scale, and yet here they were.

"They fight," he murmured to himself, "even when it's not their fight."

Starscream's barrage had done some damage, but it was not serious enough to incapacitate him. Stabilizing himself, Optimus fired afresh, forcing Starscream to keep his distance. At the same time, he was disconcerted to see that the Decepticon had finally detected the presence of the human craft.

"Leave them alone, Starscream," he transmitted forcefully.

Starscream had his own unique, shrill laugh. "It will only take a moment. They'll die just like you and the others," he sneered. "Well, perhaps not just like you, but perish they will." Whirling, he started to train a single weapon on the brash humans.

It was not much of an opening, but it was enough. Putting on a burst of speed so unexpected it passed unpredicted by Starscream's instrumentation, Optimus closed the gap between them before the Decepticon could react. Shooting out a hand, he grabbed his rival by the shoulder and arm and spun. Because Optimus's body mass considerably exceeded that of the Decepticon's arm, metal bent and composite screeched. Caught by surprise, Starscream flailed with his free hand and tried to escape.

"Not this time." Maneuvering to retain his positional advantage, Optimus bore down with all his strength. "And not ever again."

A surge of panic washed through Starscream when he felt Optimus grab hold. He was as conscious as Optimus of the sudden physical position the Autobot had acquired. Caught at a serious disadvantage, he could continue to fight back, or . . .

Whatever the consequences, he knew he could not allow his hatred of the Autobots to distract him from the more important mission.

When he had interfaced with the alien vessel's primitive computer system, he had taken care to download every bit of information it contained. Not all of it was directly related to their mission. He knew that the Allspark had been found and placed in a secure facility on their world. He knew that Megatron had found his way there as well and was now trapped and contained in some kind of frozen stasis. Both arrivals were being reverse-engineered to discover the secrets of their respective science. It was those efforts that had led to the design, however pale an imitation, of their ship.

There was no way he was going to allow the other Decepticons to discover any of this, far less the Autobots. The last thing Starscream wanted was for the Allspark or Megatron to be found by anyone but him. The humans and their ship had to be destroyed, along with Optimus Prime and Bumblebee at the very least.

As Optimus gave another destabilizing wrench on his arm, Starscream redoubled his efforts to free himself. The Autobots were proving to be much harder to destroy than he had anticipated. And if he and his colleagues expended all their energy in fighting them, the humans might escape. Ignoring the pain in his arm and the blows Optimus was landing on other parts of his body, Starscream fought to take aim at the alien vessel once more, intent on blowing it out of the ether. Only then could he return his full attention to his frustratingly persistent foe.

The Autobot leader must have seen what he was about to do, because Optimus suddenly spun him around and heaved him away with enough force to send the Decepticon whirling out of firing range.

As he fought to stabilize himself, Starscream saw his cohorts fully engaged in their own individual battles. None of them had taken notice of the humans' arrival. Frenzy had already been put out of commission. Desperate, he transmitted as widely as he could. Starscream ignored his injured cohort to press his own program.

"Decepticons! Disengage from the Autobots and destroy the alien vessel. It must be annihilated at all costs!"

From the *Nemesis,* the badly injured but already healing Blackout responded immediately—and disconcertingly. "Why is that, Starscream?" Before he could answer, the other bot continued, "You told us it was destroyed and now we see that it is not. What else are you hiding, Starscream? What is the significance of the alien ship?"

Starscream cursed silently to himself. Despite having been shown the error of his ways, the single-minded fool would not let the matter go. Now he was providing an unnecessary distraction at a critical time. Well, Starscream had already determined that he would not lose his position to Megatron's ghost. As far as he was concerned, regardless of the treacherous data contained on the humans' ship, Megatron was dead and gone. He, Starscream, had been the leader of the Decepticons for some time, he was the leader of the Decepticons now, and *nothing* was going to change that.

Offering an objection, Optimus unleashed a heavy volley in his direction, forcing him to dodge at an angle that took him even farther from the alien ship.

"I am hiding nothing," he responded in frustration. "While you repose on the *Nemesis* and lob insults, the rest of us are out here fighting."

Blackout was not intimidated. "I am doing my part. You just can't see it yet. Clearly you wanted me out of the way and silenced. Why is that?"

Starscream seethed with anger. When this was over, he was going to make a point of ripping Blackout's Spark right out of his chest. Unaware of the mental conflict that threatened to consume his adversary, Optimus fired again. This time his well-aimed salvo struck Starscream on the shoulder and spun him around.

I cannot squander any more time on this confrontational drivel, the leader of the Decepticons told himself. "Do as you will, then," he snapped at Blackout. "The rest of us have fighting to do. Decepticons, I repeat: disengage from the Autobots and target the alien vessel!"

"Maybe Blackout has a point," Bonecrusher rumbled unexpectedly.

Taking his attention off Optimus for a second, a startled Starscream turned to see Bonecrusher halt his ongoing pursuit of Ironhide.

"What!"

"You owe us an explanation," the massive mechanoid muttered.

"I don't owe you anything," Starscream retorted furiously. "We have been through this already. Now do as I command!"

"After this fight is over," Barricade declared as he dodged out of Ratchet's range and fired at Bumblebee, "you will explain, Starscream. But I agree that now is not the time. We have Autobots to fight!" Accelerating swiftly, he slammed into Bumblebee at nearly full sublight speed, sending the little Autobot spinning away.

"As you will if you must," Starscream acknowledged. "But not before time."

His momentary distraction was costly. For a second time showing unexpected speed, Optimus had summarily closed the distance between them.

"It's over, Starscream." The leader of the Autobots let loose with everything he had.

Jensen struggled to see through the ivory swirl. The blizzard had lessened somewhat, but the snow continued making visibility difficult. The Russians had tested the makeshift perimeter in several places, and so far his troops had held on.

Still, they had taken many casualties, and it was likely the next round would see the well-trained intruders break through. The perimeter was too wide, and he did not have enough men left to hold every point. He eased himself back down into the crease in the ground that he was sharing with one of the noncoms. The sergeant squinted at him.

"Sir?"

"I'm open to suggestions, Sergeant," Jensen muttered. "I don't think we have enough people to hold the line here. What do you think? Should we pull back and try to form a tighter perimeter around the Ice Man's hauler?"

The noncom considered the question for a moment, then shook his head. "If we pull back, we may as well give up and retreat toward the station. Sure, we'll have less terrain to cover, but we'll also be dangerously concentrating our own forces. If we tighten up and they bring in a mortar, they could take us out completely with a couple of accurate lobs."

Jensen nodded. "I was afraid you'd say something like that. Options?"

"I think we let them break through, sir." The sergeant voiced the opinion with obvious reluctance. "It may be the only way."

"Let them break through?" Jensen asked. "The 'only way' for what? How does that help?"

The husky noncom stuck his own head up over the lip of the crease, had a quick look around, then ducked back down. "They're on the verge of overrunning us anyway, so trying to hold them off is only going to result in more of my—of our men dying, sir. If we fall back, they'll be able to surround us. But if we wait, hold position, and let them through, they might jump at the chance to rush the trucks. If we can let them get ten or fifteen yards past us, we can hit them from behind before they get to the camp itself." He grinned wolfishly. "They won't know how many of us are behind them and how many of us are still in front. And we know the layout of the camp—they'll be coming in ignorant, through the snow."

Jensen was suitably impressed. "That's not half bad. We let them in, they'll think we've fallen back, but they won't penetrate deep enough to know for sure one way or the other." He closed his eyes and wondered what Colonel Kinnear would do.

"All right, let's do it. Start the word along the line for the men to spread out a bit and get under their winter ponchos. Man-to-man only. No radios, in case they're listening to us. We'll let our visitors pass, then when I give the signal we'll hit 'em from every direction as hard as we can with everything we've got left."

The sergeant nodded once, then moved silent and swift as a wraith to instruct the two men nearest them on their left and right. The order was passed quickly along the line in both directions. Maintaining silence, the surviving soldiers spread out, disappearing beneath the white of their winter ponchos.

Jensen knew they would only have one chance to make the strategy work, and even that chance was a small one. The Russians had landed a sizable, experienced force whose movements were not burdened by the need to protect equipment, technicians, scientists, and one very large frozen alien. Still, under the right conditions and properly sprung, surprise could be worth a full company.

He risked a glance back in the direction of the camp. The line of vehicles was more or less intact, there was no sign of panic, and everything looked pretty . . .

Then he saw the Ice Man. Beside his hauler. Standing up.

"Oh, sh—" he started to say. Before he could finish, a flash of bright headlights entered his field of view from the left and promptly smashed into the back of the alien's massive legs. This was followed by two huge explosions. A rapidly expanding fireball rose into the air, propelling the Ice Man with it.

Stunned, Jensen climbed to his feet and stared at the camp. What the hell had happened?

"Sir!" the noncom yelled. Leaping from his position, he tackled Jensen to the ground just as a barrage of bullets whizzed overhead. "Don't make yourself a target."

"Yeah, yeah," Jensen replied, almost absently. "Thanks." He jerked his head in the direction of the camp. "So much for surprise."

Another barrage of rifle fire split the night air—but this burst caused the senior sergeant to break out in a huge grin. "Those aren't AK-47s—those are M16s!"

Both men peered over the edge of their hiding place. In the dim light, white-clad figures were rising and turning to fire behind them. There was no mistaking what was going on: the Russians were being attacked from behind.

"Can't be that many." Hope shot through Jensen like a gulp of twenty year-old bourbon. "Or they'd have been heard moving up."

The noncom thought furiously for a second. "There was a squad of Rangers training back at the base. Maybe they were sent for us."

"I don't care if it's Santa's elves protecting their turf," Jensen exclaimed. "Pass the word to hit the Russians now, while they're preoccupied."

"Yes, *sir*!" Leaping to his feet, Martin sounded a piercing whistle that carried over the falling wind. "Attack!" he yelled.

Rising en masse from their hiding places, the transport team's soldiers jumped up from beneath their ponchos and charged forward. Rifle fire erupted from multiple locations. Caught by surprise from behind and counterattacked in front, the Russian assault dissolved into chaos. Jensen would have taken part, but other responsibilities and concerns took precedence. Turning in the opposite direction, he broke into a run as he headed back toward the camp.

If the Ice Man was now mobile, they would have to find a way to stop him and get him back under control. Compared with the Russians, the giant alien machine posed unknown problems the lieutenant preferred not to contemplate—except that reality was forcing him to do exactly that.

Leaping over a mound of snow, he hit a patch of iced-over road and nearly went down. Somehow he managed to keep his balance. As he approached the first of the hastily erected tents, his eyes were drawn to a dark, irregular line in the snow. Frowning, he knelt for a closer look. With widening eyes, he rose and followed the still-moist trail.

It led him to the seriously wounded Kinnear. The colonel was slowly dragging himself forward in the direction of the hauler that had been carrying the Ice Man. Leaning against a nearby truck was a battered and bloody Lieutenant Colonel Nolan, his arms wrapped around his chest as if once he let go, his insides might spill out. Both men looked on the verge of death, yet were still trying to fight. For the first time in his career, there in the arctic snow and dark, the real meaning of the word *soldier* impressed itself irrevocably on Jensen's soul.

His attention was drawn away from the two badly injured senior officers to the far side of the hauler by the screech of rending metal and a deep, horrific electronic growl. Jensen felt the hair on the back of his neck stand on end.

The Ice Man may have gone down, but he certainly wasn't out.

Chris Smythe rubbed his aching forehead. Why the hell did Nolan have to take off and leave him in charge of this mess? He closed his eyes and pushed his glasses up onto his forehead, trying to think.

"Chris?" a voice asked. "Hey, Chris?"

The communications director answered without opening his eyes. "Yeah?"

"I'm not getting through to them." The voice belonged to Brad Conncarry, one of his best communications techs. Conncarry was a rotund middle-aged man with thinning brown hair, eyes that were too close together, a nose like a macaw, and a fondness for cobbling together telephones with no obvious practical applications. "No response at all."

Fighting to organize his thoughts, Smythe reminded himself not to clench his teeth. The base dentist had already bawled him out for what was unarguably a terrible habit.

"Is the alien communicator still responding?"

"Yeah, we're still picking that up," Conncarry replied. "But no matter what we send, *Ghost One* isn't responding to us."

"Son of a—what are they thinking?" Smythe complained. "Why did I have to give Walker the damn code? I should have just told them to get home." He considered for a moment, then ordered, "Ping their equipment."

"Just a ping?" Conncarry was clearly confused. "Why?"

"Look, if the connection still exists, that means the

ship isn't destroyed, right?" He continued quickly, not wanting to give Conncarry a chance to object. "So they signed off. Okay. Maybe they shut down communications deliberately for reasons we can't imagine. Or maybe they're receiving but they can't reply for some other reason. But if we get a ping, we'll at least know that the system is still functioning."

Conncarry turned to go, then stopped and turned back. "Suppose we get a ping. Do you want to try to send something? Besides asking them to acknowledge?"

The communications director thought a moment, then nodded. Screw protocol. Nolan wasn't here and he, Smythe, was in charge. That made Walker and the crew *his* responsibility. If afterward he had to face some kind of covert kangaroo court because of his decision, well—at least his conscience would be clear.

"Tell them—SSAB Command to *Ghost One*. Authorize priority code override. Come home immediately, regardless of prevailing circumstances. What's the word from the science desk on wormhole stability?"

Conncarry's expression was grim. "Last I was told it continues to deteriorate rapidly. Maybe twenty or thirty minutes at most."

Smythe nodded. As far as he was concerned, interstellar physics had made the decision for him. "Send that message. Send it right now."

Conncarry looked uncertain. "Are you sure you know what you're doing, Chris? They'll fire you for this, you know. And maybe worse. We got our orders."

"I don't care," Smythe snapped. "I'm in charge and I am not leaving those people to die out there on account of a postulated 'maybe.' It's all speculation and more than a little fiction. This call is my responsibility. Now send the message."

Conncarry nodded, smiled, and left. As soon as he was gone, Smythe leaned back and stared at the insulated ceiling, trying to see beyond it. Way beyond it.

"Come on, Maria," he murmured to himself. "Get the message and tell Walker to get the hell out of there."

The spatial clock was ticking. If the crew of *Ghost 1* didn't make an attempt to reenter the wormhole soon, it wouldn't matter how much they wanted to come back.

He closed his eyes again, hating the waiting almost as much as he had begun to hate Sector Seven and the inescapable burden of its overriding, perfidious secrecy.

Walker looked on as Thompson maneuvered *Ghost 1* into position behind Optimus Prime. Having come to the conclusion that they were all going to die out here, the captain wanted to be certain that they took at least *one* of the duplicitous Decepticons with them. Bearing in mind the manifest differences in technology and fighting ability, he was also reasonably certain he and his crew would have only one shot at doing so.

The view out the foreport bordered on the unreal. Two huge mechanoids, Optimus Prime and Starscream, were weaving and firing at each other while off to the right other Autobots and Decepticons fought and flew for their very lives. Despite the ferocity of the ongoing combat, so far there was only one apparent casualty. A smaller Decepticon drifted, alone and motionless, on the edge of bedlam.

"How do you want to play it, Captain?" Thompson spoke without looking up from his console.

"See if we can get behind Starscream while he's occupied with Optimus Prime. Even the engineering team that installed the weapons system on *Ghost* doesn't know everything it can do. Maybe we'll have a chance at a good shot."

Thompson started to reply, only to be interrupted by a suddenly energized Gonzalez. "I've got something!"

Walker turned to look at her. "What is it, Maria?"

"We just got a message from SSAB Command," she told him excitedly.

Walker's tone indicated that he was less than pleased. "I thought I told you to shut down our communications via the alien transmitter."

"I did," she replied. "I don't understand." She was staring down at her console. "The system *is* turned off."

Walker shifted attention to his engineer. "Explain."

"Maria shut down the transmitter, and the communications system went into standby mode," Clarkson speculated. "Our receiver isn't offline completely, and they pinged it to make sure it's still operational. Pretty slick."

"Could you maybe keep it down back there?" Thompson wrenched the *Ghost* to port to avoid a wild blast of energy from the distant Decepticons battling the defenders from the *Ark*. "I'm kind of busy here."

Walker turned back to Gonzalez. "What does the message say?"

She glanced at her readout. "SSAB Command to *Ghost One*. Authorize priority code override. Come home immediately, regardless of circumstance." She looked up at him. "They're saying we can come home."

Walker's response was curt. "No, we can't."

Gaping at him, Clarkson gestured at Gonzalez's main screen. "Are you crazy, Sam? SSAB just authorized us."

"Captain," Maria started to say, but Walker held up a hand to silence her.

"No," he declared steadfastly. "We're not going anywhere until this clash between the Autobots and the Decepticons is over. I won't take the risk of going back through the wormhole and leading them straight to Earth."

"Come on, Captain!" Clarkson was shouting now. "We're in the clear. Let's get out of here while we've got the chance."

"I said no!" Walker yelled back. "My decision is final. We stay until it's over. Do I make myself clear, Craig? And might I add that casting aspersions on your commanding officer's sanity while in the course of a mission is a poor way to ensure the continued viability of your retirement fund."

Resentment filled the other man's eyes, but Walker found that he didn't care. As mission commander he did not have the luxury of caring. In countermanding the printed code someone back on Earth was second-guessing the experts, even if by so doing it was for the perceived benefit of the *Ghost* and its crew. Walker knew he was making the right decision. He returned his gaze forward.

"Stay with it, Jake," he murmured quietly.

"Yes, Captain," Thompson replied, then added reflexively, "Look out!"

He yanked the controls, forcing *Ghost 1* sharply down to avoid a random blast that nearly hit them dead-on. As they changed course, another bolt of plasma headed straight at them. Optimus Prime must have predicted and reacted to the blast because he cut in front of them and caught the powerful energy discharge flush on his chest. It flared as it splashed across his armored front, knocking him backward.

"Jesus," Thompson muttered. "That would have cut us in half."

"Then don't get hit," Walker ordered. "Keep maneuvering to get behind Starscream."

"You think we can actually harm him with what we have on board?" Thompson continued to work *Ghost 1* around toward the rear of the skirmishing Decepticon leader.

"Starscream may be intelligent and independent, but he's still a machine," Walker pointed out. "And every machine has a weak spot." Turning, he eyed Avery and Clarkson. "That's going to be up to the two of you. Mike, I want you analyzing his frame. See if you can find anything that looks like a weak spot in his armor. Craig, you know more about this ship's weapons systems than anyone on board. Concentrate on determining how we can make the best use of them."

Avery nodded that he understood. Clarkson hesitated briefly, then turned furiously back to his console.

Let him focus his resentment on his work, Walker mused. If the irate engineer could channel half as much anger toward Starscream as he was feeling toward his commander, then they might actually have a chance to do some damage to the leader of the Decepticons.

XVI

Struggling into the back of the hauler, Nolan kept one eye on the snow and section of ditch where the Ice Man had fallen. The giant's arms and legs were twitching and jerking, and his eyes—if they actually were eyes and not simple photoreceptors—flickered a dull, angry red. There was no question in Nolan's mind that after long years in stasis, the alien was starting to come around. His level of apprehension was about as high as the temperature was low. Shoving loose and broken gear out of the way, he began a frantic search.

The specially constructed, heavily insulated container that had been mounted on the hauler had suffered substantial damage when the vehicle had jackknifed and slid off the road. In the course of his flailing about and efforts to stand, the Ice Man had damaged it further. Nolan's search turned up plenty of equipment—all of it bent, busted, or both.

His gaze settled on a composite-covered hose an inch in diameter that was tipped with a bright metal nozzle. Unable to see where it led, he picked it up by the end and gently lifted it free of the snow. Even through his gloves Nolan could tell that the hose was colder than the air surrounding it. Using it as a guide, he worked his way up the length of the tube to where it terminated in a large cylindrical tank. He could make out lettering on the metal, but ice and snow had accumulated to the point that he could not read it. He called over to where Kinnear lay panting on the ground.

"Tom? I think I've got a functional tank and hose here."

Kinnear struggled to look up. "No way. The tanks all ruptured in the crash." As he replied he reflected on how difficult it was trying to talk with blood in one's throat.

"Maybe not all. This one looks okay. Is it full of what I think it is?"

Kinnear wheezed, choked, coughed. "Mix of anhydrous ammonia and liquid nitrogen—pretty stable. If it's still functional and if it's full, there might be enough to refreeze the Ice Man. Or at least slow him down." He coughed some more, aware that he was growing weaker by the minute.

Great, he thought feebly. *It's so cold I can't even tell if I'm dying or not.*

"I'm going to see if I can get it to work!" Nolan was yelling to him.

He turned back to the tank and studied the controls. Though chemistry had never been one of his strong suits, he was damn sure he didn't want this stuff anywhere on him. The valves were simple turn-ons. A quarter turn at a time, he carefully opened the one in the middle. The tank sputtered and coughed. Nolan made sure the nozzle was aimed away from his own body.

A thin stream of strong-smelling liquid smoked out of the nozzle. He watched as it made contact with a piece of twisted titanium plating. The exposed metal iced over in seconds.

"It works!" He shut down the flow by flipping the control bar on the side of the nozzle. "Hang in there, Tom."

Pulling on the hose, trying to accumulate as much slack as possible, he walked it over to the other side of the hauler bed. Upon reaching the edge, he squinted out into the darkness and the snow. Before he opened the switch he wanted to make sure his aim was perfect. The tank was not that large, and he couldn't afford to waste any of its essential supercooled contents. Snow swirled around him as he struggled to relocate the recumbent Ice Man. After a couple of minutes it struck him why he was having so much trouble.

He could not see the Ice Man because he was no longer where he had fallen.

With a sinking feeling, Nolan turned and began to scan the icy landscape. The screech of metal on metal forced his head around so quickly that he actually felt the tendons twang in his neck.

The Ice Man had regained his footing and was now standing on the other side of the hauler's back end, peering into it with hate-filled eyes.

Anthropomorphic tendencies be damned, Nolan resolved. Those eyes were incontestably malevolent.

A massive hand began to descend toward the near-paralyzed Nolan. Metal fingers gleamed in the light from a truck burning itself out nearby.

Nolan stumbled backward. For some reason, he still gripped the end of the hose tightly in his gloved hands. As those glowing eyes and that monstrous hand came closer he found himself wondering why he should bother to resist. Now that the Ice Man had revived, the night's outcome was inevitable. The alien was going to kill him.

He was going to kill them all.

Time slowed to a crawl for Lieutenant Jensen. In his mind's eye he saw the dead soldiers, Russian and American both; the flames from the makeshift camp as explosions tore through first one vehicle, then another; the trail of blood Colonel Kinnear had left behind as he had crawled away from the dead body of the Russian infiltrator. Jensen saw them as clearly as he could recall the way the sky looked after an Arctic storm had passed or how his breath, labored and hard, left his lungs to crystallize almost instantly in the frigid night air.

But the image he knew would never leave him for the rest of his days was that of the Ice Man glaring down at Lieutenant Colonel Philip Nolan as he stood in the back of the hauler, the fires flickering around them turning the huge silvery body a deep orange-red. The alien looked like some mad surrealist's vision of Lucifer himself, come forth to bring all the terrors of Hell to Earth and to mankind. Seconds stretched into what felt like hours as he paused to take in the scene.

Nolan was backing away a step at a time, the end of a hose from one of the liquid nitrogen tanks hanging loosely from his right hand. The Ice Man was reaching down for him, ready to crush him like a bug. Unable to think of anything to do, anything he *could* do, Jensen stood motionless, waiting for whatever was going to happen next.

From behind the Ice Man there sounded a cry of rage and pain. Stunned though he was, Jensen recognized the voice. Somehow overcoming the pain from his injuries, Colonel Kinnear had slipped behind the alien.

The cry came again. Momentarily distracted, the Ice Man slowly turned to see the tiny creature behind him.

Jensen wanted to start forward, wanted to run, but his legs refused to obey the commands his brain kept sending out.

"Come on, you ugly metal bastard," Kinnear was screaming. "Look at me!"

As the Ice Man completed his turn, the colonel opened fire with the machine gun he had recovered from a nearby truck. At point-blank range, he fired into the Ice Man's armored chest. Slugs ricocheted in all directions, bouncing off the armor-plated body while Kinnear yelled and carried on like a wild man. Jensen expected some kind of reaction from the alien, but it simply stood there until the clip was empty.

Dropping the empty weapon, Kinnear continued cursing violently at the alien. As Jensen looked on in horror, it reached down with one massive hand and picked up the badly wounded colonel as if he weighed nothing at all.

For Jensen, the entire world was suddenly still and quiet, and had anyone ever asked him later, he would have sworn on everything he held sacred in life that he heard Kinnear say two more words. They reached him as a whisper, but they carried all the force of a bomb.

"Mission accomplished."

That's when Jensen saw the wire leading to the pack the colonel had somehow managed to strap across his back. He never learned what it contained. Gelignite, perhaps, taken from the engineering team's truck. RPGs. Or maybe just a case of the oval, fist-sized, fruit-shaped devices like the one from which Kinnear now extracted a metal pin as he lunged forward toward the Ice Man's chest.

Jensen heard Nolan yell, "Tom, no!"

Time started up again and Jensen heard himself scream, "Phil! Get down!"

He dropped, burying his face in the cold, wet snow, and had not counted to five before the grenade went off. An instant later so did the entire contents of the backpack Kinnear had been wearing. The sudden, shocking fireball was not nearly powerful enough to penetrate the Ice Man's armor—but it was strong enough to knock the still only partially recovered alien backward into the bed of the hauler. Raising himself up, spitting out dirt and ice, Jensen yelled, "Colonel! Do it now!"

Nolan had been stunned by his friend's sacrifice—but he had not been stunned insensible. Even as he scrambled back to his feet, he turned the nozzle on full blast. Gushing from the special hose, supercooled liquid splashed the stunned Ice Man and instantly froze more solid than any of its immediate surroundings. Gigantic arms and legs flailed as the giant fought to regain his feet. Splashing across his body, spurts of liquid N_2 instantly froze joints and limbs.

Tossing aside the charred fragments of what had moments earlier been Colonel Thomas Kinnear, the Ice Man started to reach for Nolan anew. Bringing his own rifle off his shoulder, a reenergized Jensen took aim and opened fire.

"Hey gruesome!" he yelled. "Eat some of this!"

His thumb flicked the switch to full auto and the Ice Man turned in his direction. Freezing on contact with metal and composite, the liquid nitrogen was forming a solid coat and seal around the alien form. The enormous body was now emitting a peculiar squeaking sound as it struggled to move.

The alien was emitting some incomprehensible high-pitched shrieking that could only be translated as the equivalent of hate-filled promises of vengeance. He took one step forward, another—and halted as the freezing liquid began to lock up his joints.

From inside the hauler, Nolan's voice could be heard very faintly. "You called it, Tom."

The final few rounds emptied from the M16's clip and Jensen dropped it to one side. His ears were ringing from the gunshots and the explosion. Out of ammo, he looked on as the giant machine coming toward him slowed, slowed—and finally stopped. From the back of the hauler Nolan continued to drench it in the special liquid nitrogen solution. The red glow of the monster mechanoid's eyes faded, blinked once, and went dark.

From out of the darkness that still dominated the camp's perimeter, two figures came running toward the lieutenant. He recognized Sergeant Martin and one of the other Rangers. Breathing heavily, his breath fogging the air in front of him, Jensen slowed to a halt. He did not salute, and Martin did not call him on the omission.

"Really, really glad to see you, Sergeant. What's the situation?" Jensen looked past the two men, trying to see into the darkness.

"The Russians are in full retreat, sir. Running for their subs." Tired as he was, Martin still managed a triumphant grin. "We've got them beat."

"Anybody still out there making sure they don't change their minds? " Jensen wondered.

"A couple of my guys, some of the transport team," the Ranger told him. "We figure we'll chase them a ways, just to make sure they don't stop until they're all the way back to Vladivostok."

Jensen nodded. "All right," he said. "Well done."

Looking past the lieutenant, Martin took in the bizarre scene and the tattered remnants of the camp. "What happened here?" he asked.

"We checked in at the end of the world and almost jumped off," Jensen explained without going into detail. "Fortunately, we stopped in time. Colonel Kinnear is dead." He looked back in the direction of the hauler. "Lieutenant Colonel Nolan was badly wounded, mortally by the look of it. Set up the perimeter on minimum guard and bring the rest of our people back into camp. We'll get this place cleaned up, get everyone warmed up, then hold tight until sunrise."

"What happens at sunrise?" Martin wanted to know.

Jensen looked up at the sky and took a deep breath. The air was cold, sharp, and tasted of ash and burned rubber, but it was the best breath he had ever taken in his life. Silently shifting flowing waves of green tinged with pink were visible through widening breaks in the clouds—the aurora borealis.

"Looks like the storm is passing. By the time the sun comes up, maybe we'll be able to raise help on the radios. In any case, there are sure to be aerial patrols out to check on us."

"What happens then, sir?" the Ranger inquired.

Jensen looked back at the irregular lump of ice that contained the body of the Ice Man. Nearby was the frozen body of Nolan who, like Colonal Kinnear, had made the ultimate sacrifice, and may well have saved the planet. But there would be no ticker tape parade for these heroes. "I'm going to finish this mission," he declared, surprising himself with the intensity of his response. "As planned, if not exactly on schedule, that thing over there is going down to a bunker in the U.S., and the base up here is going to be shut down. If I'm reading the signs right, Sector Seven is going one hundred percent black. There won't be any more overt military involvement, but if they'll let me I think I'll stick around." He thought of Kinnear, and Nolan, and what they had done. "I owe people."

"Finish the mission?" Martin exclaimed. "We were lucky just to make it through the night."

Jensen laughed. "Come on, Sergeant. That's what we're paid to do. Finish the mission." He gestured in the direction of the perimeter. "So let's get to it, all right?"

The Ranger took a step back, saluted. "As you say, sir." Then he and his companion hustled off to get the rest of the fighters back into camp.

Bending, Jensen picked up his rifle and slung it back over his shoulder. A great deal needed to be done before Operation Ice Man could get moving again, but he knew he could do it. He wanted to do it. He had worked with the very best, and the idea of helping to see the project through appealed to him now more than ever. Appealed to him almost as much as knowing that he was trading the cold of the Arctic for the searing heat of southern Nevada.

Give me coyotes and jackrabbits over seals and polar bears any day, he thought. Not to mention the fact that the Russians were not likely to give Sector Seven any trouble once everything had been safely relocated to a site that was only a short drive south of Las Vegas.

Nothing could ever threaten the project there, in the heart of the American Southwest.

Optimus Prime could see that Starscream had become obsessed with destroying the humans and their ship. The Decepticons kept trying to disengage from battle even as Ratchet, Bumblebee, and Jazz worked to press their advantage. In the meantime, he had his hands full keeping himself between Starscream and the humans' ship.

It would be better if the intrepid organics simply ceased maneuvering and settled on a fixed position—or better yet left the area entirely. Why they had not already done so eluded him, but he was too preoccupied with Starscream to pause and engage them in conversation.

On the move once more, the human vessel began to circle to his right. Detecting the change of direction, Starscream tried to close the distance between them. Jumping on the sudden, unexpected opening, Optimus accelerated swiftly, firing as rapidly as he could. Forced to respond, the Decepticon leader altered course as he returned fire. The humans fell back, safely out of range, and Optimus felt a sense of relief pass over him.

It was short-lived. His periodic area scan happened to fall on the *Ark* just as the hangar bay doors blew apart and went flying out into space. A multilimbed, non-bipedal metallic shape was just visible at the top of the now gaping cavity.

Scorponok! How had the creature managed to sneak aboard the transport?

"Ratchet! Fall back and secure the *Ark*. Scorponok's on the ship!"

"What!" a confused Ratchet responded. "How did he manage that?"

"Does it matter?" Jazz blurted fretfully. "Get over there! I'll cover for you." While the quicker Autobot engaged the other Decepticons with a ferocious flurry of shots, Ratchet pulled away from Barricade and headed for the ship.

A distracted Optimus managed to notice that the human vessel had at last circled all the way behind Starscream. In all likelihood their weapons would be useless against him while their reckless repositioning would only ensure their rapid destruction.

"No!" he tried to transmit to the small ship. "Move back, get away!"

Too late. The humans unleashed a modest salvo of simple, self-propelled projectile devices. These missiles seemed to crawl across the firmament. Even had they been impelled by more advanced means it was doubtful they would have had a chance to strike their intended target. Starscream was faster than most of his kind.

His scanners detected the primitive attack almost immediately. Whirling, he let loose with his defensive weaponry. The lightning-fast barrage of plasma blasts obliterated the archaic projectiles before they got anywhere near him.

"Irrational animals," the Decepticon leader murmured. "You have left your guardian too far away." He was preparing to eliminate the pesky organisms when a violent scream broke over all communications frequencies.

"Get off our ship!"

Spinning to assess the situation, he saw that Ratchet had arrived in the hangar and grabbed Scorponok by the intruder's dangerous metal tail. A single powerful yank sent the startled Decepticon spinning away from the *Ark*. Not satisfied with merely removing him from the ship, Ratchet followed in hot pursuit, weapons blazing.

Scorponok struggled to control his trajectory. In a weightless environment he was virtually helpless without Blackout's aid.

"Come back and fight!" Ratchet roared as he closed the distance between them.

Accelerating from the vicinity of the *Nemesis,* a partially repaired Blackout hurriedly rushed to the rescue of his vulnerable symbiote. Optimus felt a touch of unavoidable pride as he watched Ratchet carry the attack to the enemy. Turning, he prepared to engage Starscream once more.

He never completed the turn.

As the leader of the Autobots had tried to keep track of Starscream, the movements of the defenseless human vessel, and Ratchet's pursuit of Scorponok, Bonecrusher had slipped in close enough to send his long, piercing tail smashing through Optimus's left side. Circuitry shut down, and there was the distinct feel of metal splitting and twisting. Struggling to twist sideways he fought to line up a weapon on his foe, or at least put himself in position to physically engage the Decepticon so he could not use his immensely powerful pincers.

I could be in trouble, he thought.

Then he saw Starscream starting to close the distance between them.

I am in trouble.

Starscream had just locked in on the human ship when that ridiculous mechanoid Ratchet surprised Scorponok. Blackout had been telling the truth when he had claimed earlier that he had succeeded in slipping the ferocious symbiont aboard the *Ark*. The devious multilimbed Decepticon had managed to do some real damage before he himself had been surprised.

Scanning the entire field of battle, it struck Starscream that a golden opportunity had presented itself.

His attention focused on the suddenly endangered *Ark*, Optimus Prime had not seen Bonecrusher floating up cautiously beneath him. Somehow the huge Decepticon had managed to break away from the ongoing fight with the other Autobots without his absence being noticed.

Over a closed and coded frequency, Starscream snarled, "Take him, Bonecrusher."

Without responding, the behemoth sensibly continued his steady approach until he was in perfect position. In the distance, Ratchet was teaching the unmaneuverable Scorponok a lesson in humility. Starscream saw Blackout leave the *Nemesis* as if his internals were on fire. All a sideshow, Starscream knew. What mattered was what was about to occur much closer to his present position.

Bonecrusher struck savagely and effectively, spearing Optimus Prime through his side armor. Letting out a cry of pain and surprise, the leader of the Autobots tried to turn to face this new enemy, but the huge Decepticon had struck deep. Starscream was convinced that Optimus Prime's reign over the Autobots was about to end once and for all.

Aligning his weaponry, he took careful aim. At this range and with his quarry otherwise occupied, there was no way he could fail to strike a lethal blow. He would make an effort not to destroy the head. It would constitute a fine trophy—and an excellent reminder to all other Decepticons.

"Farewell, Optimus Prime," he whispered to himself. "Time for Endspark." He prepared to fire . . .

. . . just as the missile smashed into his back. It should not have harmed him. It was too simple, too primitive, too slow. The creatures who had built it were made not of resistant alloy and complex composite but of water barely held together by a few aberrant sticky proteins. But there was nothing slow about the chemical reaction the warhead unleashed or the effect this had on the sensors in the lower half of his body.

Emitting a screech of outrage, Starscream whirled to face the human vessel that, instead of continuing to flee, had turned around to unexpectedly close the distance between them. Doing so had placed it within easy reach of his own weapons. As soon as he completed his turn, he would annihilate them utterly.

Outrageously refusing to acknowledge this self-evident fact, they had the temerity to fire at him again.

"Don't miss, Jake," Walker tersely urged his copilot. "We'll probably only get one chance. We're lucky to still be here at all."

"I just hope Craig got the coordinates right." Thompson concentrated on instrumentation he never thought he would have the opportunity to actually utilize. "Otherwise all we're likely to do is make him mad."

Avery laughed from his chair. "He's already mad. For some reason, he hates us like poison."

Walker smiled humorlessly. "The feeling's mutual. I had a toaster once that no matter how I adjusted it, it burned the bread every time. Ended up kicking it clear across the kitchen." He nodded at Thompson. "Let's do some serious kicking."

From his seat Clarkson reported very quietly, "The wormhole is gone, Captain. Imploded, is my guess."

"Not like it's a surprise." Strange how little effect the engineer's news had on him, Walker mused.

"Then let's really make this count," Thompson avowed. "I don't want to die out here for nothing."

Walker reached over to squeeze his friend's shoulder, then turned to face the crew one last time.

"None of us is dying for nothing. We're dying to make sure our whole world stays safe. I guess that makes us . . . "

"Always wanted to be a hero," Thompson finished for him as he fired the last missile.

It struck the leader of the Decepticons precisely at the point Clarkson had designated.

Looking on, Walker knew he had made the right choice. With the wormhole gone, humankind would be safe. For a while, anyway. He wanted to believe that, even as the massive alien spun around to face them once more. His outraged screech reached them over the ship's open communications system. The tenor of the shriek was such as to render the need for a translation utterly moot.

He was—mad.

He heard a voice praying softly in Latin. Turning, he saw Gonzalez murmuring to herself even as she continued to monitor the ship's communications instrumentation. Seeing him looking at her, she paused to smile in his direction.

"You did what you had to do, Captain. You made the right call. I'm just glad I wasn't the one who had to make it."

Walker closed his eyes. He did not especially want to see the final consequences of that call coming.

Starscream's primal metallic howl was sufficiently intense to make even Bonecrusher pause to see what had happened. As he looked on, small explosions continued to erupt from within the depths of the fiery glow that had enveloped the Decepticon leader's lower body.

Optimus struggled to free himself, knowing as he did so that despite his efforts there was no way he was going to be in time. As he looked on helplessly, the enraged Starscream unleashed everything in his individual arsenal. The humans never had a chance. Their ship disintegrated under the barrage, obliterated in a ball of iridescent flame.

With a final twist and heave Optimus managed to free himself from Bonecrusher's tail. As the huge Decepticon reached for him, the leader of the Autobots flashed away, firing repeatedly to cover his retreat. Given the damage he had suffered, he knew that if Bonecrusher came after him with help, a second escape would prove far more difficult.

"Decepticons, withdraw!" The unexpected general call came from—Starscream. "Bonecrusher, help me back to the *Nemesis*."

Though he intercepted the transmission cleanly, at first Optimus refused to believe it. The leader of the Decepticons was calling for a retreat just when the Autobots were all but beaten.

"Retreat?" Barricade exclaimed in disbelief. "Now?"

"Yes, you unperceiving slag heap," Starscream responded swiftly. "Fall back! I have incurred serious damage and require immediate repair. This fight is over—for now."

Optimus's scanners followed the gathering of Decepticons as they obediently turned and raced back toward their ship. One by one he was soon rejoined by the other Autobots.

Ironhide's perceptors were also tracking their fleeing enemies. "Do we go after them, Optimus?"

"Now might be the time," Jazz pointed out.

Turning, Optimus found himself scanning the last coordinates that had been occupied by the humans' ship. There was nothing there. The space that had formerly been filled by the humans and their vessel had been replaced by a rapidly expanding sphere of particulate matter whose simple component parts in no way indicated the significance of the former whole. He shook his head. "No. We return to the *Ark* to continue our quest for the Allspark."

"They saved you, Optimus," Ratchet murmured. "I saw it all. What fascinating, contradictory creatures. They must have known that at that range Starscream would blow them to bits."

"I'm certain they did," Optimus replied. "But they did it anyway. A demonstration of courage and sacrifice unknown among organics. Perhaps—perhaps we'll encounter their kind again one day."

"Who can say?" Jazz ventured. "We know they have come across Megatron. Maybe they've even got the All-spark on their world, too!" He laughed at what surely was a completely ludicrous notion.

Optimus apparently found it less so. "If that is the case," he declared somberly, "they didn't mention it. We can only hope that the same thoughts don't occur to Starscream."

"Even if they did," Ironhide remarked, "he wouldn't go there. He wants Megatron to remain lost and forgotten, Optimus. Otherwise he doesn't remain leader of the Decepticons."

Optimus stared at the retreating mechanoids, paying particular attention to how Bonecrusher was assisting Starscream. The humans had made a lasting impression on the leader of the Decepticons, too. Ironhide's assessment notwithstanding, he wondered how long it would be before Starscream sought out their world for the sake of vengeance. He was not one to forget what would be a lasting insult.

"I have a feeling, Ironhide, that he'll be compelled to look for their home eventually. Let's get back to the ship."

As they started toward the *Ark*, Jazz inquired, "Where do we go from here, Optimus?"

"For various reasons I would myself like to visit the humans' world. If Megatron is still there and still immobilized, it would offer us an unprecedented opportunity to eliminate him once and for all." He gestured toward the distant stars. "It's not as if we are strangers to searching."

The understatement prompted laughter from every one of his companions.

Safely back aboard the *Ark*, Optimus used the ship's powerful ranging instrumentation to follow the path of the *Nemesis* until it engaged its main drive. It was of course impossible to discern what path they had chosen. Such a determination would have been immaterial even if it could have been plotted, since it was a given that the Decepticons would employ multiple course changes to conceal their true intentions.

There was no avoiding the choice that lay before them, Optimus decided. He and his colleagues would have to find the humans' world—Earth, they had called it. And they had to find it before the Decepticons. Knowing Starscream's nature as he did, he knew that if the leader of the Decepticons found that inoffensive planet first, he and his callous cohorts would wreak a terrible vengeance on its populace for the affront he had suffered at the hands of a few of their kind. To do less than prevent that from happening would be to refute all that made him and his friends Autobots, and everything that had led to him being designated Prime.

As the humans had proven beyond doubt, size wasn't everything.

He sighed internally. Though Jazz had voiced the thought in jest, it was not out of the realm of possibility that in addition to Megatron, the Allspark had also fetched up on the humans' world. The universe was full of stranger coincidences. What else, after all, would have drawn Megatron to such a primitive, out-of-the-way place? He pondered Megatron and the Allspark, together on the same world. Not a good thought, even if the former was powerless and the latter, unrecognized. Yes, he and his companions would definitely have to seek out the unfamiliar world that was home to the surprising humans. Besides, it was as likely a place to find the Allspark as any other uncharted system. Unhappily, the same thoughts would doubtless occur to Starscream; if not immediately, then while he was recovering from his injuries.

In the interim, this corner of the galaxy would see peace of a sort. Optimus knew it would not last forever.

As long as Autobots and Decepticons vied for control of the Allspark, it never could.

TRANSFORMERS
THE GAME
SUMMER 2007
TransformersGame.com
Licensed by:
Hasbro
Properties Group
Paramount
A VIACOM COMPANY
DREAMWORKS
ACTIVISION
activision.com
RATING PENDING
RP
CONTENT RATED BY
ESRB
Visit www.esrb.org for updated rating information.
HASBRO and its logo, TRANSFORMERS and all related characters are trademarks of Hasbro are used with permission. © 2007 Hasbro. All Rights Reserved. © 2007 DreamWorks LLC and Paramount Pictures Corporation. Game © 2007 Activision Publishing, Inc. Activision is a registered trademark of Activision Publishing, Inc. All rights reserved. The ratings icon is a registered trademark of the Entertainment Software Association. All other trademarks and trade names are the properties of their respective owners.

TRANSFORMERS
COMICS
COMING JULY 2007
All new stories written by *Transformers* legend Simon Furman
Exclusive artwork by an amazing artist line-up!
HE ENDLESS WAR CONTINUES.....
UK ☎ 0844 844 3797 Eire ☎ 01795 414642
www.titanmagazines.co.uk
sformers © 2007 Hasbro. All Rights Reserved.
07 Dream Works LLC and Paramount Pictures Corporation.
DREAMWORKS PICTURES

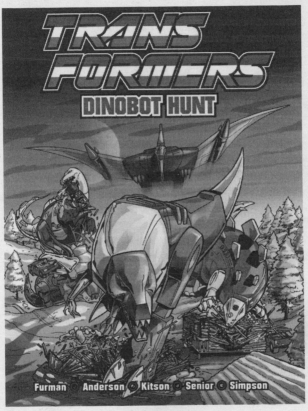

TRANS FORMERS
PREY
Furman Anderson Reed Senior Simpson

TRANS FORMERS
SECOND GENERATION
Furman Anderson Kitson Simpson Stokes

Transformers US comic collections now available from Titan Books!

Dark Star
Limited Edition Hardback
ISBN: 1 84023 975 1
ISBN-13: 9781840239751

Dark Star
Paperback
ISBN: 1 84023 960 3
ISBN-13: 9781840239607

Last Stand
Limited Edition Hardback
ISBN: 1 84576 009 3
ISBN-13: 9781845760090

Last Stand
Paperback
ISBN: 1 84576 008 5
ISBN-13: 9781845760083

WWW.TITANBOOKS.COM

Transformers Energon comic collections now available from Titan Books!

Energon Vol. 1
ISBN: 1 84023 932 8
ISBN-13: 9781840239324

Energon Vol. 2
ISBN: 1 84023 959 X
ISBN-13: 9781840239591

WWW.TITANBOOKS.COM

Pocket-sized Transformers UK comic collections now available from Titan Books!

Aspects of Evil!

ISBN: 1 84576 055 7
ISBN-13: 9781845760557

Pocket-sized Transformers UK comic collections now available from Titan Books!

Way of the Warrior
ISBN: 1 84576 059 X
ISBN-13: 9781845760595

Fallen Star
ISBN: 1 84576 060 3
ISBN-13: 9781845760601

Earthforce
ISBN: 1 84576 061 1
ISBN-13: 9781845760618

Perchance to Dream
ISBN: 1 84576 062 X
ISBN-13: 9781845760625

WWW.TITANBOOKS.COM

Benjamin Cobbina

TRANSFORMERS

GHOSTS OF YESTERDAY

TRANSFORME
GHOSTS OF Yesterday

Ben

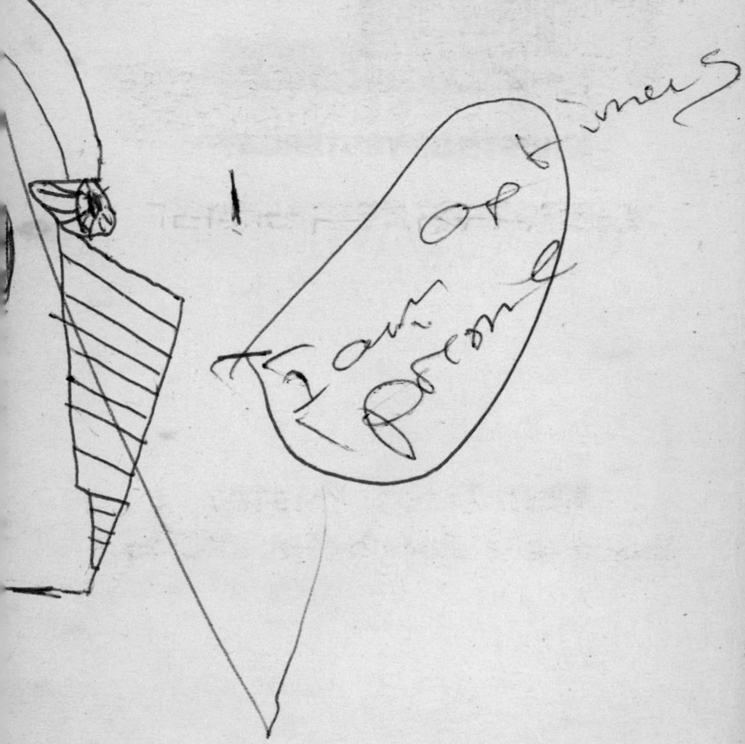

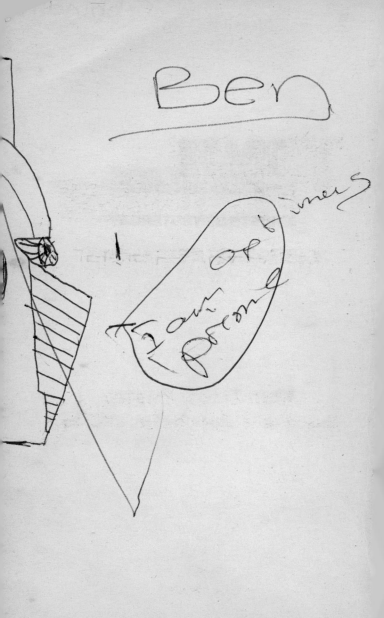

Benjamin Cobbinah

TRANSFORMERS

GHOSTS OF YESTERDAY

Alan Dean Foster

Based on a story by David Cian

TITAN BOOKS

Transformers: Ghosts of Yesterday
ISBN 1 84576 602 4
ISBN-13 9781845766023

Published by
Titan Books
A division of
Titan Publishing Group Ltd
144 Southwark St
London
SE1 0UP

First edition April 2007
10 9 8 7 6 5 4 3 2 1

Transformers: Ghosts of Yesterday is a work of fiction. Names, places and incidents either are products of the author's imagination or are used fictitiously.

Published by arrangement with Del Rey Books, an imprint of The Random House Publishing Group, a division of Random House, Inc., New York.

www.titanbooks.com
www.transformersmovie.com
www.hasbro.com

Did you enjoy this book? We love to hear from our readers. Please e-mail us at: **readerfeedback@titanemail.com** or write to Reader Feedback at the above address.

To subscribe to our regular newsletter for up-to-the-minute news, great offers and competitions, email: **booksezine@titanemail.com**

A CIP catalogue record for this title is available from the British Library.

Printed and bound in Great Britain by Cox & Wyman, Reading, Berkshire.